Creative Strategy

Creative Strategy

Reconnecting Business and Innovation

Chris Bilton
and
Stephen Cummings

WILEY

A John Wiley and Sons, Ltd, Publication

This edition first published in 2010
Copyright © 2010 Chris Bilton and Stephen Cummings

Registered office

John Wiley & Sons Ltd, The Atrium, Southern Gate, Chichester, West Sussex, PO19 8SQ, United Kingdom

For details of our global editorial offices, for customer services and for information about how to apply for permission to reuse the copyright material in this book please see our website at www.wiley.com

The right of the author to be identified as the author of this work has been asserted in accordance with the Copyright, Designs and Patents Act 1988.

Reprinted November 2010, August 2011

Wiley also publishes its books in a variety of electronic formats. Some content that appears in print may not be available in electronic books.

Designations used by companies to distinguish their products are often claimed as trademarks. All brand names and product names used in this book are trade names, service marks, trademarks or registered trademarks of their respective owners. The publisher is not associated with any product or vendor mentioned in this book. This publication is designed to provide accurate and authoritative information in regard to the subject matter covered. It is sold on the understanding that the publisher is not engaged in rendering professional services. If professional advice or other expert assistance is required, the services of a competent professional should be sought.

ISBN 978-1-4051-8019-1 (P/B)

A catalogue record for this book is available from the British Library.

Typeset in 9/13pt Kuenstler by Thomson
Printed and bound by CPI Group (UK) Ltd, Croydon, CR0 4YY

To Anna and Noelle

Contents

Acknowledgements

We would like to thank all of those who generously agreed to be interviewed or gave up their time and opinions to help us with this project over the past four years. In total, they are too numerous to name here but you will see their names and their influence throughout *Creative Strategy*. We would, however, like to give particular thanks to everybody at The Royal Shakespeare Company who allowed us access to their rehearsals and commented on the draft. We are very privileged to be able to present their story as the cornerstones of *Creative Strategy*.

Working from opposite ends of the earth has been challenging but ultimately extremely rewarding and surprisingly efficient (with the time-zones and 21st century Internet communication being very much in favour of our nightly 'baton changes'). This has, however, meant that we have worked with two quite distinct support groups whom we acknowledge below.

Chris would like to thank Richard Twyman, Michael Boyd and everybody in the Histories company at the RSC, together with Vikki Heywood, Liz Thompson, Liza Frank, Lyndon Jones and Jane Ellis, for being generous with their time and their ideas. Thanks to Nick Hornby, not just for the interview but also for his helpful comments on an early draft; to students on the MA in Creative and Media Enterprises at Warwick for their interest and good humour when test-driving parts of the book; to Paul Kohler, Claudia Chibici-Revneanu, Gonzalo Soltero and Hsiao-Ling Chung for being a lively and inspiring group of PhD students; to friends and colleagues at Warwick, Oliver Bennett for his trust and his critical nudging, Tim Walker of the Strategy Room for his many insights on the music industry and Ruth Leary for all her input and support along the way. At the risk of vicarious self-congratulation, he would also quite like to thank his co-author for what has been a truly enjoyable collaboration which took us both out of our comfort zones as well as across continents. Thanks to Richard Huntington, Tim Supple and Clive Lindop for giving their time and their ideas. Above all thanks to Anna Wright for her editorial skills, love, support and encouragement – and for everything else. And thanks to Kate, Laurie and Rob for letting him use the computer in the attic.

Steve would like to thank Sophia Lum and Luisa Acheson at Victoria Management School for their administrative support, tolerance and friendship; Todd Bridgman, John Brocklesby, Urs

Daellenbach and David Stewart in the Management Group at Victoria University; Terry Bowe and Rebecca Bednarek who were set many unusual research tasks along the way and always came back with something interesting; Deb Cumming from Massey University's School of Design; also Sheila Frost, Janet Biddle and Duncan Angwin for being excellent points of contact at Warwick Business School; to Chris (for his patience, diligence and good humour); Caithi and Oisín for putting up with frequent absent-mindedness; and particularly Noelle Donnelly for endless love and understanding.

Together we would like to thank Sam Hartley, Michaela Fay and Jo Golesworthy at Wiley UK. We give special thanks to Louise Cheer and the team that worked on the cover for this book, for whom we were not the easiest of authors to work with, and whose better judgement (thankfully) prevailed over ours.

Finally, we thank David Wilson who played a very active role in sponsoring this project at the outset and whose interest, advice and support along the way have been extremely welcome and helpful.

But, especially, we would like to thank Rosemary Nixon, our editor at Wiley. Without her patience with a project that started out as one thing (how creative and strategy are different) but ended up another (how good creativity and good strategy aren't so different), and her courage to support and champion this book as our support led us to change track and deadlines to sail by, this book would not be.

PROLOGUE: WHEN STRATEGY MEETS CREATIVITY

1

False Separations and Creative Connections

'One fine day in the middle of the night
Two dead men got up to fight.
Back to back, they faced each other,
Drew their swords and shot each other'

Anonymous

C reativity and strategy are much discussed but poorly understood. And whilst there is no shortage of advice on how to apply innovation in business or on how to apply strategic thinking to creative enterprise, much of this is poorly directed. Too often it relies on stereotypes which ignore the complexities and interactions of real creative and strategic processes. Or else it amounts to little more than window-dressing, talking up a particular business idea as 'creative' or a creative initiative as 'strategic'. Most damagingly though, creativity and strategy are seen to be at odds, with out-dated conceptions facing off and taking pot-shots at one another, much like the two dead men in the poem above.

This book aims to peel away these stereotypes and misconceptions to reveal how creativity should be at the heart of strategy and how strategy should be at the heart of creativity. The approach or framework we develop in this book is at once a creative approach to strategy and a strategic approach to creativity.

Having surveyed organizations with concerns ranging from theatre to computer games, from novels to noodles, from baseball to barcodes, from fashion to fighting, we have found that the most successful of these are both creative and strategic. And, moreover, the processes that drive effective creativity and strategy in these diverse organizations are very similar. Rather than appearing like comical combatants, strategy and creativity should be bedfellows.

During our investigations of 'creative strategy' across these many domains, we have discerned a process that applies, more or less, across them all. This process is based on a series of inter-related and paradoxical couplets. Whereas 'paradoxical thinking' is established as a key element in creativity, strategy has tended to pursue clarity and simplicity at the expense of paradox and complexity. In this book, we will consider the paradoxes which lie behind the four generic elements of creative strategy: innovation, entrepreneurship, leadership and organization.

First though, we must establish the parameters for the book as a whole. We offer a three part definition of creativity, we consider why strategy has tended to be 'uncreative', we offer a broader view of strategy, and finally we explain what we mean by *creative* strategy. But before we get to that, we must dispel five false separations, or imagined differences, which have obscured a more integrated understanding of strategy and creativity and we will identify five creative connections that we believe will drive successful organizations in the 21st century. It is these false separations and new creative connections that give purpose to this book.

Overcoming Five False Separations

The first false separation that *Creative Strategy* seeks to dispel is the notion that strategy is a stand-alone business discipline, much like accounting or marketing. We believe that this view may be traced back to the very first texts that sought to define what strategy was. The approach of early pioneers, such as Chandler and Ansoff, was to see strategy in terms of what was happening 'over and above' the operational units of a corporation. Viewing organization as a triangle, as was the norm, strategy was seen to exist at the top, to be the 'capstone'. There were then two approaches one could take: the first was that strategy was about the fruitful integration or bringing together of an organization's parts, business units or functions or regional offices, so that the whole might indeed be greater than the sum of those parts. The second view (and the one that prevailed) was that strategy was something separate that was done at the highest level of an organization just as marketing and accounting were discrete activities performed in other parts. The distinction is subtle, but its effects have been damaging.

After much mental effort, there are now many different philosophies or schools of thought as to what a distinct strategy process should be (rational, cultural, deliberate, emergent, and so on). But none of these focusses on the practicalities of strategy as being that which connects and gives purpose to an organization as a whole. As a result, strategy can be (and often is) disparaged as where 'the rubber meets the sky' (to twist a popular phrase). We believe that it would be useful to reconnect with that first view of strategy: to recognize that strategy only starts to make practical sense as an approach that integrates and gives collective creative purpose to the many and varied aspects and philosophies that co-exist in an organization. In other words, we think it would be better to think of strategy not as the capstone but as the *keystone* that coordinates and makes the organization create in concert.

This brings us to a second false dichotomy: the idea that creativity and strategy are fundamentally different modes. Business leaders often equate creativity with novelty, individualism and originality – an unplanned, spontaneous eruption of new ideas.

This view, when taken to its extreme, suggests that the two ways of thinking even occupy different sides of the brain. Creativity is unfettered, dynamic, borderline-crazy, right-brain thinking; strategy is stolid, rational (even overly-rational), left-brain. Creativity is mythologized as Dionysus (or Bacchus); Strategy is Apollo.

But we argue that any substantial creative act requires the incorporation and integration of both of these types of thinking. Creative flights of fancy generally only amount to anything when framed by a series of more rational and deliberate thinking styles. This is not an original claim, it follows a thesis put forward by Friedrich Nietzsche nearly 150 years ago. And in perhaps the first book in modern times to seriously investigate human creativity, Arthur Koestler similarly concludes that invention or discovery takes places through the combination of different ideas and angles. 'The Latin verb cogito for "to think"', Koestler informs us, 'means "to shake together" ... the creative act, by connecting previously unrelated dimensions of experience is an act of liberation [and] defeat[er] of habit.'

Creativity, we believe, is another keystone. It integrates aspects of experience and intuition that might otherwise go unconnected in order to change human experience. Koestler describes this as 'bisociation'. The act of creation is productive or enjoyable because it comes from and results in a different way of seeing the world around us. In its process and in its outcome, creativity makes a connection. A creative act reverses what a physicist might see as the natural entropy of things – just like a strategic act.

Of all the areas of business then, strategy should be especially wedded to a 'creative' approach. Strategy is (if we accept the argument above that strategy is an integrative keystone not a stand-alone discipline) the realm in which all of the myriad parts of an organization come together, clash and compete, compromise and work to solve collective problems to move forward. But, unfortunately, we are inclined to see creative and strategic thinking (and 'creative' and 'ordinary' industries) as polar opposites, with 'strategists' and 'creatives' facing off like the two dead men at the start of this chapter. And rather than combining and learning from each other, an earnest pursuit of what is perceived to be 'creative' or 'strategic' has driven them further apart. Why?

It could be that they have both been looking in the wrong direction. Artists and creative professionals tend to equate strategy with systems of control and accountability, while underselling the importance of decision-making and strategizing in their own work. Business leaders see creativity as a metaphor for inspiration and unpredictability, without analysing some of the analogies between creative and strategic thinking. On both sides, 'creativity' and 'strategy' are seen as extraordinary opposites, rather than as integral to each other. We look for them outside our experience, rather than recognizing them in our own reflections.

Consequently, 'creative' and 'strategic' initiatives are too often framed as external interventions. In the so-called creative industries and in the arts, 'strategic' frameworks and strategic management styles have been imported from business, often at the behest of senior managers or external stakeholders. 'Strategy' in the arts thus comes to be resented as an external imposition, rather than acknowledged as an integral part of the creative process. Similarly, 'creativity' in business tends to be seen as peripheral rather than integral to core strategic processes. It is not unusual for a business to invite an arts organization to run training workshops to improve discretionary motivation or presentation skills among the sales and marketing team. But 'creativity training' tends to be individualized and compartmentalized rather than applied to the overall running of the organization. Despite some apparent interest and enthusiasm, such initiatives promote a feeling that strategy and creativity are alien, exotic or extraordinary to each other. Managers and artists mimic each other's language or dress codes without exploring the underlying substance; and strategic and creative thinking remain sharply divided.

Rather than marking out the differences between 'creative thinking' and 'strategic thinking', we argue that all industries are creative and all creativity is, in some way, strategic. This book will attempt to uncover some of the underlying similarities and sympathies between creativity and strategy in the arts, in business and in sports, in order to demonstrate that 'creative strategy' can add value to *any* organization.

The tendency to treat creativity and strategy as peripheral to each other encourages the notion that creativity and strategy will be less important (or different) in times of recession than in times of growth. The third false separation we seek to dispel in this book is the assumption that recession and growth require radically different strategies.

In macro-economic theory, growth and recession are stages in a continual cycle of creative destruction. Just as unplanned growth can trigger recession, a recession can open spaces for innovation and eventual recovery. Whether markets are contracting or expanding they are always changing and this change creates opportunities for any organization, whether a big multi-national or a small start-up, to think creatively about how they might go about their business more effectively. Indeed, it may be that a recession causes greater entropy or stagnation; as established firms pull back into more defensive positions, markets converge and contract around them, opening up gaps in between. These spaces provide *new* opportunities (and *new* impetus) for creative strategizing. When asked how the recession might change the relationship between the 'creative' and the 'commercial' in his industry, Aaron De Mey, artistic director at Lancome, said: 'I think [it will] separate talent from mediocrity. It [will actually] motivate people to be more creative, original and focussed'. A recession can help reconnect business and innovation.

A fourth division that needs to be surmounted is the popular view that 'young people today' somehow form a separate generation (sometimes referred to as Generation Y, the Millennials or the Net Generation) that is fundamentally different from, or opposed to, the mindset of previous generations. A corollary of this is the idea that this generation is not so interested in things like business, strategy, entrepreneurship and organization. For example, a recent article coined the phrase 'antipreneurs' to describe an emerging group of young people who want to promote sustainability, eco-consciousness and fair labour practices. However, we argue that it would be much more accurate to describe this new group as entrepreneurs who are seeking to use their entrepreneurial energy to further different aims from those normally associated with past models.

This generational split reinforces our previous dichotomy – young people are seen as creative and spontaneous, leaving the older and presumably wiser heads to worry about strategy. We argue that creativity and strategizing are fundamental characteristics of all generations. The failures and successes of the Net generation are often attributed to their 'creativity' and their disrespect for the rules of strategy. While it is true that more recent generations have grown up with new technologies that may cause them to operate in ways that appear unique, they are still, we believe, using these tools to integrate creative ideas and strategic methods. Indeed several recent commentators have argued that the Internet encourages personal interaction and integration – the kind of things that we argue facilitate creative and strategic mindsets – to a greater extent than the one-way communication provided by broadcast television and other mass media. They may go about it in particular ways, but creative or strategic thinking cuts across the generations. In this book we will combine recent and historical examples to illustrate that 'creative' or 'strategic' approaches cannot be separately attributed to a particular generation or period.

The last separation that we challenge might be better described as an artificial specialization. This specialization has seen aspects that should contribute to creative strategy dissected and treated as specific disciplines in their own right. Search for books with Innovation, or Leadership or Entrepreneurship in the title and you'll find thousands. The biggest surprise to us, when we started researching this book, was that there wasn't one called Creative Strategy already.

This book builds out from a fundamentally different approach: any substantial or lasting approach must view creative strategy as an integrative cycle of elements that are often viewed in isolation, a cycle whereby *Innovation* creates the potential to add value to people's lives, but for Innovation to effectively 'get to market', *Entrepreneurship* provides the necessary impetus; but in order to build upon the Entrepreneur's market beachhead, *Leadership* must convert short-term opportunities into long-term direction; but for Leadership to be developed the right *Organization* must provide a framework for connection and change; and for that Organization to be refreshed, Innovation is required. And so the cycle begins again. This book does not aim to offer the last words on any of these four elements, but to offer a guide as to how an effective orientation to each in combination with the others can help an enterprise to survive and thrive into the future.

---

5 FALSE SEPARATIONS THAT *CREATIVE STRATEGY* COLLAPSES

- *Strategy is a discipline distinct from other business disciplines* We don't think so: Strategy should not be thought of as a discrete 'over and above' capstone but as an integrative keystone.
- *Creative thinking and strategic thinking are very different* We don't think so: Creativity and strategy are more similar than different, they are both integrating processes. All creativity is potentially strategic; and all strategy should be creative.
- *Growth and Recession call for fundamentally different approaches* We don't think so: Creative Strategy is important in times of growth and in times of recession.
- *Generation Y is essentially different from everybody else* We don't think so: All generations (if such a categorization actually makes sense) have an interest in creativity and strategizing.
- *Innovation, Entrepreneurship, Leadership and Organization are separate domains* We don't think so: Creative Strategy is about the effective integration of such pursuits.

Five Creative Connections for the Future

One of the characteristics which marks the transition from modernity to postmodernity is an acceptance of paradoxes and contradictions which in a modernist era we might have attempted to choose between or resolve. So, instead of discovering whether the world is globalizing or becoming more locally oriented, we might now begin to appreciate that both things are happening (looking at how the 1980s phrase 'think global' has morphed into 'think global, act local', to Coca-Cola's mantra in the late 1990s, 'think local, act local,' to Toyota's more recent 'learn local, act global' provides a nice insight into how we may be moving from either/ors towards appreciating paradoxical both/ands). Is technology leading to a dumbing down or a wising up? Probably both. Does technology provide greater freedom now than ever before? Yes. And no.

If the ability to embrace apparent contradictions is characteristic of a postmodern approach, then *Creative Strategy* may be described as a postmodern book. It attempts to show how creative strategy, paradoxically, requires incorporating what might have once been seen as incompatible approaches to the same thing. Having cleared away some of the assumptions and misconceptions identified with the five false separations set out above, we can turn to the emerging connections which underpin and give purpose to *Creative Strategy*.

The last of our five disconnections – the false separation which sees innovation, entrepreneurship, leadership and organization as separate domains – provides the starting point for our five connections. The success of a creative strategy cannot be attributed to an exciting innovation any more than it can be attributed to a solid organization (or, indeed, good entrepreneurship or leadership). Creative strategy means innovation *and* entrepreneurship *and* leadership *and* organization. Then, there are paradoxical connections to be embraced within each of these integral parts.

While there has been a great deal of debate about whether *innovation* is more likely to be borne out of an active emphasis on creation or a more passive focus on discovery, we argue that innovation is advanced by both approaches in concert.

Next, we argue that creative strategy is furthered by an approach to *entrepreneurship* that requires the seemingly contradictory characteristics of focussed diligence and a meandering or unfettered dilettantism.

Further, the sort of *leadership* required to build something from an initial innovative and entrepreneurial spark into something more lasting requires an ability to both envision and communicate simple pictures of the future, and to lead by doing what might be seen as the smallest of practical tasks in the present. (We also question the popular debate about whether leaders are born or made and add a third alternative to this 'either/or' choice.)

And, lastly, we posit that the sort of effective organization required to ensure that an innovation is not a one-hit wonder, to create an environment where the original innovation will be refreshed or new innovations created, requires an ability to simultaneously loosen and tighten the organizational reins.

THE 5 CONNECTIONS THAT *CREATIVE STRATEGY* BUILDS UPON

- *Creative Strategy requires the integration of innovation <u>and</u> entrepreneurship <u>and</u> leadership <u>and</u> organization.*
- *Creative Strategy incorporates an approach to Innovation that harnesses both creation <u>and</u> discovery.*
- *Creative Strategy utilizes an approach to Entrepreneurship that promotes both diligence <u>and</u> dilettantism.*
- *Creative Strategy draws upon an approach to Leadership based upon being able to envision the big picture for the future <u>and</u> interact in the present.*
- *Creative Strategy involves an approach to organization that focusses the activities of others <u>and</u> encourages them to roam into pastures new.*

In summary, we argue that the key to creative strategy lies in the recognition and reconciliation of apparently contradictory or opposing characteristics or capabilities: a process that we call 'bisociative', and we propose a bisociative thinking framework that can aid the development of creative strategy. But, having outlined how this book is different and where we would like to take the reader, there is a danger of moving ahead of ourselves. We shall expand upon these paradoxes and bisociative thinking soon. However, before leaping any further we should step back and look more closely at the nature of creativity, the reason why strategy may not have been as creative as it should have been in the past, and at the subsequent gap that *Creative Strategy* seeks to fill.

What is Creativity?

I n Chapter 1, we noted that one of the causes of disconnection between creativity and strategy was a lack of understanding as to what creativity is. This is not just a problem for 'business people'. Many in the creative industries too would struggle to articulate more than a superficial view of creativity. In order to get beyond this we devote Chapter 2 to clarifying the concept.

We define creativity as a temporal system with three levels:

creativity's *content*,
creativity's *outcome*, and
creativity's *process*.

The *content* of creativity describes the basic elements contained in a working definition of creativity. The *outcome* of creativity is a more pragmatic assessment of the impact or output of creativity, without which a creative act has little meaning. Finally, the *process* of creativity describes the dynamic processes and interactions through which creativity occurs.

1. Creativity's Content: Innovation + Purpose to Add More than Individual Value

Most contemporary definitions of creativity as content combine two elements or criteria. Creative ideas or products must be novel, and they must also be valuable. But the nature of an innovation (from the Latin *nova*, or new) depends upon context – I may have a 'new' idea, only to discover somebody else has got there first. Margaret Boden makes a useful distinction here between that which is new to the individual ('P-creativity') and that which is new to the world ('H-creativity'). For the purposes of this book, we argue that creative acts should aim to have a more than personal significance, they should be new or surprising in a broader social context.

The element of value in creativity has been expressed in terms of 'fitness for purpose', problem-solving or other given criteria, and is added to innovation in order to distinguish creativity from 'mere novelty'. Novelty without purpose or value might, by accident, result in a creative outcome, but is not in itself creative. For example, some schizophrenics have produced art work which has impressed expert observers. Yet we would be unlikely to consider a schizophrenic patient as 'creative' (even if their pictures were valued as such) unless he or she were deliberately directing the artistic outcome. It is also less likely that a work of art will happen to meet external criteria of value if the artist has no knowledge or intention regarding those criteria. Schizophrenia may result in a 'novel' or innovative way of seeing, but the idea that creativity can be defined in terms of mental illness overlooks the role of intention, purpose and self-awareness in the production of value.

Nevertheless, the critic John Carey reminds us that we should not construct our definitions of creativity around the intentions of artists and inventors. The road to creative failure is paved with good intentions – and plenty of breakthrough moments in art and science have arisen from happy accidents; the absence of purpose does not make the result any less novel or valuable in the eye of the beholder. Carey likewise observes that value, like novelty, depends upon context – the value judgements of creators themselves, of those around them, and of the broader social context. Attempting to define creativity purely in terms of content – without regard to context – is thus a slippery business. Some creativity theorists, notably Robert Weisberg, prefer to remove the notion of value from definitions of creativity as overly subjective. For our purposes it may be easier to define the value of creativity (and its novelty) in terms of outcomes rather than intentions. This leads us to our next question – what is the outcome of creativity? Perhaps we can assess the novelty and value of creativity by its results, not so much for what it is, but for what it does (or claims to do).

2. Creativity's Outcomes: Transforming Contexts and Redefining Problems

Moving beyond the content of creativity, a more pragmatic definition of creativity requires a focus on its *outcomes*. Simply put, the outcome of creativity must be change (or the 'destruction of habit' to use Koestler's more poetic language). More specifically, change occurs through a reorganization of the existing elements into a new and surprising pattern that is more than fleeting.

Valuable innovations subsequently transform the context or framework within which they occurred. Henry Moore changed the way we think about sculpture. The Dyson vacuum cleaner changed the way we think about domestic appliances and household cleaning. Margaret Boden describes this as 'transforming the conceptual space'; a genuinely creative solution does not simply solve a problem, it subsequently redefines the questions that we might ask.

Creativity is sometimes associated with an anarchic disregard for rules or structure. Yet, creative practice (and creativity theory) takes place within clearly defined rules, conventions and constraints precisely in order to re-structure them. A Picasso painting, or a John Cage composition, work within an awareness of the traditions of the art form and a mastery of their craft, even as they seem to break (and then remake) conventions. Creative thinkers are also strategic thinkers, planning, making choices and evaluating and positioning themselves and their work according to a range of external and internal parameters. Creative change reconfigures the way we see a problem or scenario, but it is also valuable because it reconstructs the values inherent in that problem or scenario. Creative transformation is paradoxical – we see the same things, but structured in a new way. This takes us to another level, from which we might encounter new problems that we never considered before.

While it is interesting to define what a creative act is and what its outcomes should be, if we wish to foster and develop creativity it is more useful to understand the creative process that leads to these actions and outcomes.

3. The Creativity Process: Tolerating Contradictions Enables Bisociative Thinking

We defined the content of creativity as novelty + value, or 'valuable innovation'. This combination in the content of creativity connects with a combination in the creative *process*. In order to arrive at something both novel and valuable, more than one type of thinking is necessary. The creative process involves an ability to make connections between apparently contradictory frames of reference, or 'bisociation'.

Cognitive theories of the creative process emphasize that creative thinking is a complex process encompassing multiple stages and thinking styles. These cognitive theories can be seen as a reaction against previous 'trait-based' definitions which attempted to define the creative process as a set of singular steps taken by a set of idealized individuals or creative 'geniuses'. As these lists of steps or characteristics expanded, contradictions emerged between them. In order to encompass such diverse elements, creative individuals and organizations came to be recognized as those who cultivated their ability to tolerate contradiction and paradox. Cognitive theories of creativity consequently make contradictions integral to our understanding of the creative process which is now regarded as incorporating apparently contradictory ways of seeing and thinking.

Instead of listing personal characteristics or competences, cognitive theories of the creative process encourage us to trace the movements between them. These movements on a human scale may be related to those movements between mental regions or the hemispheres of the brain. Five hundred years ago the opposing characteristics and processes between which an individual's 'psyche' moved were charted as 'humours'; today they are reproduced in encephalograms mapping hemispheric activity and synaptic connections inside the brain. Neuroscientific research has revealed some of the surprising connections which are made between different regions of the brain during the creative process.

Brain scans show that all people use both left and right brain hemispheres for creative tasks, further adding weight to the idea that you need to work across many parts of the brain to make the novel associations from which creativity springs, and undermining earlier popular views that creativity existed in the right hemisphere. Indeed, one interesting recent study found that a category of people called schizotypes (who demonstrated greater levels of bilateral brain use without the debilitating symptoms associated with schizophrenia and other mental illnesses, although they are prone to psychoses) made more novel associations than the average 'normal' person. Creative luminaries like Vincent Van Gogh, Albert Einstein, Emily Dickinson and Isaac Newton are believed by many psychologists to have had schizotype personalities, but we can all experience higher levels of bilateral brain activity during creative phases of our lives.

Whereas mental illness traps the sufferer in one mode of thinking, the schizotype is able to switch between them. It may be for similar reasons that accounts of creativity among the mentally ill suggest that the most intense periods of creative activity are more likely to occur immediately after mental illness, in the periods of recovery or transition between mental states. Wordsworth and Coleridge claimed that poetry was composed in the reflective tranquillity after intense emotion, or else in those lucid moments between sleeping and waking; the spontaneous and the deliberate phases were equally important to them. Koestler described creative thinking taking place 'on the mind's marshy shore', on the cusp between differing mental and emotional states, allowing the mind to flick between alternative ways of seeing and thinking.

The paradoxical nature of the creative process is reinforced by *sociological theories* of creativity which examine the social interactions, dependencies and contexts which lie behind individual creativity. Again these theories move us away from a person-centred or trait-based model of creativity towards a process-based definition encompassing multiple sometimes contradictory elements. When we translate 'innovation + value' into a social setting, it is clear that there may be significant conflict between individuals and groups. One person's job may be to dream up new ideas, while another's may be to test the value of these ideas in terms of costs and benefits. In organizational settings, these contradictions may be exacerbated by cultural and hierarchical differences. Innovators and managers end up arguing about the relative importance of novelty and value, and organizations are split between so-called 'creatives' and 'suits'. Yet genuine creativity requires a tolerance for contradictions on both sides and an ability to switch focus and perception and be changed in the process. Hence, while we have presented the traditional divisions between artists and managers in negative terms, the ensuing conflict or interaction between them can also be a positive source of creativity.

The definition of creativity as a process which tolerates contradictions and paradox allows us to draw together opposing theories of creativity which have developed in different cultures and at different times. The mythology of genius highlights the spontaneous, irrational or transgressive aspects of the creative process. Conversely an opposing intellectual tradition argues that creativity conforms to certain rules and conventions, and is rooted in memory, logic and an understanding of tradition. These opposing arguments can be traced across time, beginning from the opposing positions of Aristotle (rational imitation according to the rules of nature) and Plato (irrational 'divine madness', against the rules of sense and order). The debate continues into discussions of the relationship between neurosis or eccentricity and 'originality' from Freud to De Bono, as well as in contemporary psychological perspectives on creativity. In a global context, we can recognize these philosophical arguments embedded in different cultural traditions. The Western emphasis on individualism and originality as the essence of creativity contrasts with a belief in continuity, order and tradition in Confucian and Buddhist philosophies.

Interestingly, while intellectual arguments have swung from pole to pole, the definition of the creative process as an ability to move between contradictions recurs constantly in creation myths. Almost every pre-modern creation myth requires the intermingling or coming together of opposing forces. Cosmos and chaos, personified by the gods Apollo and Dionysis (Bacchus) for the Greeks and Romans, the Norse mythology of Northern Europe, and the Chinese myths of ying and yang – all feature a collision of opposites, between the forces of chaos and of order. The box overleaf provides an example of how this ancient thinking is still played out in offices today. In a similar vein, we argue that creative processes are based on an ability to move between, or bisociate, rational (inductive) and irrational (intuitive) thinking styles.

THE POWER OF BISOCIATION

A recent paper by Jennifer George and Jing Zhou in the prestigious *Academy of Management Journal* shows that workers are most creative when they experience positive and negative perspectives at the office, as long as their boss is supportive. The negative mind-set encourages scepticism and a focus on addressing problems, while positive moods promote a sense of confidence. Either one alone, they said, is less effective in enhancing creativity.

These findings recall work done a decade or so ago. *Creativity – Flow and the Psychology of Discovery and Invention,* by Mihaly Csikszentmihalyi, published in 1997, found that the personalities of the creative people similarly incorporated opposite moods or characteristics:

- Creative individuals have a great deal of energy, but they are also often quiet and at rest.
- Creative individuals tend to be smart, yet also naive at the same time.
- Creative individuals have a combination of playfulness and discipline, or responsibility and irresponsibility.
- Creative individuals alternate between imagination and fantasy at one end, and rooted sense of reality at the other.
- Creative people seem to harbour opposite tendencies on the continuum between extroversion and introversion.
- Creative individuals are also remarkably humble and proud at the same time.

(Continued)

(Continued)

- Creative individuals to a certain extent escape rigid gender role stereotyping and have a tendency toward androgyny.
- Generally, creative people are thought to be rebellious and independent.
- Most creative persons are very passionate about their work, yet they can be extremely objective about it as well.
- The openness and sensitivity of creative individuals often exposes them to suffering pain yet also a great deal of enjoyment.

This brings us to *Creative Strategy's* definitional framework of creativity ... As shown in the figure below, we define creativity as something containing *innovation* and *value*, which *transforms* the context in which it occurs (and thus how we may think and live), and which results from a process of paradoxical *bisociative* thinking. Each of these elements in our definition of creativity is connected, or part of a system. The transformative outcome of creativity is linked to the ability to switch between and connect together apparently contradictory concepts, thinking styles and frames of reference. The same process of paradoxical thinking results in a product which is both novel *and* valuable. The combination of innovation and value results in an innovative solution which transforms the way we think and live taking us to another level of problems and opportunities for further creativity. And so the process of creativity is engaged once more.

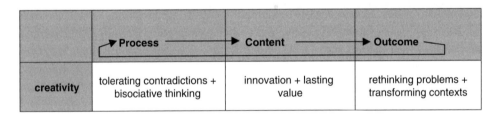

	Process	Content	Outcome
creativity	tolerating contradictions + bisociative thinking	innovation + lasting value	rethinking problems + transforming contexts

Figure 2.1 A definitional framework of creativity

As we have already stated, strategy should be well suited to integrating in this bisociative fashion, and so be well predisposed to creativity. Why it has not made these connections is the subject of the next chapter.

WHAT IS CREATIVITY? THREE BISOCIATIVE LEVELS

- The creative *process* requires us to connect together unfamiliar frames of reference and utilize different types of thinking (left-brain and right-brain). It might also require us to connect with different types of people.

(Continued)

- The *content* of creativity should be both novel and valuable. In order to evaluate whether something meets these criteria, we must connect ideas with applications, and locate creativity in a context of intentions, actions and outcomes. Mere novelty is not the same as creativity.
- The *outcome* of creativity connects with the field or domain within which it occurs. Creative ideas transform the context or 'conceptual space' around them, opening up new possibilities for future creativity. Individual creative insights have collective consequences.

CHAPTER 3

Uncreative Strategy

Before considering the possibilities for making strategy more creative in the future, we should explore why strategic management may have failed to employ greater creativity in the past. In this chapter, we outline ten reasons why the dominant logic of strategic management (a set of assumptions and practices which have come to dominate thinking about strategy in businesses and business schools) may have got in the way of more creative approaches to strategy.

1. Creativity Can't be Planned Directly . . .

. . . and strategic management has generally been associated with planning.

Early definitions of strategic management associated strategy with the plans that were made concerning the whole organization, for the longer term. But translating this plan into implementation further down the organization typically followed a predictive path of step by step planning – 'first we do A, then we do B. . .'. Such an approach undermines an integrative model of strategy and certainly does not fit with accounts of creativity. Paul Feyerabend's study of the nature of scientific creativity clearly outlined that because scientific success could not be explained in a simple way, to the point that it would be wrong and misleading to say, for example, that: 'the structure of the atomic nucleus was found because people did A, B, C. . .' (where A, B and C are procedures which can be understood independently of their use in nuclear psychics), all we can do is give *an historical account of the details including social circumstances, accidents and personal idiosyncrasies*. This does not lend itself to the logic of strategic plans and their step by step application.

This is not to say that creativity lacks structure. We have already noted that creativity is in part a structured, deliberate process, not just a product of spontaneous acts of genius. Nevertheless, creativity cannot be generalized, certainly not into a series of specific 'steps' that could be planned out in advance. There must be space in the plan for contingency and change. There must also be space for individual, unscripted departures from the predicted path. Strategy is often seen as the expression of a company's collective rationality, but, as Tait Elder at 3M famously said, 'we expect our champions to be irrational'. Or, at least, bisociatively rational and irrational.

Similarly, James Dyson argues that creative products cannot follow a planned approach to strategy because individual distinctiveness inevitably means deviating from what has been collectively agreed. 'We have focus groups', he explains, 'but I take a perverse delight in ignoring them.' Dyson points out that one of the most boring British cars ever made – the Hillman Avenger – emerged from focus groups, committees and boards, whereas the Mini, one of the most memorable, resulted from one man's (Alex Issigonis's) idiosyncratic creative processes and a vision quite at odds with what had gone before. This approach is not new. As Henry Ford once said, 'If I'd listened to customers I'd have built a faster horse.'

On the logic presented here, if an industry or organization adheres to a planned and predicted approach to strategy, the most creative response from the individual employee would be to ignore the plan and strike out alone. Strategic plans which are fixed in the boardroom require consistency and predictability in their application further down the organization. 'Creative strategy', on the other hand, would be purposeful and future-oriented, but leaves us free to discover our own individual, unplanned paths towards collective goals.

2. Creativity Requires Bisociation, Going Between Things, Seeing from the Edges, both/and Rather than either/or Thinking and Can be Thwarted by Rigid Classification . . .

. . . and strategic management has spent a great deal of time and effort trying to classify itself and separate itself out.

As discussed in Chapter 1, some early pioneers of strategic management defined strategy as an integrating component in organization, the area that brought together the many diverse actions and concerns of the company for the greater good. Continuing along this road would have led strategic management to become the most creative of business processes (by the definition we outlined in the preceding chapter). But, strategy was subsequently redefined as something distinct from other aspects, functions or levels of a corporation, especially as separate from the operational activities of an organization – no longer the keystone pulling the parts together into a coherent whole, but the capstone which is set above the rest.

A Cartesian dualism, or split, between thinking (strategizing) and doing (operations) emerged. Moreover, strategic management has come to rely upon classifying particular industries or stages of development and generalizing within them, or dividing out generic strategies and defining rules for adhering to these. Not only did strategic management thus become separated from the rest of the organization, but divided within itself into separate models or approaches. Pursuing one generic strategy would require the organization to work consistently within that strategy's predetermined boundaries and avoid switching between or mixing with other generic strategies.

But, as Kurt Vonnegut put it, being creative is about standing 'as close to the edge as [you] can without going over. Out on the edge you see all the kinds of things you can't see from the center.' Vonnegut echoes bisociative theories of creativity, requiring us to switch between categories and types of experience in order to make unexpected connections. To achieve this, Vonnegut describes a dilettante or drifter attitude at odds with classification and hierarchy. Think of Swatch's challenge to the assumption that the wrist watch was a single purchase luxury item by combining fashion industry practices with Swiss watch technology; or Cirque du Soleil's creation of something unique and extremely profitable by effectively collapsing two declining industries – theatre and circus – into one. These are two good examples of creative products born from riding or ignoring traditional boundaries. They also illustrate how a creative approach to strategy can jump from one model or method to another, rather than dogmatically sticking to the knitting.

Strategic management limits our options because it separates strategy from action and separates out distinctive positions and models of strategy which we must adhere to. 'Creative strategy' would invite us to step outside these divisions and adopt a more eclectic approach to products, organizations and industries and to switch and reconnect between multiple strategic positions.

3. Creativity Requires Plurality . . .

. . . and those in strategic management roles have traditionally been of one type: most commonly accountants, lawyers, engineers who have risen to the top of organizations.

In 1605, Francis Bacon wrote in *The Advancement of Learning* that a key 'error is the peremptory reduction of knowledge into arts and method, from which time the sciences are seldom improved; [just as] young men rarely grow in stature after their shape and limbs are fully formed'. Unfortunately, strategic management has previously been regarded as the preserve of older 'fully formed' professionals.

Worse than this, the fully formed are of one particular type. Most senior positions in organizations and consultancies are occupied by people from law, engineering and accountancy backgrounds. Such fields are concerned with compliance, with being mindful of past precedent, general standards and established practice. People from beyond these backgrounds – design, marketing, the factory floor or the laboratory – might be better able to understand the importance of plurality, bisociation, and unstructured and unique thinking. Companies would do well to bring other characters into the boardroom and enable creative thinking to emerge from having these different ways of seeing in the one room.

A good example of this, which we often like to tell our students, is the story of a senior executive from a television broadcaster who became CEO of a large information services company (whom we are not at liberty to name here). One of the first things he did was to send out an e-mail to all staff. It was two words and one question mark long: 'Any ideas?' He got about 300 responses. Around thirty of these were implemented.

One of these ideas came from an operative working in the photocopy room. He claimed that tens of thousands of dollars per annum could be saved if all documents were copied 'double-sided'. The idea was put into practice and the money was saved, just as the photocopier said it would be. But more than this, a strong signal about the company's focus on cutting costs wherever possible without compromising on quality reverberated around the company. A simple operational innovation could have strategic consequences. It is interesting to ask whether such a strategic initiative would have been proposed by somebody on the Board or a classically trained senior manager?

The professionalization of 'arts management' in the 1980s has led to a similar narrowing of backgrounds. Arts management courses are increasingly run out of business schools. Opera houses, broadcasters and arts councils are increasingly reliant on captains of industry for their strategic direction, rather than on former practitioners. When Greg Dyke was appointed as director-general of the BBC in 2000, the organization had become associated with 'management by accountants'. Dyke, himself a former television producer, attempted to challenge the senior management hierarchy by actively soliciting strategy ideas from other members of the organization. More recently the Royal Shakespeare Company's 'ensemble' approach to organization has followed a similar logic – by opening strategy up to other voices and perspectives not only is the workforce implicated and enthused in the running of the organization, we might discover some better, more creative, ideas about strategy.

Identifying strategic management with a specific professional background or an elite group within the organization cuts down the strategic options and opinions available. A creative approach to strategy would draw on a plurality of voices and perspectives.

4. Creativity Requires Mistakes and Accidents, or at Least an Acceptance of Their Value . . .

. . .strategic management, or indeed management in general (or indeed Western education), has become highly averse to failure.

In June 2007 James Dyson was asked by *The Irish Times* whether 'designers should begin their careers with an education in strategic thinking'. He replied:

> Everything is 'strategic thinking' these days. [But f]or us strategic thinking involves making lots of mistakes. I've always thought that children should be marked by the amount of mistakes they make at school because it is through these mistakes that we come up with new ideas.

Pasteur, famously acknowledged the role played by chance in creative discovery, but noted that 'chance favours the prepared mind'. William Perkin, inventor of purple dye and subsequently a series of fields within industrial chemistry, similarly acknowledged the importance of accidents, but observed that 'accident arises out of purpose'. A large part of this attitude is being prepared to risk failure or failing with a purpose. In an interesting twist on the old adage 'failing to plan is planning to fail', 'creative strategy' would require a change of emphasis: planning to fail would become a means to increase your chances of success.

One of the most widely discussed examples of 'failing in order to succeed' in this way is Honda's pioneering entry into the US motorcycle market in the 1970s. Honda's strategic analysis and research extrapolations of the US market led Honda to leave behind the little bikes it produced and sold in Japan (American motorcycle riders rode much bigger bikes) and develop bigger 'American-style' bikes for the US market.

Honda's big bikes flopped. American motorcyclists could already buy big bikes: American companies like Harley-Davidson that enjoyed great customer loyalty produced them. But then people who had never thought about riding a motorcycle before started asking Honda's couriers where they could get one of the little 50cc bikes that they were riding around US cities to make deliveries (Honda had shipped out a small number of 'Japanese-style' bikes for its employees). After this news filtered up the company, Honda quickly reconfigured its approach and took a crack at the market with its small bikes. People who were not traditional motorbike riders could see themselves using this much smaller, more fuel-efficient and less intimidating mode of transport and bought them. Once these new riders were introduced to motorbike riding by Honda, and gained confidence with them, opportunities began to emerge to sell them bigger bikes. And, over time, Honda established itself as the leading motorcycle brand in the world's biggest market.

The failure of the original strategy contained the seeds of success. Entering a foreign market always carried a risk of failure, but it was Honda's ability to recognize and respond to a failed strategy which allowed it eventually to succeed.

Creativity requires idealism and 'fast failing', continual prototyping and re-prototyping, and being at what has been called the 'bleeding edge'. Unfortunately, the rise of 'accountability', a particular type of 'risk management' where risks are to be avoided rather than managed, and the accretion of best practice benchmarking from an operational tool to a low-risk strategy guide, has resulted in strategic management developing a risk averse 'follower' mentality.

This follower mentality crept into the arts and creative industries during the 1980s and 1990s too. A combination of professionalism, escalating competition and growing dependence on external investment has made developers nervous, especially with new talent and new products. It is sometimes argued that classic British television comedies like *Steptoe and Son* or *Only Fools and Horses*, or American shows like *The Mary Tyler Moore Show*, might never have made it beyond a first series in today's more risk-averse broadcasting industry. *Variety* magazine reported an all-time record number of movie sequels in the mid-noughties. As David Koepp, co-writer of *Jurassic Park*, explains: 'Approving a sequel is a non-fireable offence. If a sequel doesn't work, they can still say, "It wasn't my fault! It was a no-brainer".' A similar logic promotes the continued investment in 'heritage' (or 'geriatric', depending on your point of view) rock music.

Yet despite these outbreaks of follower mentality, the business model of any creative industry must be fundamentally premised on being prepared to fail. Test screenings and focus groups do not predict future hits. Indeed it is said that the US cable network HBO will reject a pilot with a test screening approval rate of more than 75% on the basis that anything which fits this comfortably into current viewing habits is unlikely to be sufficiently edgy and challenging for their target audience. Some of HBO's most successful series, including *The Sopranos* and *Six Feet Under*, achieved poor initial ratings and baffled audiences at first (one focus group suggested changing *The Sopranos* to *The Family Man* because audiences wouldn't understand it), and the company prides itself on its imperviousness to audience research and ratings.

The 'creative strategy' capability of an organization would lie in its ability to recognize and adapt to unexpected failures and success rather than their ability to predict them. Why? Because strategic management's preoccupation with control and efficiency misses the correlation between success and failure: without flops, there can be no hits.

5. Creativity Requires Slack . . .

. . . and increasing efficiency became a fundamental principle in management.

'To get creative thought to emerge', wrote Carl Jung, 'one must have a special training for switching off consciousness, at least to a relative extent, thus giving the unconscious contents a chance to develop.' Similarly, some degree of what we might call 'slack' is required to foster creative thought. It is unfortunate, then, that a mechanistic definition of efficiency (as a short-term reduction of the ration of inputs over outputs) became an underlying driver in strategic management.

After Alfred Chandler's *Strategy and Structure*, Igor Ansoff's *Corporate Strategy*, published in 1965, is the second most revered founding document in strategic management. When finalizing his model of the firm, on which he would base his model of strategy, Ansoff concluded that seeing as: 'there is no general agreement on a proper philosophical basis for business objectives . . . our framework for formulating objectives was made adaptable to a variety of different management attitudes, so long as the underlying concept of the firm is that of an efficiency-seeking organization'. The underlying concept of efficiency turned out to be a singular limitation.

A good example of promoting slack rather than efficiency is 3M's most famous product – Post-It Notes. These emerged in the mind of a research scientist who took advantage of the long-standing 3M policy of allowing research staff to spend 15% of their time to think on their own ideas and projects. In this time, the researcher in question had been experimenting with glues, unsuccessfully (they didn't stick very well), but a bit of lateral thinking turned the failed glues into the first Post-It prototypes. Google's policy of giving staff one day a week off to work on their own projects is based on the same philosophy. Freeing the mind, or decoupling from the pursuit of greater efficiency, helps in entering an unthinking zone where new ways of doing emerge. However, a good deal of management practice appears to increasingly demand a focus on accounting for every minute or associating this with immediately productive work. Much creative work occurs outside the office, in the pub or in the bath; one successful games developer claims that he gets his best ideas by going out bowling.

As we will see later, focus and a loosening slack both have a part to play in creative processes. But strategic management's emphasis on efficiency, especially the efficient use of time, takes us too far in one direction by closing down creative possibilities too quickly. 'Slack time', despite appearing inefficient, allows us to make the unexpected connections which lie at the heart of creative strategy.

6. Creativity Correlates Strongly with an Expectation that one Should be Creative . . .

. . . and the 'suits' who do strategy are generally perceived to be the opposite of the 'creatives' who do creativity.

If there is some truth to the view 'that we become what we imagine ourselves to be' (to quote Vonnegut again), and by definition we do not become what we do not imagine ourselves to be, then there is a further convention that limits the development of creative strategy. This is that 'the management' (and by association strategic management) has for so long been seen as the opposite of 'the creatives'. Just as strategists were traditionally separated from operational staff by the colour of the collars (white collar versus blue collar), the creative's uniform features an even starker contrast. The 'creative class' is now often referred to as 'black collar' or 'no collar'.

In a survey of cultural entrepreneurs in Vienna, Erich Poettschacher notes that the self-perception of being creative is allied to the cultural entrepreneur's feeling that they are different from traditional organizations – not just 'business as usual' – even if their differences are more perceived than real. Whereas many business consultants, along with Freud (who roots the creative impulse in childhood play, arguing that artists have simply failed to repress these childhood urges in adult life), might consider such self-perception as an infantile failure to adjust to the new (commercial) reality, for Poettschacher however, this self-perception is the key to their creative drive. Indeed, self-perception or self-belief has been identified by Abraham Maslow, Teresa Amabile and Albert Bandura as fundamental to the intrinsic motivation possessed by creative individuals. Bandura argues that 'self-efficacy beliefs' are developed back in formative childhood experiences. Amabile presents a similar argument, but suggests that this inner drive can also be undermined by external interventions, notably the wrong type of encouragement or the imposition of inappropriate incentives and targets. A composer of our acquaintance claims that his career started to take off when he described himself as a 'composer' in his passport; as with Poettschacher's Viennese cultural entrepreneurs, even if the claim is impossible to prove, in terms of motivation, perseverance and drive, the self-perception of creativity was enough.

In the last decade or so when creativity has come to be seen as having strategic value, managers have mimicked the style of creativity (the no-collar workplace, the celebration of charismatic individual 'genius'), but still presented creative processes and people as something extraneous and exotic. By viewing creativity as something done by other people, strategic managers have undermined self-belief in their own creative abilities and kept creative thinking at arm's length from core strategic processes. Consequently, the self-perception of 'uncreative management', mirrored in the stereotype of 'unmanageable/spontaneous creativity', has become a self-fulfilling expectation.

A few years ago we were running a training workshop for managers on the theme of 'creative management' and the organizers warned us to avoid the word 'creativity' as this might alienate the participants. Training in 'creative' thinking skills may likewise do more harm than good, convincing managers of their inadequacies as artists or performers rather than revealing their inner creative drive.

Having worked for some time with other incentives and targets, strategic management tends to assume that creative thinking is something done by artists and not by managers. Starting with a different set of expectations would, we argue, lead to more creative strategies. A 'creative strategy' might begin from a recognition of the creative elements within strategy and within our own experiences.

7. Imagery is More Likely to Stimulate Creative Thinking than Language on Its Own . . .

. . . and corporate strategies are generally expressed in large tracts of text, thirty or forty page long reports.

We have known for some time, thanks to educational scholars such as Jerome Piaget and Jerome Bruner, that effective learning is more likely to be achieved if threefold stimulus is utilized: if *concrete* learning by physically doing is combined with *pictorial* examples and combined with written *textual* expressions. Management in general, and strategies in particular, are often represented in text (how many have felt their heart sink with the thud of a lengthy strategy plan being dropped on their desk! There is an acronym to describe what becomes of these tomes: SPOTS, Strategic

Plan on Top Shelf). Companies may also sometimes encourage 'operatives' to learn a strategy by doing it, but they are not so good at showing a strategy in images or pictures.

Pictures, as opposed to the other two modes of conveying knowledge, are easier to conceptualize than concrete doing and easier to manipulate, 'play around with' or adapt than a text document. Just think of how much more motivated you are to step up to a whiteboard and re-draw something than you are motivated to substantially edit a large document.

In the words of Aristotle: 'It is impossible to even think without a mental picture.' Or as Einstein, who recognized that his great ideas only sparked interest when they were 'geometrized', put it: 'If I can't picture it, I can't understand it.' Strategy would be more understandable, more involving, more dynamic, more bisociative, and more *creative*, if it spoke in pictures. (We offer suggestions in this regard further on in the book.)

8. Creativity is Often Spurred on by a Competitive Tension . . .

. . . but one of the objectives of strategic management in the past has been to unify an organization, either through shared plans or a 'strong' (i.e., unitary) corporate culture.

Probably the biggest (or at least longest lasting) buzz-word in management over the past twenty-five years has been 'culture'. In 1972, Blake and Mouton's groundbreaking study of organizational cultures differentiated between sound cultures that 'stimulated efforts to produce' and unsound cultures where 'beliefs and values bear little relationship to productive achievement or profit seeking'. Indeed, it has been argued that the fervour with which researchers attempted to understand organizational culture may be linked to the belief that certain forms of ideal culture correlated with effectiveness or efficiency.

Building upon Blake and Mouton's findings is a long list of research that has correspondingly shown that 'good cultures' were those that were 'cohesive and tight-knit', 'congruent', 'integrated', 'aligned', 'stable' or having a high degree of commonality. These cultures were described using synonyms such as 'strong', 'sound', 'powerful' or 'positive'. Relatedly 'unsound', 'weak' or 'negative' organizational cultures were those composed of pluralities, disparate differences and clashing sub-cultures. But, as we have seen, these are precisely the characteristics likely to promote creativity. Indeed, according to studies of creative cities, a creative culture appears linked to its capacity to tolerate opposing values and beliefs rather than its capacity to integrate or reconcile them. In places like Manchester, Paris, Hong Kong, Wellington, Cape Town, Jamaica, New York or London, creative activity flows from disparate sub-cultures, not a unified ethos, culture or brand. Business leaders have been slow to acknowledge the importance of cultural diversity and have tended to see it as a problem to be solved rather than a resource to be developed.

Strategic management has identified strategy as part of a process of developing a 'strong' or unified, corporate culture and mission. A creative strategy would require a more open and diverse organizational culture which juxtaposes different ideas and values rather than attempting to reconcile them.

9. Strategy is Often Associated with Heroic Leadership by Individuals . . .

. . . and our understanding of creativity has moved beyond individual genius.

While our first reason why strategy is often not creative emphasized the importance of maverick individuals (with particular reference to Alex Issigonis), it would be wrong to take from this that creativity is the exclusive domain of the heroic genius leading from the front. As James Dyson, admits, while 'some people think designers have Eureka moments where they come up with a brilliant idea and the rest is easy. . . the reality is far less glamorous; it's the step by step process of testing your ideas, making mistakes, learning from them and starting again'. And this, generally, requires a team. Or, to be bisociative again, an individual *and* a team.

But scan the business bookshelves and you will only see the strategy heroes: the Iacocca's, Welch's, and Branson's who have long since made it. You will not so easily find the stories of the 'backroom boys and girls' that make up the teams that combine their talents to create.

Take, for example, the emphasis placed on Michael Schumacher even in the business press. Schumacher left the Benetton Formula 1 racing team, which he had helped to unprecedented successes, to join the world's most powerful team Ferrari in 1996. Many thought the world's best driver combined with the richest team would be invincible, but it was not to be. In 1996 Schumacher only recorded three wins and the team finished second behind Williams. The next year the story was much the same: Williams first, Ferrari second. But something very important happened at the end of that season. Ferrari lured technical director Ross Brawn and chief designer Rory Byrne from Benetton. The old Benetton creative team was reunited. It took some time for the Brawn-Byrne-Schumacher team to bed in to the Ferrari community, and while 1998 was encouraging, Ferrari still finished second. But in 1999 things began to click. Ferrari went on to win every Formula 1 championship from 1999 to 2005, and by increasingly grand margins. Listen to Schumacher being interviewed and there is no doubt as to where the credit should be placed with regard to productive creative strategy: he will always credit the team, the relationships, the innate combinations, the camaraderie, the instinctive knowing what each other needs and what must be done to create the best set-up.

Heroic leadership is another example of strategic management's tendency to adopt the style of creativity rather than its underlying substance. As we discussed in Chapter 2, cognitive and sociological theories of creativity have moved us away from the myth of the individual creative genius. According to Keith Sawyer, since the 1990s the dominant paradigm for understanding creativity has been a sociocultural model based on teams and networks, not individuals. Strategic management's tendency to focus on just the hero may be yet another reason why creativity and strategy do not gel as well they might.

10. Strategic Management, Like Management in General, has been More Enamoured with Innovation as Opposed to Creativity . . .

. . . and, as we have seen, they are not the same thing.

Creativity may incorporate novelty, but it is not the same as innovation: innovation emphasizes the new (remember it has as its root the Latin *nova*); creativity emphasizes substantive change. New approaches to strategy are thus not necessarily creative approaches.

Strategic management appears to be fatally attracted to new ideas and fashions. It has been argued elsewhere that the field of management's obsession with the new has hindered its ability to make substantial creative advances. The quest for the latest new approach and the assumption that management as a field is always improving upon the past has left the field and its students with little interest in its history (in stark contrast to thinkers in other fields like medicine, architecture and philosophy). As discussed in the book *Recreating Strategy*, the most popular 'new' theoretical framework for thinking about strategy at the end of the 20th century – Business Process Re-engineering – was remarkably similar to F.W. Taylor's principles of 'scientific management' at the century's beginning. But most of the users and advocates of BPR had little or no knowledge of its history – the perception that this represented a 'new' approach reinforced its popularity.

A key to creativity can be to take commonly used ideas and recombine them in elegant new ways. The emphasis on the novel and quick change in management often distracts us from realizing that substantive change often requires a good look around (rather than just a look ahead) at all that we have at our disposal. As Paul Feyerabend explains: 'The first step on the way to a new cosmology [is often] a step back: apparently relevant evidence is pushed aside, new data are brought in by ad hoc connections, the empirical content of science is drastically reduced.' And only then may minor incremental development be replaced by leaps. Some of our most innovative musicians and performers, from the Beatles to Bowie and Madonna, have reinvented themselves by raiding their own back catalogues; a new idea, image or identity results from a twisted reflection of the past.

A recent study in the journal *Science*, titled 'Electronic Publication and the Narrowing of Science and Scholarship', offered proof that the increasing use of electronic data mining was narrowing (homogenizing) the range of referencing (by leading people into similar pathways or tracks of papers) and that this was becoming detrimental to creative thinking. Similarly, a recent study of a database of 2400 strategy papers written on strategy over the past forty years found that many approaches considered as 'new' (ethics, for example), were well covered decades ago, and that thinking might advance more quickly if it were to take the time to rummage, with an open mind, in the archives a little.

Creative strategy is as likely to result from an awareness of our history as an enthusiasm for new ideas. Strategic management has a tendency to ignore its own history, focussing on the recipes and rhetoric of the latest best practice.

If any of these ten failings strike a chord, you may want to use the summary table below – a reminder of 'the ten habits of highly uncreative strategizers' – as a checklist of assumptions to avoid when seeking to develop creative strategy in your organization.

10 REASONS WHY STRATEGY HAS NOT BEEN PARTICULARLY CREATIVE

- *Creativity can't be planned directly...*
  ... and strategic management has generally been associated with planning.
- *Creativity requires bisociation which can be thwarted by either/or classification...*
  ... and strategy has spent a lot of time classifying itself and separating itself.
- *Creativity requires plurality...*
  ... and those in strategic management roles have traditionally been of one type.
- *Creativity requires mistakes and accidents, or at least an acceptance of their value...*
  ... strategic management has become highly failure averse.
- *Creativity requires slack...*
  ... and increasing efficiency became a fundamental principle in management.
- *Creativity correlates strongly with an expectation that one should be creative...*
  ...and the strategy 'suits' are perceived to be the opposite of the 'creatives'.
- *Imagery is more likely to stimulate creative thinking than language on its own...*
  ...and corporate strategies are generally expressed in large tracts of text.
- *Creativity is often spurred on by a competitive tension...*
  ...but one of the objectives of strategy has been to unify an organization.
- *Strategy is often associated with leadership and heroic individuals...*
  ...while creativity research has moved beyond the 'myth of individual genius'.
- *Strategy has been more enamoured with innovation as opposed to creativity...*
  ...and they are not the same thing.

In this chapter we have highlighted some of the blindspots which have prevented a more creative approach to strategy in the past. Many of these pitfalls are associated with an approach to 'strategic management' as a narrowly defined, specialized and self-contained discipline, which is intolerant of external perspectives and ideas. Given these constraints on strategy's ability to be associated with creativity in the past, the first step toward a more creative future might be a broader view of what strategy is or what it can be – the subject of our next chapter.

CHAPTER 4

A More Creative View of Strategy

S trategic management and theories of strategy have evolved, and the conventions that were criticized in relation to creativity in Chapter 3 have been, and are being, challenged. We can begin to address some of the limitations highlighted in the previous chapter by building on emerging perspectives on strategy. In this way Chapter 4 presents a broader view of strategy, based on three levels of definition:

1. the *content* of strategy, or what strategy is about;
2. the *processes* by which this broader notion of strategy is formed;
3. a focus on what strategy is aiming toward (or its *outcomes*, to borrow the language used to define creativity in Chapter 2).

Using a definitional model similar to the content-process-outcome framework of creativity in Chapter 2 will allow us to develop an integrative and bisociative view of strategy. It will also help us to explore the relationship between creativity and strategy, as we build toward a working definition of 'creative strategy' in the next chapter.

Strategy's Content: Plans, Patterns, Positions, Ploys, Perspectives

Our view of what strategy can be has been expanded in many ways over the past two decades. Perhaps the best framework for thinking beyond strategy as being just about planning is also the earliest: Henry Mintzberg's 'Five P's for strategy'. Here strategy can contain the following five elements (or, indeed, a combination of them):

Plans – consciously intended guidelines or sets of guidelines determined in advance of action.

Patterns – consistent streams of action over time that define a course. For example, if over time a series of actions by key players to reduce costs become a part of an organization's culture, then it can be said that the organization has a low-cost strategy. In this way, strategies can be seen to emerge over time rather than be planned or intended.

Positions – here strategy is about matching organizational capabilities and aspirations to a particular part of the market environment, or niche. By concentrating its efforts over time the organization should become better adapted to the environment that it has specifically placed itself in than its competitors.

Ploys – a strategy can be as much about what the competition thinks a company might or could do than what it actually does. This emphasizes the fact that organizations do not, generally, exist in a vacuum; they are jostling with other organizations; and it emphasizes that organization are human: competitive, dynamic, clever and inventive. One only needs to look at the way companies react to news that a potentially valuable acquisition is on the horizon. Often firms will act as if they are interested in buying such a company when they are not really interested, or they may feign indifference when they have every intention of making a bid: just to keep others on their toes. In the same way film companies will often option a book, even if they have no intention of filming it, simply to pre-empt a competing project.

Perspectives – here strategy is about a company's way of looking at the world, or more particularly business opportunities or the market. Apple's view of blending design and technology is a perspective, as is Ryanair's or SouthWestern's view of how air travel should be. Similarly, characters like Richard Branson and Anita Roddick, or Phil Knight's celebration of the spirit of Steve Prefontaine, or Jack Welch (and subsequently Jeff Immelt), embodied a vision that others in their organization followed. Thus the strategies (plans, positions, ploys, and patterns) of Virgin, Body Shop, Nike or General Electric were led by these characters and their perspective on life.

A more flexible or wide-ranging view of strategy as about a *combination* of elements and the interplay between them helps get us beyond some of the limitations to strategy being creative, outlined in the previous chapter. But our view of strategy can be broader still, by considering not just a plurality in thinking through *what* strategy is; but by going on to consider a plurality with regard to *how* strategy develops.

The Process of Strategizing: Designing, Planning, Positioning, Learning, Emerging, Entrepreneuring, and so on

Another expansion in our view of strategic management has come from those who have recognized that the content of a strategy can be better understood if we understand the process that has led to its formation. In Europe, Andrew Pettigrew has been at the forefront of this movement. In America, Henry Mintzberg has greatly advanced understanding in this regard. And his book, *The Strategy Safari*, may be the best exploration of the many types of strategy processes.

Mintzberg's safari begins with the well-known tale of six blind men each holding a different part of an elephant and arguing that they each have a quite different beast. Mintzberg and his co-authors argue that strategy has become a lot like that elephant. And like the blind men at the start of our book, competing theories of strategy have grappled in the darkness rather than working together towards a bigger picture. Since Mintzberg and others had broadened out the view of what constitutes a strategy from the late 1980s and 1990s, the field had been characterized by heated debates about whether strategy was about planning or emergence, design or opportunism, and so on. The introduction to *Strategy Safari* puts this to rest by arguing that it is not an either/or debate. Strategy (or strategizing to make the term a verb) is a multifaceted beast, like the elephant, and we are mistaken to take just one part and assume it to be a single essence.

HENRY MINTZBERG'S STRATEGY PROCESS SCHOOLS

The **Design School** sees strategizing as the result of senior managers using conscious rational analysis to design a fit between organizational strengths and weaknesses and environmental opportunities and threats.

The **Planning School** reflects most of the design school view except that strategizing is decomposable into distinct steps delineated by checklists and supporting frameworks like the Value-chain or the 5-Forces of Industry.

The **Positioning School** views strategy as a process of selection from generic options or frameworks (e.g., The Generic Strategy Matrix) based on the formalized analysis of the specific industry and market situation.

The **Environmental or Impositional School** concentrates on the environment's influence in steering firms toward or mitigating strategic options. Unlike the first three schools, senior managers are seen here to have far less agency and control over strategic decisions. They are 'imposed' upon by the 'movers and shakers' or 'industry dynamics'.

(Continued)

(*Continued*)

The **Cognitive School** is concerned with understanding the mental processes of the strategist that lead to particular strategic decisions. Kenechi Ohmae's *The Mind of the Strategist* is written in this vein.

The **Learning School** views the strategy development process as emerging incrementally over time through trial, error and learning. Strategists and other influences on strategy can be found throughout the organization, great attention is paid to environmental shifts and questioning present assumptions.

The **Cultural** or **Ideological School** concentrates on the influence of culture in promoting particular strategic choices.

The **Consensus School** is similar in nature to the cultural school. However, unlike the cultural school where consensus is established around a common belief system, the consensus school views strategy as emerging from the mutual adjustment of a company's key stakeholders as they learn from each other to establish a common strategic perspective.

The **Power School** sees strategizing as influenced by *micro-power* (which suggests that the strategy process is entirely political, involving bargaining, persuasion and confrontation between various interested parties) and *macro-power* (which relates to the power dynamics that exist between the whole firm and its strategic partners and other networks).

The **Entrepreneurial School** represents a move away from precise designs or plans, towards looser notions such as 'visions' and 'perspectives' – typically articulated through metaphorical statements or a 'sense of mission' embodied by the CEO or Senior Management.

The **Process School** sees the strategic role of senior managers as defining and controlling the processes by which strategy is developed. The determination of actual strategies is left to others at lower levels.

The **Configuration School** views organizations as coherent but time-varying 'states' or clusters of resources, characteristics and behaviours. The strategic development process then becomes one of defining a desired end state (configuration) relative to the current state, and mapping out a series of steps to move from one to the other. The configuration school can be seen to draw upon many of the other schools.

Strategy Safari then goes on to explore the many types of strategy processes out there in 'the jungle'. Unlike Mintzberg's earlier work, which highlighted five content focussed Ps, what was found amounted to thirteen 'schools of thought' with regard to strategic management relating to the processes by which strategy is made. The *design school* believes that strategy comes from a conscious rational process of design; the *cognitive school* sees the most important processes occurring in the minds of corporate leaders; the *learning school* focusses on strategy as an incremental process of trial, error and subsequent learning, and so on (the full gamut is summarized in the box above).

Obviously, *how* strategy is developed will influence *what* sort of strategy stems from that production process. But of more importance to our discussion here is the possibility that an expansive acceptance of multiple perspectives on the strategy process will encourage the sort of bisociative interplay and debate critical to creativity.

The Outcomes of Becoming Strategized: Orientation, Animation, Integration

If we bring back the diagram we worked toward in Chapter 2, we can begin to align this broader view of strategy with our working definition of creativity. But in order to fill the missing section, strategy's *outcomes*, we must reconsider current definitions of strategy as process.

Whereas strategy used to be about making plans to achieve future goals, it has come to be more about setting up processes in advance of decisions. Beyond Mintzberg and others' delineation of a number of schools of strategy has come the view that there may be as many strategy processes as there are organizations. The shift toward looking at strategizing processes rather than the content of a strategy has produced some interesting results. One is that writing on strategy has increasingly gravitated toward musing on what happens prior to what we might call 'the point of decision': things like winning cultures, organizational structures, and best practices, the things that lead toward good plans, positions and so on. A second consequence has been that we now have a much broader view of what might be considered strategic and an appreciation of how organizations may do strategy differently. However, there are two potentially negative effects. Firstly, it has become increasingly difficult to differentiate strategy from anything else, or to know what we are talking about when we talk about strategy: if everything happening in an organization is strategic, then maybe nothing is. Secondly, we have taken our eyes off the future. This is not to say that strategy should just be about decisions in the present for the future, but recent studies have shown that the neglect of the future may be just as detrimental to an organization as a neglect of strategy process.

But we believe that we can address these negative consequences, and at the same time usefully fill the *outcomes* box for strategy in the diagram above. While we could say that strategy outcomes are as many and varied as organizations are, this may not help us toward a definition of what

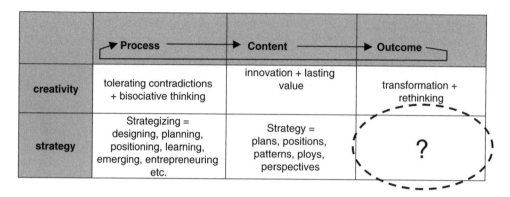

Figure 4.1 The beginnings of a definitional framework for strategy

is strategic and what isn't. A better response may be to retain an open-minded view of strategy process while also focussing on developing generic outcomes that all good strategies can be seen to lead toward; or develop, in other words, a 'teleological' view of strategic management.

Teleology is the idea that individuals and objects can be defined in terms of the purposes they characteristically have within them, at core, or the outcomes they are expected to fulfil. Perhaps the best known proponent of teleology was Aristotle but it was a mainstream view in pre-modern times. On this view, for example, the object of a knife cannot be defined independently of the concept of a good knife, a concept that can only have meaning by thinking of an associated general future outcome: a 'good cut'. Because we understand that, generically speaking, the purpose of a knife is to cut things we can draw the general (but not universal) conclusion that a sharp knife is a good knife.

What we need for a teleological understanding of strategic management to be helpful is to identify some general purposes shared by (almost) all strategies. We suggest three general purposes or positive future outcomes of any strategy. The first two borrow from Karl Weick who argues that greater *orientation* and greater *animation* are two manifestations that may be more useful focal points for thinking about what is important in strategy rather than focussing only on contents or processes. Orientation may be defined as the direction or focus of interest and resources. Animation may be defined as the motivation, vigour and activity toward a particular orientation.

To these two general outcomes of good strategy, we may add a third: that good strategies, generally speaking, lead toward greater integration. In some ways this is an old idea, it connects to an earlier, but much neglected, view that strategy is about the decisions that require input from many of the functional areas of a business, and/or 'join' or coordinate many such areas, which we described in Chapter 1. Adding integration to orientation and animation as our generic outcomes of strategy also helps mitigate against an overbalance of either orientation or animation. We have probably all witnessed these organizations: one that becomes stagnant as an overly heavy emphasis on orientation leads to thick planning documents that wear down animation; or another whereby a frenzy of animation overwhelms any orientation as an organization's employees or departments head every which way. A focus on effective integration is often necessary to guard against excess.

Three generic outcomes of a good strategy might then be greater orientation, greater animation, and more effective integration. The things that contribute to these outcomes in an organization (and they may be different from organization to organization: for some a brand may integrate and animate, for others a particular performance measure or design philosophy may orient and animate) may be defined as strategic.

The figure below illustrates how an organization might become strategized by moving toward the outcomes of greater orientation, animation and integration of effort. An event (X) may spark off some animation in a group (it might be an encounter with a customer, a competitor's move, a new employee, a change in the industry environment, etc.); their interactions (through research, communication, planning, etc.) lead to a greater sense of orientation; which creates greater animation and integration of effort; which leads to clearer orientation, and so on. This is not so much about having a *strategy* in the present or *strategizing* over time but about aiming toward the outcomes of *becoming strategized*; or about developing and maintaining progress toward generic outcomes like greater animation, orientation and integration, which are at once achievable and constantly moving as the environment moves.

Hence, elements beyond those that relate to traditional strategy contents can easily be incorporated into this view of what is strategic, depending on the particular organization in focus. At the same time, not every customer interaction need be considered strategic, only those interactions, patterns, plans, or whatever, that will likely impact on the orientation of an organization and animate individuals to act beyond present circumstances and integrate two or more parts or aspects of an organization.

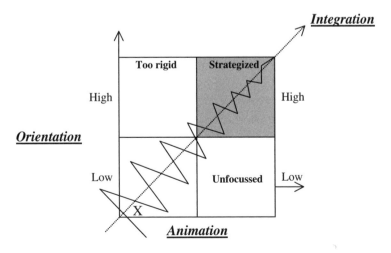

Figure 4.2 Orientation, animation and integration as the outcomes of strategy

Having developed an expanded view of strategic management, incorporating content, process and outcomes, we are now in a position to define it in a similar setting to our definition of creativity. This is shown in the figure below. What remains to be done is to bring creativity and strategy together to form a view of creative strategy.

	Process ➔	Content ➔	Outcome
creativity	tolerating contradictions + bisociative thinking	innovation + lasting value	transformation + rethinking
strategy	strategizing = designing, planning, positioning, learning, emerging, entrepreneuring etc.	strategy = plans, positions, patterns, ploys, perspectives	becoming strategized = moving toward greater orientation, animation, integration

Figure 4.3   A definitional framework of strategy

CHAPTER 5

Creating and Discovering a Creative Strategy Process

We began *Creative Strategy* by describing how strategy and creativity, despite being logical bedfellows, have never really fully engaged: they are hampered by five false separations and fully appreciating creative strategy requires joining five paradoxes. Chapter 2 then developed a rounded definition of creativity, before Chapter 3 examined ten reasons why strategic management may not have engaged with creativity to the extent that it should have. Subsequently, Chapter 4 updated a view of strategy in order that it might be fruitfully combined with our understanding of creativity.

Placing together the two systemic definitions, of creativity and strategy from previous chapters, enables us to define the content of creative strategy and its likely outcomes (see the figure overleaf) without too much trouble. The contents and outcomes columns that emerge here are relatively uncontentious. Numerous academic commentators, management gurus and practising managers agree on the need for radical, innovative strategies which transform markets, change the rules of competition and redefine businesses. What is less clear is an understanding of how the content and outcomes of creative strategies are formed – or *what might be the process of creative strategy formation*. Attempting to fill this gap in our understanding provides the impetus for this book.

	Process	Content	Outcome
creativity	tolerating contradictions + bisociative thinking	innovation + lasting value	transformation + rethinking
strategy	designing, positioning, learning, emerging, entrepreneuring etc.	plans, positions, patterns, ploys	orientation + animation + integration
creative strategy	?	innovative plans, positions, patterns, perspectives and ploys that add value	orientation + animation + integration that results in transformation and rethinking within an organization and beyond

Figure 5.1   The beginnings of a definitional framework for creative strategy

To simply combine the relevant rows and say that the process of how creative strategy might be produced involves tolerating contradictory strategy processes and bisociation would be rather vague and somewhat uninspiring. While this might be a start toward developing an awareness of the creative strategy process, it is hard to know what one should do toward it in practical terms.

Rather than just simply working down the process column, adding the boxes to fill in the 'missing link', we concluded that we should instead do two more substantial things in concert. Over the past four years we have simultaneously put a great deal into thinking backwards from creative strategy's outcomes and contents in order to *create* a working definition of creative strategy. And, at the same time, we have set out to *discover* how creative organizations do what they do, and by creative organizations we don't just mean organizations from the so called creative industries, but a whole spectrum of organizations that successfully create things that people value, from baseball clubs to Bollywood; from fashion houses to flower auctions to frozen foods; from Ford to *My Big Fat Greek Wedding*, from Alessi to Amazon to Apple, from Tata to Radiohead.

Innovation is required, as is added value; as is a new, or renewed, orientation, animation and integration that transforms an organization and its markets. But what has emerged from our investigations is a slightly more complex 'helix'. The achievement of creative strategy or becoming strategized in a way that embraces creativity, appears to require a process with four key inter-relating elements: an innovative element; an entrepreneurial element; a leadership element; and an organizational element. And we have found that each of these elements, in keeping with our process definition of creativity, requires bisociation, or the integration of paradoxically passive and active approaches which may be described as four distinctive bisociative characters. Hence:

1. The innovative element requires the character of a *creative discoverer*
2. The entrepreneurial element requires the character of a *diligent dilettante*
3. The leadership element requires the character of an *envisioning actor*
4. The organization element requires the character of a *focussed freer*

The interrelationships between these elements and their bisociative characteristics can be better understood by mapping them on to a matrix with regard to their lightness and heaviness of 'touch', combined with whether they tend toward an internal looking or external facing 'locus'. This reveals a figure eight, or 'creative strategy helix', whereby the creative strategy process begins with innovation as the combination of dexterous and introspective discovery and active attempts to create by thinking broadly and combining ideas; moves to an entrepreneurial realm where a flitting and free-ranging dilettantism interacts with a hard-nosed diligence when an idea and a corresponding market potential is seized upon; develops into a leadership focus that is partly about envisioning desired futures and partly about leading by doing or active interaction; and then into an organizational context where creative strategy can be maintained and sustained through both focussing minds and letting them loose.

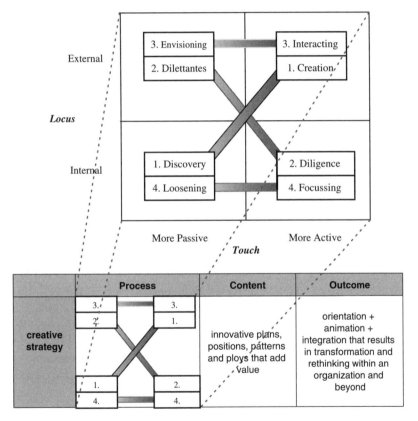

Figure 5.2   A definitional framework for creative strategy (incorporating the creative strategy helix)

This helix is our best approximation of what an effective creative strategy process looks like. Subsequently, we would place it in the empty box from the previous table, as shown in Figure 5.2, fleshing out our definition of creative strategy. The remainder of this book is arranged according to the form of the creative strategy helix and is summarized in the paragraphs that follow.

In Part I of *Creative Strategy*, we explore the nature of the *innovative* element of creative strategy. Being oriented and animated to develop the new requires a combination of single-minded observation and contemplation toward *discovering* what may have always been the case but which had not hitherto been revealed; *and* an active bouncing around with other people and ideas to absorb and combine influences in order to *create* the new. We investigate why strategic innovation is at the heart of creative strategy and why it generally involves a combined emphasis on both discovery and creation – or 'creative discovery'. We identify six different degrees of strategic innovation, illustrate these with examples from what might be described as creative and 'normal' industries, and outline a framework for aiding the discovery and creation of these six degrees. We then develop an 'innovation generation matrix' that can aid the discovery or creation of innovative approaches to lift thinking and action beyond what are considered to be current best practices.

In Part II we investigate the *entrepreneurial* element of creative strategy. We describe how taking innovations out into the market in order to extract value, change the market and maybe even the world requires a combination of a *dilettantic* travelling, playing and light-hearted dabbling in search of the interesting and new and a *diligent* attention to detail and perseverance when something interesting and marketable is hit upon. We highlight five general phases or 'angles' of this bisociative entrepreneurialism and outline ways you can develop your ability along these lines in your endeavours. Then we examine three entrepreneurial journeys: one about a British author bringing new forms of writing to a wider market, one about taking New Zealand fashion labels to the world, and one about games designers marrying up technological expertise with imaginative play.

The *leadership* element of creative strategy is addressed in Part III. Here we describe how being able to integrate the forces and resources necessary to achieve the innovator and entrepreneur's potential requires a combination of being able to *envision*, or picture, a desirable future in a way that orients, animates and integrates others; and an ability to lead through taking action and interacting with others, by enacting, in other words, the behaviour that will lead toward the achievement of what has been envisioned. Despite widespread debates about whether leaders are born or made, we find that this kind of leader is neither born nor made: creative leaders *mature*. Despite the myth of genius (described earlier in relation to creativity, but often associated with leadership too) we find that the characteristics that appear to underlie this biosociative approach, characteristics such as humility, sincerity, frankness and patience, are qualities that all people have the potential to embody, particularly as they mature (which may happen at a young or an advanced age). We describe this creative strategy of leadership as 'leading from the middle', having the ability to move to, to draw upon, and to inspire involvement from all levels of an organization and beyond. And we develop a framework, or 'leadership keypad', to help you consider how best to conceptualize and perform this sort of leadership.

Part IV then brings creative strategy full circle toward examining how structures can be developed or put in place to ensure that the innovation that began the creative strategy process is built upon or developed anew. This is the *organizational* element of creative strategy. Creating the environment within which the forces and resources required to pursue and achieve creativity, and maximize the value from this creativity, requires, once again, a bisociation of seemingly paradoxical forces. An intensity and *focus* that keeps current projects on the boil (without boiling over); *and* some cutting of slack or *loosening* of reins, clearing out the space, in the organization or in individuals' minds, for new innovations to bubble up. We consider how this combination of looseness and focus can be embodied, developing an approach whereby the seven organizational 'virtues' associated with creative strategy are each seen to exist between two 'vices', and how one might seek to steer between them.

The key processes behind creative strategy, as the remainder of this book will demonstrate, require keeping an organization actively interacting across the four bisociative filament strips that constitute the creative strategy helix described above; to keep, as it were, the whole figure 'lit up and humming'. The examples that we have chosen to illustrate this process and the elements within it are suitably diverse, in keeping with our finding that organizations in what were once perceived as 'creative' and 'non-creative' industries are actually far more similar than different, and that, in any case creativity stems from a broad and bisociative view. Sometimes themes have emerged. Part I on innovation blends examples from conventional businesses with those from music, film and television. Part II on entrepreneurship combines the conventional with a focus on writing and publishing. Part III on leadership adds sporting organizations and military practice. Part IV, on organization, which draws the elements together, uses examples from all of these contexts.

To connect together the different parts of this book, we have developed a capstone (or, we should say, 'keystone') case that follows the Royal Shakespeare Company (RSC) – an organization that spans and transgresses the traditional distinctions between the creative and the commercial. The case, and its relationship to the book, are introduced below; subsequent episodes or 'acts' follow at the end of each part of the book. By looking at how innovative ideas, entrepreneurial attitudes, leadership qualities and organizational systems evolve in the RSC, we illustrate how the four elements of creative strategy run together as a continuous relay. The first leg in this relay is innovation, generating the ideas which feed through the rest of the Creative Strategy Helix. This will be the subject of Part I.

THE ROYAL SHAKESPEARE COMPANY PROLOGUE

In writing this book we wanted to include a single case study to show how the different aspects of creative strategy connect together. In each subsequent section of this book we will consider how the Royal Shakespeare Company enacts innovative ideas, entrepreneurial attitudes, leadership positions and organizational virtues, and how these feed off each other both in the rehearsal room and the boardroom.

The case study derives principally from our observations of the company in rehearsal for a production of *Richard III* in late 2006, supplemented by interviews with Michael Boyd and Vikki Heywood in 2009 and observations and interviews from other theatre directors. The remainder of the case is presented in four sections or 'acts', each relating to a different aspect of creative strategy. These acts are located at the end of each part of the book. In this prologue section we will briefly introduce the case and its relationship to creativity and to strategy.

In June 2008, the Artistic Director of the Royal Shakespeare Company, Michael Boyd, outlined his approach to ensemble theatre in a speech at New York Public Library. In his speech Boyd commented on the values which informed a cooperative, collective approach to theatre (summarized in the box below). This approach had been applied both to the practical task of uniting a diverse group of actors over an extended rehearsal period working on several projects at once, and more broadly to the business of running the RSC (Royal Shakespeare Company) as a complex, multi-divisional organization. Creative thinking and strategic thinking would share a common vocabulary and a common set of values.

The values and behaviours of ensemble according to Michael Boyd:

- Cooperation: the intense, unobstructed traffic between artists at play and the surrender of self to a connection with others, even while making demands on ourselves.
- Altruism: the moral imagination and the social perception to realize that the whole is greater than the sum of its parts. The stronger help the weaker, rather than choreographing the weak to make the strong look good.
- Trust: the ability to be appallingly honest and to experiment without fear.
- Empathy: caring for others with a forensic curiosity that constantly seeks new ways of being together and creating together.
- Imagination: keeping ideas in the mind long enough to allow them to emerge from the alchemy of the imagination and not the factory of the will.

(Continued)

- Compassion: engaging with the world and each other, knowing there may be mutual pain in doing so.
- Tolerance: accommodating differences and allowing mistakes.
- Forgiveness: allowing and recovering from big and potentially damaging mistakes.
- Humility: the expert who has nothing to learn has no need for creativity, because the answer is already known.
- Magnanimity: the courage to give away ideas and love, with no thought of transaction or an exchange in return.
- Rapport: the magic language between individuals in tune with each other.
- Patience: this is only really possible over years. Art can be forced like rhubarb, but it tends to bend in the wind.
- Rigour: dancers and musician take life-long daily training for granted, and theatre could do with catching up.

Source: The Stage, 2 April 2009.

Boyd's approach to theatre reinforces the connections we outlined in this chapter. The ensemble approach relates initially to the process of theatre making but also to the audience and the wider community. Boyd describes theatre as a collective embrace between actors and audience, and sees the collective experience and sense of connection between them as essential to the vitality and humanity of good theatre. But Boyd extends this idea of connection to community and educational work beyond the performances, even to the 'community-minded architecture' of the new building. Above all he and the RSC's Executive Director, Vikki Heywood, have applied ensemble principles to the organizational culture of the RSC and to managerial tasks such as recruitment, financial management and strategic planning.

Arts organizations are often divided between 'creatives' and 'suits'. This division is exacerbated by the project-based and specialized nature of creative work which encourages a narrow focus on the immediate and the personal. 'Ensemble' was a way of breaking down barriers and rebuilding connections between the acting company and the other departments of the RSC, couched in an imaginative language that would not alienate the workforce with bureaucratic 'management-speak'.

The ensemble approach fits our definition of a creative approach to strategy in its *content* as something new and valuable. Artistically the idea of working with the same group of actors for a 30-month rehearsal period is novel, particularly in the UK. This novelty rests on a connection between familiar ideas in unfamiliar contexts. Boyd had worked in Russia and Eastern Europe, where ensemble theatre had been developed first by Stanislavski in Moscow, and then by Brecht with the Berliner Ensemble. Ensemble was also part of the RSC's history, under the earlier leadership of Peter Hall. Applying these methods to a 21st century British theatre scene increasingly dependent on star casting, short rehearsal periods and rapid turnover of quick-fire projects was highly unusual. Extending that artistic method into organizational structure and strategy took this connection further and turned what we have referred to as 'mere novelty' into an 'original' or radical innovation with far-reaching consequences. (We will say more about the difference between the 'new' and the 'original' in the next chapter.)

The RSC ensemble meets our second criterion of creative content by being valuable as well as new. Whilst Boyd and Heywood are reluctant to be drawn into a purely financial evaluation of their methods, Heywood notes that ensemble accounting – delegating budgetary control to departments (rather than to a centralized financial directorate) – yielded savings of £1 million over a 12-month period. Beyond financial returns, the success of the ensemble as an organizational strategy can be measured in the engagement and commitment of the workforce – a recent survey of staff attitudes demonstrated a genuine engagement with the company's values and the ensemble 'project'. More broadly, the company has successfully negotiated a series of major changes, moving out of deficit, overseeing a multi-million pound building project and working from a temporary building whilst still sustaining artistic output and morale. Artistically the value of the company's first major ensemble project, the Histories cycle, was reflected in the three Olivier awards won by the ensemble in 2007, and in the enthusiastic notices and sell-out crowds in Stratford and London.

The ensemble approach has also been transformational in its *outcome*, not just in terms of changing the internal culture of the RSC, its approach to theatre and its relationship with audiences, but also in terms of the broader context of theatre. Heywood notes that one of the challenges for herself and Boyd has been to embed the changes they are making in the collective culture of the organization so that it is no longer dependent on the charisma and vision of their individual leadership. She comments that it would be extremely difficult for the RSC board to appoint an autocratic successor to herself or Boyd, or to reinstate a more hierarchical management structure, even if they wanted to. She also suggests that the RSC ensemble has had repercussions beyond the company, affecting other theatre organizations 'like a virus'. When creatives and staff have experienced working in this non-hierarchical, collective culture, they are likely to demand similar rights and responsibilities in other organizations. Heywood notes that recent interviewees have become more likely to ask employers about culture and ethics, preferring – even in a recession – to work with an organization where they can identify a common set of values. RSC actors, staff and associates are able to carry the company's ethos into other organizations, especially at the point of recruitment.

Finally, the *process* of the ensemble is bisociative, both in its connections between artistic and managerial practice, but also in the connections it makes between individual and collective processes. We will explore the creative process of rehearsal and management in the remaining sections or 'acts' of the case. The next act will examine the generation of new ideas in the rehearsal room, showing how innovation in rehearsals alternates between collective discovery and individual creation. Act Three will consider how this innovative process depends in turn upon an entrepreneurial attitude to risk, shaped by a dilettante's openness to new ideas and a diligent application of technique, craft and effort. Act Four will examine the role of the director as the leader of the rehearsal process, envisioning and interacting with the actors, and 'leading from the middle' to both initiate and follow a creative process. Act Five will look at the organizational structure of the ensemble as it is manifest firstly in the rehearsal room and also in the wider organization of the RSC, providing a framework within which innovation can occur and so returning us to the start of the cycle.

Creative Destruction: work begins on the Royal Shakespeare Theatre with the demolition of the old building

Boyd and Heywood are uncomfortable with the notion of the RSC ensemble demonstrating 'best practice' for other theatres or other types of organization. Our aim with the RSC case is not to present a new management paradigm but to show how various aspects of creative strategy can connect together. As we will see, the cycle of innovation, entrepreneurship, leadership and organization requires a continual cycle of reinvention. Ensemble is presented not as a model but as a set of principles which can orient and animate a strategy, providing a framework for individuals to achieve extraordinary things – in Boyd's phrase 'to turn playfulness into virtuosity', and to connect individual creativity to collective purpose.

The demolition and reconstruction of the Royal Shakespeare Theatre in Stratford, pictured above, is a vivid metaphor for this cycle of renewal. Breaking down the old assumptions and hierarchies which divide creativity and strategy, and rebuilding the connections which join them, is the first step in the creative strategy journey.

'SPARK-NOTES'

- The RSC case does not represent 'best practice' – every organization will be different. A creative strategy approach opens up options rather than closing them down, inviting us to experiment and take risks rather than follow rules. The 'spark-notes' at the end of each 'act' should only act as a memory aid and spark your own creative thinking: they are not meant to capture an essence that should then be followed.
- Since 2005, the Royal Shakespeare Company's ensemble project has attempted to apply the principles of ensemble to both the acting company (actors are contracted to the organization for 30 months and work together on a sequence of plays) and to the organization (the actors and the office workers are made to feel part of the company's creative and strategic direction).
- The ensemble approach to rehearsal and to organization fits our definitions of **creative strategy**.
  - the ensemble is **bisociative in its process**, bringing together different perspectives from the whole cast/whole organization in both rehearsal room and boardroom.
  - the ensemble is **novel and valuable in its content**, generating new insights but testing and applying these ideas to add value and meaning to the play and to the organization as a whole.
  - the ensemble is **transformative in its outcomes**, changing the way that the ensemble's members think about themselves, the organization and the field they work in, but also changing the RSC's relationships with audiences and communities.
- Breaking down the division between creativity and strategy at the RSC requires **demolishing** familiar assumptions and **rebuilding** connections.
- In the remaining four parts of the book, we will consider how the creative strategy of this 'ensemble' is applied to innovation, entrepreneurship, leadership and organization.

PART I

THE INNOVATIVE ACT: DISCOVERY AND CREATION

6

The Bisociations of Strategic Innovation

Without innovation art is a corpse.

Winston Churchill

The rhetoric surrounding the dramatic phrase 'innovate or die' may be new, but the principle is not. Francis Bacon, most famous for the expression 'knowledge is power', put it thus over 500 years ago: 'He that will not apply new remedies must expect new evils.' By the same token, there is increasing evidence to suggest that organizations that do not innovate will be over-taken and left behind. Indeed, global competition and technological change place increased pressure on organisations to have innovation at the core of their strategy. While we argue that for that innovation to be effective, or strategic, it must be developed with one eye on the other elements of the creative strategy – entrepreneurship, leadership and organization – without innovation this whole enterprise is bereft. Hence, the heart of creative strategy must be strategic innovation.

Using the three-part definition developed in previous chapters, this part of the book examines the content, outcomes and process of strategic innovation. In this chapter we explore why there is a greater need for strategic innovation now and introduce theories suggesting that this innovation is driven by bisociative *contents* of

- newness and originality, and
- creation and discovery.

Chapter 7 outlines six generic *outcomes* of strategic innovation:

- added value,
- reduced cost,
- increased volume or capacity,
- better market relationships,
- the redrawing of conventional boundaries or
- better learning.

Chapter 8 explores a process with five components that will encourage a biosociative strategic innovation mindset and help generate the six outcomes listed above:

- supporting diversity
- encouraging curiosity
- promoting naivety
- creating urgency
- moving beyond a best-practice mentality

Throughout these chapters we illustrate these concepts by drawing on examples from so-called traditional and 'creative' industries, with a particular emphasis on music and film.

The Importance of Being Innovative

While innovation has always been important, there are reasons to suggest that it is more important now than ever, in both the arts and in strategic management.

In the arts, information technology and targeted global marketing have made good acts more ubiquitous than ever, beyond national boundaries. Thirty years ago, a homogenization of demand and the realities of geographic distance led most countries that considered themselves developed or developing to seek, find and regard without cynicism, their own replication of Elvis Presley (or Constable or the Bolshoi Ballet). It was possible to carve out a respectable career by providing only a pale imitation of an innovative artist, provided the original was far enough removed by distance.

Figure 6.1 The Adoration of the 'Elvi': Britain, France and New Zealand's responses to Elvis Presley

Nowadays such expressions would seem odd. While there are many 'tribute bands', these are treated as obvious parodies and figures of fun. Copying or importing a style from abroad is dismissed as inauthentic, to be an artist now one must be true to oneself and one's location and *innovate*. Of course repetition and imitation, some of it illegal, remain rife in the creative industries, but this is unlikely to hold consumers' attention for long. As a result of the speed and ubiquity of access to cultural content around the world, much of it available for free, consumers will pay a premium for the authentic experience, and expect to get the copy for nothing. We might make an exception for an innovative imitation which reinvents rather than merely replicates, but to be seen as a leader one must be truly different from everything else on the planet. One's response to another's success can no longer be simply to copy.

Historically, we can see how the rise in global communication firstly led to people seeing (and hearing) musicians or products from all parts of the world and when they saw something good they wanted something similar. Many experts extrapolated that this convergence in global tastes would lead to the extinction of local individuality. Theodore Levitt in 'The Globalization of Markets', published in the mid-1980s, famously predicted the progression toward the same standard product for all, with efficiency and economy of scale as *the* universal criteria. Levitt went on to criticize those who had been 'thoughtlessly accommodating' in 'willingly accepting vestigial national differences, not questioning the possibility of their transformation, not recognizing how the world is ready and eager for the benefits of modernity, especially when the price is right'. He claimed that the 'accommodating mode to visible national differences [wa]s medieval' or like paying homage to an 'obsolete institution'. By contrast, Levitt's 'Corporation of the future' would:

> constantly drive down prices by standardizing what it sells and how it operates. It treats the world as composed of few standardized markets rather than many customized markets. It actively seeks and vigorously works toward global convergence. It . . . accepts and adjusts to. . .differences only reluctantly, only after relentlessly testing their immutability, after trying various ways to circumvent and reshape them.

But what actually happened next was a little more complex. Certainly, the globalization of demand led to a rise in multi-national companies doing similar things in different places. Some products and services did become more homogenized as reverse engineering became easier and less costly. But, at the same time, technological advances also made customization more cost effective, and companies began to recognize the value of doing things differently (think how car design converged in the 1990s to the point where all the main makes looked extremely similar before companies like Renault, Fiat and Volkswagen attempted to go back to their essential brand characteristics and exploit the differences in the 2000s). And, again at the same time, the rise of the Internet, and the rise in the number of consumers seeking to be different and express this sense of difference through what they consumed, led to a phenomenon that has been branded 'the long tail'.

In a 2004 article in *Wired* magazine, Chris Anderson argued that while globalization may have led to a greater frequency of demand that could be grouped together (or placed in the centre of a bell curve), what was more interesting was that the tail of that curve was getting longer and longer. Demand here was becoming increasingly difficult to categorize. The article struck a chord and Anderson followed it with a book, *The Long Tail: Why the Future of Business is Selling Less of More* (in 2008 he followed this with another edition called *The Longer Tail*).

And there is now much evidence to back up Andersen and others' claims – evidence that suggests that good margins and critical acclaim are to be had by innovating and differentiating rather than copying and homogenizing, whether one is aiming at niches along the long tail or even seeking to meet bigger demand categories.

Both Levitt and Anderson recognized the competitive advantage of differentiation but disagreed on its relative cost and on how far along the value chain (from production to distribution) innovation could or should be applied. Levitt saw market-led innovation as mere 'tinkering' which distracted from the fundamental innovation of the core product. Writing twenty years later, Anderson recognized that costs of differentiation in production and distribution were drastically reduced by digital technologies and consumers could call the shots, driving producers to seek out and respond to diversity of demand.

Beyond these differences, both Levitt and Anderson recognize the benefits of innovation. Their arguments on the consolidation and fragmentation of markets can be seen as stages in the evolution of markets in a global economy and as point and counterpoint in a cycle of innovation. Standardized products and services open up new opportunities for customization. Customization and diversification open up new opportunities for consolidation, aggregation and intermediation. Perhaps the most striking change in our understanding of innovation in a global market, to which we will return in the next chapter, is that innovation can now be initiated (at affordable costs) at numerous points along the value chain – not just in the design of an original product or service at the start.

While these may sound more economic than artistic arguments, they also help explain why music did not evolve into a single global master genre or band (or brand), and why global superstars and cult artists continue to co-exist alongside each other. They also may explain why market-centred innovations, changing the ways in which products are packaged, delivered and consumed, have become at least as important as Levitt's preferred strategy of product innovation, not least in the creative industries.

Without innovation then, art dies. And the same is increasingly true for business. Within industries where the copying of 'best practice' has become widespread, financial performance may actually decline over time. While 'benchmarking' in this regard may have seemed logical at first, when one thinks it through it is obvious that this might lead to diminishing returns. While copying should at the outset lead to either reducing costs or increasing value-added, over time, if this copying is widespread, products or services homogenize. Homogenization makes it difficult to differentiate the qualities of a product or service; hence, customers will seek to buy on price. This leads to a price war. Prices fall and margins deteriorate – until somebody starts to innovate again (which can be difficult to do if ordering best-practice copying has led to a decline in motivation and capability, or a 'dumbing-down', within your own organization).

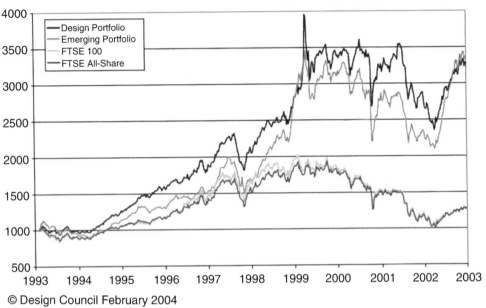

Chart 1: Performance over ten years 1994–2003

© Design Council February 2004

Figure 6.2 Creative design outperforms the norm

Authors like Philip Nattermann have begun to publish research that bears this out: showing how a decline in differentiation in an industry, linked to the widespread adoption of best practice copying, leads to financial performance declining at a similar rate. And where the worlds of art and business collide, in design, for example, there is increasing evidence to suggest that innovation pays. The UK Design Council recently produced a stock market index of firms which had won design awards. A significant separation occurs in the late 1990s where companies with design at the heart of their strategy start to streak ahead of the norm. In the ten years to 2004 the sixty-one companies in their 'design index' rose by 263%, compared to the FTSE 100's 57%. The chart above is a graphic illustration of how it is only innovative design led firms that can keep pace with the lower cost driven performance of organizations from developing economies.

Other evidence in support of these arguments now includes:

- In 2001 a study of Dutch firms found that integrating a design focus into new product development projects had a significantly positive influence on an organization's turnover, export sales and profit.
- Whyte, Salter, Gann and Davies in 2002 found that half of actual export sales made by winners of the UK's Queen's Award for Exports could be attributed to their investment in design.
- In 2003, the Danish Agency for Enterprise and Housing conducted a wide-ranging survey of Danish companies and found that companies where design was seen to be a core strategic issue performed better on a range of economic measures. The design focussed group's growth in gross revenues across a period of five years, for example, was 22% higher than the average of all companies.

- Further studies carried out by the UK Design Council in 2005 found that rapidly growing companies attached greater weight to creative design than average growth companies. They also found that a much lower percentage of design-intensive firms than the average (just 21%) were driven to compete primarily on price.

If we accept that design is a useful indicator of innovation, such studies suggest that investing in innovation – even during difficult financial times – can lead to strategic differentiation and better financial outcomes.

Defining Strategic Innovation: Discovering and Creating the New and Original

Definitions of innovation typically refer to the application of novel ideas in order to generate value. The value of innovation, in purely financial terms, has been referred to in the preceding examples. But for an innovation to be a strategic innovation, it should also be transformative in its outcomes. Put differently, a strategic innovation, and by this we mean an innovation that has effect beyond itself, should be bisociatively *new* and *original*.

We often use this sort of definition for innovation without realizing that the new and the original are quite different but related characteristics. The notion of an innovation being 'original' relates back to earlier definitions of the terms that associated innovation with revolution – in the sense of circling us back to an essential state of understanding but at a higher level or in a new context. In this way, a strategic innovation will be not only *new* in a localized context, it will reveal something underlying or fundamental about the world around us, and subsequently, it will become or re-ignite a point of origin for other new developments.

A strategic innovation will be new and original in bringing forth a fundamental shift:

- Picasso's work was a strategic innovation, in the sense that it had never been seen before while being original in the sense of unearthing fundamental emotions while becoming an origin for further new works and styles of art.
- The double helix was a new discovery but it too became a point of origin by creating wave after wave of further discoveries.
- American Airlines' launch of frequent flyer miles was a new means of exploiting something fundamental about human beings (we like to get things for free) and it became the origin for any number of point collection/redemption schemes across many industries.
- An *original* film – like *The Blair Witch Project* or *The Bourne Identity* – will not only be new and unexpected on its own terms, it will draw comparison with older 'classic movies' and redefine the genre ('horror' or 'action movie' respectively) and spawn a new sub-genre of its own.

The beneficiaries of original content may not be the originators – film studios and investors are not always impressed by claims to originality and tend to prefer a proven formula. 'Original' films and film makers may be influential rather than financially successful. Hollywood has thus tended to follow a strategy of repetition rather than innovation. Copying a successful formula offers a low risk, low cost option for the studios, allowing them to build on an existing fan-base.

But there are signs that this might be changing. As in the music industry, the rapid cloning of successful formats in other media makes mere repetition a game of diminishing returns. Customers with more choices are increasingly savvy about paying for a sequel which does not contain some new elements. Successful sequels or movie franchises – like the James Bond franchise – succeed in reinventing the character or genre and reigniting the surrounding 'buzz' (particularly when it comes time to choose the 'next James Bond'). There is accordingly a pressure to innovate even within the constraints of a specific genre or film series.

Hence, many 'franchises' like *Pirates of the Caribbean*, *Shrek*, *Spiderman* and *Ocean's Eleven* have offered greatly diminished returns once they reached their third instalment. *Terminator 2* did well creatively and financially because it was an imaginative reworking of the original *Terminator* film in a way that later versions were not. There may also be a suggestion here that, in an increasingly competitive environment, finding tomorrow's originals becomes more significant than recycling yesterday's innovation: a genuinely original prototype opens up more opportunities for later innovations.

While it can be difficult to know at first whether something new will come to be a point of origin for other developments, or a strategic innovation, we have found it to be particularly useful to think in terms of whether a proposed innovation has the power to inspire further innovations when seeking to think creatively in organizations.

The assumed dichotomy between creative industries and other industries described at the beginning of this book mirrors a dichotomy often drawn between the arts and the sciences. And it is this opposition which often leads us not to recognize the second bisociative loop that contributes to strategic innovation.

The dichotomy established between the arts and sciences has led to a disassociation of what we argue are the two fundamental bisociative elements of any form of strategic innovation: *creation* and *discovery*. We refer to inventing (or making) new ideas from the imagination as 'creation', and finding and adapting ideas from the world around us as 'discovery'. These two elements are implicit in any discussion about where innovation comes from, but the tendency has been to privilege one at the expense of the other depending on one's point of view.

In Western thought, pre-modern or Aristotelian mimesis or sympathy (in the sense of getting inside the being of what one was seeking to know) stressed the importance of discovering and adapting ideas from nature. But the rise of what we call modernity, and the subsequent Western humanist tradition, privileged the notion of innovative ideas being created *ex nihilo* by human rationality and imagination.

'Creation', once the preserve of the gods, is a concept associated with the rise of individualistic and secular cultures in Europe from the Renaissance, and was subsequently articulated in Romantic theories of art and the imagination in 19th century Europe, from Kant's theory of genius to the Romantic poets' descriptions of the transforming power of the individual imagination. Conversely 'discovery' has been variously linked to Eastern cultures and religions, where the individual artist is expected to work according to social and religious values and beliefs, and to older pre-secular Western traditions of religious or folk arts, for example the medieval craft guilds.

At the same time, with the arts taking the 'creative' high ground, the empirical sciences were differentiated in no small part by being related to discovery. Henceforth, since the late 19th century, art = creation; science = discovery. And, as the fledgling field of management emerged in the early 20th century and sought to define itself as a science, it too has been placed on the opposite side of the fence from the creative arts.

The false dichotomy is kept alive because we focus on, and make value judgements about, the outputs of artistic, scientific and business endeavours, and the assumptions that underpin them, rather than focussing on their purpose and value as innovative acts.

It is true that the assumptions that underpin the development of the sciences, the arts and business are quite different. And, it is true that if one compares, say, Picasso's Guernica with a double-helix, or with a SWOT analysis, the differences are stark: the first looks like a divine apparition, the next the discovering of something that has always been, and the last a categorization to aid the uncovering of pre-existing phenomema. Because of these surface differences, in terms of creative merit we are able to ascribe higher values to certain innovations. Guernica or the double-helix, depending on your perspective, will be seen as vastly superior to a SWOT, but the fundamental intention is the same. The arts and sciences and business are seeking to develop and communicate novel and original truths about their worlds – to effect what we have called strategic innovation. And they achieve this by combining discovery and creation.

Theories of creativity focus on the cognitive act that underpins innovation in all artistic and scientific and business endeavour. According to these theories, discovery and creation can be seen as different phases or competences of strategic innovation, connecting to the paradoxical nature of that process as highlighted in the first part of this book. Here, discovery and creation precede and follow each other to the point that it becomes difficult to separate them in practice. What is discovered must be acted upon or recreated by the creative imagination; the act of creation draws upon and adapts to the discovered world around it.

Along these lines, creativity theorists like Boden and Weisberg remind us that what appears to be spontaneous individual creation in the arts is very often rooted in a practice of discovery, imitation and experimentation. And, conversely, the history of scientific discovery demonstrates that the most radical discoveries require individual creation to bring them alive.

- Picasso's style of painting was informed by his 'discovery' of African tribal art and by the work of his peers; individual artistic creation was rooted in discovery of older, less individualistic traditions.
- Watson and Crick may not have been the only or even the first scientists to discover the molecular structure of DNA, but they were able to connect the information together and

articulate it in a brilliantly simple model and drawing. Their scientific 'discovery' was also an act of creation, bringing together the discoveries of other scientists into a new frame of reference. The same is true of other ground-changing scientific innovations like penicillin.

- Likewise, those who worked on the BCG matrix at the Mead Paper Corporation and their Boston Consulting Group advisors drew on their experience and intuition to create the form of the model based on what they had discovered over time from working in multiple business contexts.

Not only are discovery and creation in all innovative endeavours linked, but they are symbiotic. Without discovery, creation becomes locked into its own esoteric patterns, disconnected from sources of meaning and value; without an act of creation, discovery provides only the raw material for new ideas, disconnected from an expressive communicative framework. The great scientific challenges of the future, from global warming to the spread of diseases, cannot be solved by scientific discovery alone; creative communication and interpretation of scientific data are needed to mobilize the cultural change and public understanding necessary to act upon scientific knowledge.

Creation and discovery lock together in cycles of innovative development, application and renewal. Overlapping and interdependent, they converge in strategic innovation in the development of novel and original ideas and activities. Creation, discovery, novelty and originality become necessary components of what we call the strategic innovation loop that we simplify in the figure below and which should be at the heart of creative strategy.

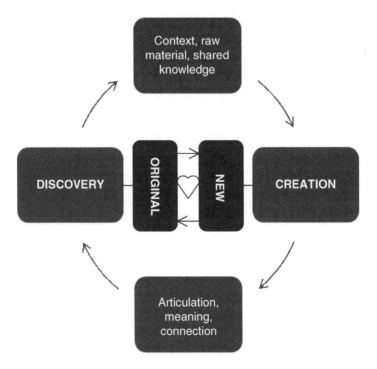

Figure 6.3 The bisociative strategic innovation 'double-loop'

Discovery feeds creation, providing new sources of energy and inspiration for the creative imagination and offering a framework of shared understanding within which we can generate innovative ideas and make sense of them. Creation acts upon discovery, by articulating and framing the discovered idea and connecting this material into meaningful propositions. Through the mutual interaction between discovery and creation, innovative ideas are continually replenished through adaptation and renewal to create something that is at once new and original.

Discovery and creation are interconnected, and one may enter the strategic innovation loop from either angle. Indeed, great minds often don't think alike on where to begin. The famous fall-out between Thomas Edison and Nikola Tesla may be traced to their opposing views on this starting point and their intolerance of the other's method. Edison's most famous phrase, that innovation was 99% perspiration, was true, for him: a relentless discoverer who believed that the truth was out there. Assuming that all electricians, as they were then called, were like him, he explained that 'All electricians work in the dark. They grope and they grope, catching on to the slightest clue, which they work upon until its fallacy or use is demonstrated, and then if useful they follow it persistently until the results are accomplished. There's luck in it, and in truth, we electricians are discoverers not inventors.' Tesla put up with this for as long as he could while he worked for Edison. But in the end he could stand it no longer. Tesla was an idealist with an incredible ability to create an innovation in his head and refine it there before drawing it out fully formed. Of Edison's 'empirical dragnets', Tesla would scoff, 'If Edison had a needle to find in a haystack, he would proceed at once with the diligence of a bee to examine each straw until he found the object of his search. I was a sorry witness of such doings, knowing that a little theory and calculation would have saved him ninety percent of his labor.' For his part, while he got great value from Tesla while he was in his employ, Edison came to regard Tesla, disparagingly, as a theoretician and an egghead.

The reason that Edison succeeded as a strategic innovator whereas Tesla, a great inventor certainly, did not, was that Edison continued to surround himself with others and an organization that balanced out his particular tendencies. Tesla, after he left Edison, was increasingly lost in his brilliant mind and disconnected from reality, lacking any sort of grounding yin to balance his creative yang.

Strategic innovation combines the qualities of novelty and originality and the acts of discovery and creation. Without this bisociative balance at its core, innovation is less likely to deliver on its promise where it matters most – in its outcomes.

CHAPTER 7

The Six Outcomes of Strategic Innovation

A colour is well suited to the eye if its bright and agreeable tones stimulate and refresh the vision, and in the same way we ought to apply our intellectual vision to those models which can inspire it to attain its own virtue. [Such a model is] no sooner seen than it rouses the spectator to action, and yet it does not form his character by mere imitation, but by promoting ... a dominating purpose.

Plutarch, Life of Pericles

While our double-loop at the end of the previous chapter points out key elements in the act of strategic innovation, it does not specify how this innovation might be promoted. To aid this we would do well, as we explained with creativity and strategy in the prologue of this book, to give purpose by focussing minds around the potential outcomes of strategic innovation and think about the processes that might precede and encourage it. This chapter outlines six generic outcomes of strategic innovation, the next chapter deals with the practical steps that can be taken towards a process to promote these outcomes.

There are many books on innovation that specify a best practice approach outlining the steps that should be taken to generate innovations and providing examples from great companies to back this up. However, as we indicated in the previous chapter, even if one could reduce innovation to a series of steps its widespread imitation would actually lead to a decline in innovation through the 'law' of widespread homogenization of best practice, leading to diminishing returns.

So, we do things a little differently here. First, we try to vary the formula by mixing a few examples of innovation which are familiar (e.g., Apple) with many which are not (e.g., Mauve, Radiohead, the humble barcode). Second, we do not suggest that the 'mere imitation' of any of these examples or of our categories will make you a strategic innovator. Much as Plutarch saw the point of his stories of the achievements of great leaders as being to inspire his readers to develop their own ideas and style, we have collated these stories to rouse, stimulate, refresh and give purpose to your own thinking: to spark off your own creations and discoveries.

We develop a framework for doing this here by 'shaking together' some new and classic strategic management thinking, and add to this combination with a creative mindset.

The something new that we'll consider in this chapter is the idea put forward in the recent book *Blue Ocean Strategy* by Renée Mauborgne and W. Chan Kim. Mauborgne and Kim's research shows that while 86% of business or product launches are line extensions, or incremental improvements, they only account for 62% of corporate revenue and 39% of profits. The remaining 14% of launches account for 38% of revenue and 61% of profits. These highly profitable product launches fit with our definition of strategic innovation, and focus on providing added value to customers rather than just novel inventions which may or may not add value. Mauborgne and Kim suggest that these strategic innovations can be advanced in four dimensions: creating, raising, reducing and eliminating, by asking structured questions like:

- Which factors should be introduced or *created* that the industry has never offered the customer?
- Which elements could be *raised* above the standard?
- Which product/service elements could be *reduced* below the industry standard?
- Which factors could be *eliminated* that an industry has taken for granted?

The something old that we 'shake together' with *Blue Ocean Strategy*, is Michael Porter's value chain. The value chain is now over thirty years old and there is no framework more ubiquitous in strategic management than its simple shape outlining the elements that might be employed to add value to, or support, inputs to create an output of greater value or benefit than what it cost to achieve the transformation.

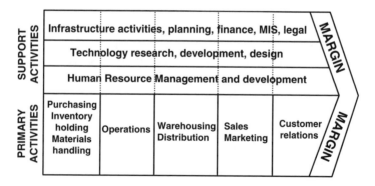

Figure 7.1   The generic value chain (Source: Porter (1985))

A criticism often levelled at the value chain is that innovation is nowhere to be seen in the chain. If it is so important (as we argued in Chapter 6), why is there no box ascribed to innovation, or, for that matter, creativity in the value chain? And, does this lack mean that the value chain is of little use in addressing our need for greater innovation?

We argue that this is precisely why the value chain is valuable in developing strategic innovation. Innovation is nowhere to be seen, but because of the white-space and malleability of the chain, it can be used to rouse, stimulate, and give purpose to discussion in every direction and this broad and malleable categorization of space can inspire discovery. If one adopts the right mindset, seeing the chain as a useful starting point rather than a constraining end, then we can use it to conceive and communicate many degrees of strategic innovation. With this attitude, the lack of innovation prescribed in the chain prompts the viewer to contribute it.

By building upon Mauborgne and Kim's four types of innovation and using the broad expressive qualities of the value chain, we have identified six main ways in which innovation can be sought, or what we call six degrees of strategic innovation.

The first two degrees relate closely to the Blue Ocean categories:

1st degree: Creating or extending the chain, or *value innovation*

2nd degree: Shortening the chain, or *cost innovation*

The first degree of strategic innovation relates to Mauborgne and Kim's *creating* and *raising*; the second to *eliminating* and *reducing*. However, using the value chain with a creative mindset enables us to articulate four other degrees of strategic innovation:

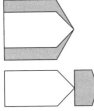

3rd degree: Widening the chain, or *volume innovation*

4th degree: Recasting the chain closer to customers, or *marketing innovation*

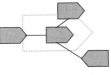

5th degree: Blending the chain, or *boundary innovation*

6th degree: Adapting the chain through product/service interactions, or *learning innovation*

These six degrees apply equally to strategic innovation in the arts or in business, and there is much to be learned from examples from both spheres. In the pages that follow we shall explore some examples as a means of further rousing, refreshing and inspiring your own strategic innovations. As a further stimulus, we provide sixty-nine strategic innovation questions to the side of the main text. These relate to the discussion as it is progressing and we have found them to be extremely useful in inspiring debate and discussion about strategic innovation in organizations.

The 1st Degree of Strategic Innovation: Value Innovation

The 1st degree of strategic innovation – value innovation – is perhaps also the best known. It is about discovering something of new or greater value to customers or constituents. It comes in a variety of forms, from the most obvious – the new invention that creates a new value chain or even a new industry (there's a list of these in the box below) – to the more common – innovative additions, combinations or reconfigurations of existing inventions or many minor incremental additions and tweaks of existing value chains. Value innovation is about discovering and meeting unmet needs or creating something new to generate a new type of demand. The best value innovations provoke consequent value chain reactions, realizing significant added value for consumers or stakeholders; they are both new and original. We will explore some inspiring examples of value innovations and the acts of discovery and creation that made them possible below.

99 INDUSTRY SPURRING INVENTIONS SINCE 1900

Paperclip, 1900; Brownie Box Camera, 1900; Escalator, 1901; Disposable Safety Razor, 1901; Alkaline Rechargeable Razor, 1901; Tea Bag, 1904; Domestic Electric Dishwasher, 1906; Model 'T' Automobile, 1908; Neon, 1910; Automatic Washing Machine, 1910; Zipper, 1913; Refrigerator, 1913; Brassiere, 1914; Sneakers, 1916; Band-Aid, 1921; Insulin, 1921; Rubber Condom, 1921; Electric Guitar, 1923; Kleenex, 1924; Television, 1924; Talking Motion Picture, 1927; Penicillin, 1928; Recliner Chair, 1928; Sliced Bread, 1928; Flash Bulb, 1930; Electric Kettle, 1930; Scotch Tape, 1930; DIY Hair Dye, 1931; Tampon, 1931; Stereo System, 1931; Detergent, 1933; Nylon, 1935; Tape Recorder, 1935; Kodachrome Film, 1935; Fluorescent Lighting, 1938; Computer, 1938; Jet Engine, 1939; Ballpoint Pen, 1943; Photocopier, 1944; Microwave Oven, 1946; Ready-Whipped Cream, 1947; Vinyl LP, 1948; Instant Camera, 1948; Security Alarm, 1950; Transistor radio, 1950; Instant Coffee, 1950; Liquid Paper 1951; Carbon Nanotube, 1952; Saran Wrap, 1953; Solar Power, 1954; Polio Vaccine, 1955; Velcro, 1957; The LEGO Brick, 1958; Skateboard, 1958; Pop-Top Can, 1959; Barbie Doll, 1959; Contraceptive Pill, 1960; Vibrator, 1960; Soft Contact Lenses, 1961; LED light, 1962; Lava Lamp, 1963; Touch-Tone Telephone, 1963; Computer Mouse, 1964; Laser Printer, 1965; Snowboard, 1966; The Internet, 1969; Quartz Wristwatch, 1969; Video

(Continued)

Cassette Recorder, 1969; Floppy Disk, 1970; Fax Machine, 1971; Global Positioning System, 1973; Tanning Bed, 1979; Handheld Electronic Calculator, 1971; Food Processor, 1973; Cell Phone, 1973; Rubik's Cube, 1974; Digital Camera, 1975; Rollerblades, 1979; Walkman, 1979; Handheld Video Game, 1979; Post-It Note, 1980; Pac-Man, 1980; Polartec Synthetic Fabric, 1981; Compact Disc 1981; Laptop Computer, 1981; Flash Memory, 1984; Prozac, 1989; Web Browser, 1993; DVD, 1993; Bluetooth, 1994; PlayStation, 1994; Viagra, 1998; MP3 Player, 1999 (iPod arrived in 2001); Xbox, 2001; Memory Stick, 2002; Wii Console, 2005; Blu-Ray Disc, 2007; iPhone, 2007...

A recent issue of *The Irish Times* provided a list of the 10 greatest inventions of modern times: the cell phone, the Apple Mac, the Mini, the Fax, the Walkman. But one was less obvious: mauve. The development of mauve dye was truly new and original. Moreover, it was not just one new product. It sparked a whole new industry in artificial dyes, and drove innovation in many other industries, as the processes it uncovered enabled a new wave of discoveries in pharmaceuticals, perfumes, plastics and food products.

What's our greatest ever invention, how was it sparked and what did it spark?

Englishman William Perkin derived mauve from coal tar by accident, in a makeshift laboratory that his father allowed him to build at home and in which he would tinker most evenings. The space was not unlike the more recently celebrated 'HP shed' or the 'Google garage' where young enthusiasts with a lot of passion and a little training in their subjects 'shake together' ideas and materials.

Do we have an innovation shed or garage? If so where is it? If not, why not?

'I was endeavouring to convert an artificial base in the natural alkaloid quinine', Perkin would later explain, 'but my experiment, instead ... gave a reddish powder. With a desire to understand this particular result, a different base of more simple construction was selected, viz. aniline, and in this case obtained a perfectly black product. This was purified and dried and when digested with spirits of wine gave the mauve dye'.

Do we recognise and act upon unexpected discoveries, or do we dismiss them as distraction or failures?

Perkin was 18 years old at the time, and these were naïve manoeuvres. Most professional chemists would not have followed the process that led to the red powder. If they had, they would have thrown the powder away and started again. It was Perkin's wide-eyed enthusiasm and curiosity that led him to play around further. But it was a mark of his ability as a chemist that he was able to separate out the 5% of the 'perfect black' that contained his colour. Perkin's bisociative combination of curiosity and application shows how discovery interacts with creation. The discovery was fuelled by Perkin's inner creative capacity to drive forward and develop the original unplanned discovery; conversely without Perkin's initial openness to an external and potentially irrelevant event, there would have been nothing for his inner creative intent and initiative to work upon.

On the 50th anniversary of Perkin's death, a senior Courtaulds' dyer named John Boulton gave an address to the Ulster section of the Society of Dyers and Colourists. 'I have been driven to reflect upon the question of what kind of man is a Perkin. How come there are so few of them', he asked. 'A person of much greater ability as an experimentalist and with a deeper knowledge as a scientist could have easily failed to make Perkin's discovery had he not also had something of [his] make-up.' This make-up, Boulton concluded, was of one who made nothing of science/industry/art divides, but embraced it all. The sort of man who made great use of the things that happened to him.

What are the main divides in our organization? Who crosses them and what could we learn from them?

Timing played a part in Perkin's discovery too. A few years earlier or a few years later and he would not have been looking in the manner that he did: John Dalton had recently theorized that atoms combine with others in definite numbers, leading to the establishment of chemical formulae. On the other hand, much still remained unknown. The combination of emergent knowledge and uncertainty was reflected in Perkin's experimental attitude, and made possible his productive error with quinine.

What are the areas of new knowledge and uncertainty in our own industry?

Sometimes the timing of an innovation is less favourable. In 1973 Federal Express founder, and then college student, Fred Smith could not have seen a value chain piecing together a potential market demand for secure individualized package delivery together with the various technological and regulatory mechanisms needed to deliver it. The mind of the professor at Yale University who famously gave him a 'C' for the term paper where Smith outlined his plan was perhaps stuck in 1970, and he couldn't see it either. As we have discussed already, value depends on context. The value of innovation also depends upon the other elements of creative strategy, including entrepreneurial attitudes and organisational open-mindedness.

What could we know about our business now that we couldn't know 20 years ago? What might we be able to know if we put our minds to it now?

Another route to the 1st degree of innovation is, rather than discovering an entirely new source of value, to take something valuable and add a further dimension to it, taking it to another level. In many cases we can conceive of this form of value innovation as like adding an adjective to a noun. For example, the Sony Walkman added *portable* to music; Swatch added *fashion accessory* to watch; Dyson and Alessi added *designer* to the vacuum cleaner and the teapot.

Could we add value by developing a new adjective in front of one of our products or services?

The Sony Walkman contained little of the cutting edge technology of the day. It simply took Sony's stereo cassette machines, the observation that people enjoyed listening to music while travelling in their cars, and sought to design a portability that would enable a tape player to be carried on their person. And it launched in 1979, just as a fitness 'craze', encouraging people to spend time walking, jogging and cycling, was sweeping the world. The Walkman, like Perkin's mauve, demonstrates a collision of external opportunity and internal logic – an openness to discovery and then a desire to create.

What 'craze' or trend are we serving? Or contributing to?

When the Japanese recently voted on what they considered their most important 20th century innovation it was not the Walkman that won, but instant noodles.

What are we prototyping right now? Why aren't we prototyping more?

Momofuku Ando's breakthrough came in 1958 after a year of prototyping. He didn't invent noodles, he simply devised a way to prepare them quickly and easily. He added *instant* to noodles. Prior to this his life had been something of a mess (more on the value of mess in the next chapter). He had sold fabrics, then engine-parts. Then prefab houses and socks. He presided over a credit association, until that went bust. And he launched a scholarship scheme for students which failed and

What might we learn on a walk through the city, or country?

landed Ando in jail for tax-evasion. Walking home one cold night, he saw people shivering around a street stall waiting for noodles, and was inspired to seek a method of flash-frying cooked noodles in palm oil, like his wife's vegetable tempura. In 2005, 86 billion servings of instant noodles were eaten around the world. Elvis Costello's 20th album, named *Momofuku*, contains the following dedication: 'remembering Momofuku Ando (1910–2007). He fed those who study.'

While the stories above relate big and singular new value propositions or additions, value innovation can emerge from hundreds or thousands of little persistent increments. Dyson's dual cyclone cleaner was the result of 5127 prototypes. As Thomas Edison said, 'The only difference between me, that's supposed to be lucky, and the fellows that think they are unlucky [is that] most fellows try a few things and then quit. I never quit until I git what I'm after'. Just as

Which of our products/services have we improved the most and how did we do it?

chance favours the prepared mind, discovery favours those who are actively creative – and behind the unexpected breakthrough discovery we can often discern a deliberate, incremental process of creation which makes discoveries more likely and recognizes and exploits them as they occur.

In a typical year Toyota employees will suggest over 750,000 areas for improvement. In some years the company will implement or develop over 80% of these. While most suggestions are small and incremental, they add up to a lot of added value. Just as important is the byproduct: a culture of value innovation, a culture that Professor Stephen Speer of MIT describes as one that assumes

What do we swarm around?

that problems and opportunities will be 'swarmed from every direction to create high-speed, low-cost discovery and learning.'

Competitors like General Motors and Chrysler attempted to mimic this approach to innovation without the underlying culture that allowed it to evolve: an open vulnerability among senior managers based on a belief that they didn't have all the answers, and a subsequent trust in employees at all levels to come up with very good ideas. As a recent article in *Time* explained: 'the top down culture of the Big Three could not absorb that kind of trust.' Instead, they

What are the top three companies in our field least good at?

kept searching, in vain, for the big hit from the top: the breakthrough design, the clever diversification, the killer advertising campaign, the big bail-out. Again we will see that strategic innovation cannot be

Who is trusted as an innovator in our organization?

separated from other aspects of creative strategy – in this case, leadership and organization.

Even this distinction between Toyota and its rivals may miss the mark. Toyota is a great innovator because it is bisociative: paradoxically swarming for little increments *and* pursuing the big breakthroughs. Like all automobile manufactures they have sought to create a car that would be more fuel efficient and environmentally friendly. They had two choices: seek to improve the traditional internal combustion engine or develop a completely new hybrid engine. The Prius is the result of taking the leap and going for the latter. Some commentators believe that this big hit gave Toyota a ten year lead on its rivals in the category that its decision helped shape. But the confidence to make the big leaps of discovery was aided by taking the smaller steps of creation.

Are we going for continuous swarming innovation, big leaps, or both?

The 2nd Degree of Strategic Innovation: Cost Innovation

The 2nd degree of innovation is about producing products, services, or experiences at a significantly lower cost than had previously been thought practical by thinking differently about what really needs to be in the chain of production. In effect, it's about thinking of the value chain as a 'cost chain'. Every time value is added, cost is incurred, so removing something extraneous or doing something differently to reduce cost is as much a strategic innovation as adding value.

Max McKeown's book, *The Truth about Innovation*, tells a story about a South American company that had established a good reputation for its meat products in the United States. The problem in the way of further growth was the cost of shipping the meat without it spoiling. The solution was to lease cargo planes that would quickly ascend to 25,000 feet where the meat would stay frozen without refrigeration. This enabled the company to significantly redesign the packaging and units for shipping as the meat now only needed to be chilled from factory to airplane and then from the destination airport to the distribution warehouse. Removing the refrigeration units from the airplane was a cost innovation.

People often look down their noses at cost innovation. They would rather associate with innovations that add value. But it is important to note that lower cost does not necessarily mean lowering quality, it is better thought of as reconfiguring perceptions of what customers consider to be valuable and what they are prepared to pay for.

Nicholas Negroponte's vision of One Laptop Per Child set out to provide cheap computers for children in developing countries, driven by a target price of $100. The project did not in the end meet this target, but it did change the way we think about personal computing and educational technology, by emphasizing certain attributes rather than those that were the norm. Reducing the costs led to a re-evaluation of how laptops add to quality of life, in ways other than simply increasing the speed and power of the processor.

What would we strip out if we wanted to develop what we do for the world's poorest countries?

While lower cost may result from lots of little increments (to use the language from our previous discussion on value innovation), creating a big gap between you and your competitors generally requires taking the initiative and leaping ahead of incremental evolution. Alfred Sloan, CEO of General Motors, described where he wanted to position his company in terms of cost innovation thus: the first era of auto production was the 'class market'. Only wealthy car-enthusiasts bought cars. The second era, which Henry Ford's pursuit of cost innovations drove, was the 'mass market'. The third, which GM in its hey-day sought to fill with its own cost innovations, Sloan described as 'the mass-market craving for a bit of class'.

One can see a cost-innovation dynamic similar to the one Sloan describes occurring in the airline industry in more recent times. The likes of SouthWest, easyJet and Ryanair worked their ways down the value/cost chain stripping out things normally associated with air travel, but superfluous to many. Ryanair CEO Michael O'Leary explained it this way: 'If people want to spend an extra 50 quid and get a cold cup of tea in a plastic cup, then they should fly British Airways.' Many people didn't. Indeed, a whole new group of people who had not previously been able to afford air travel now could, on a regular basis. The response from a number of established airlines has been to provide segments of this now mass market with little bits of extra 'class' cost effectively, much like Sloan and General Motors – not just complementary food and drink but greater flexibility on tickets and more generous baggage allowances.

Name three things we could strip out of our value chain?

Meanwhile, the car industry has been rocked by a 'new Ford' seeking to discover a new mass market for automobiles in the East – the Tata 'Nano'. Instead of taking the budget airlines approach of taking things out of a conventional product/service chain, Tata Motors' cost innovations were inspired as much from looking at a 'lesser' form of transport and working up. CEO Ratan Tata observed whole families riding on scooters, and wondered whether these families would buy a car if one could be made for a price they could afford. Setting a target price of 100,000 rupees (about $2500) Tata's design team sought to build up from a scooter and cut details out of a car that had never been cut before: one windscreen wiper, three bolts rather than four to hold the wheels on; no tubes in the tyres, gluing body panels rather than welding, cutting down on the number of tools needed to make the vehicle, arranging construction into modules that can be put together in kits, which could be transported closer to markets and assembled by dealer/entrepreneurs or franchise holders. And rather than seeking an international partner to help as has been the norm in the auto industry in recent times (and perhaps because of this), Tata came up with these ideas from within.

What's a 'lesser' product or service than one of ours? How could we build up from that?

What percentage of our innovations come from within? What would the ideal ratio be?

Rivals who dismissed the 'Nano', Tata's 'one-lakh car' (a lakh is 100,000 rupees) as impossible or too crude, are now monitoring its progress closely, and on the back-foot. Says Chrysler trend watcher Steve Bartoli, 'It's not so much the vehicle itself, it's the thought processes that went into it that's more provocative.' Perhaps the only company that took the Nano threat seriously prior to this was Carlos Ghosn's Renault-Nissan, who are now working with the Indian motorcycle maker Bajaj

What's our cost innovation process?

to develop a car to go up against it. While it will not be without its teething problems, the Nano shows how the business context can be changed by an intensive process of strategic cost innovation.

At the other end of the scale, a number of luxury fashion houses, spurred on by opulence not being such a good look during a recession, have found that they can achieve as much from investing in more interactive websites as putting on lavish fashion shows, if not more (think of how much more useful information that can capture).

How might the recession provide 2nd degree opportunities for achieving strategic innovations?

Cereality is a restaurant chain offering cold breakfast cereal at any time of day. The discovery that you can cut large chunks out of a conventional fast food franchise's cost chain (the kitchen is much cheaper to run and maintain and there are lower compliance costs in terms of health and safety) takes cost innovation to a minimalist level. Serving branded cold cereal is not an innovation about much, and it may prove a difficult advantage to sustain, but it makes you think.

More sustainable is the humble barcode. The UPC or Universal Product Code was first used in 1974 and it has not yet been surpassed. While much more sophisticated approaches have been developed they are all significantly more expensive. Says George J. Laurer who headed the team at IBM that developed the code the secret to its longevity is that it is needed, it's reliable and it's cheap.

What's the least we could do and still be fit for purpose?

Other famous cost innovations include BMW's decision to under-invest in marketing the new Mini in some markets when it launched, estimating that the buzz caused by product placement and word of mouth would be more powerful (and less costly) than conventional marketing. Nike's cost innovation, realizing that the lower cost of production in Asia would more than offset the cost of transporting products back to markets in the West, was inspired by CEO Phil Knight's Master's thesis.

How could we sell if our advertising or marketing budget was zero?

The creative industries have followed a similar path of cost innovation, cutting out retail and inventory costs through online direct distribution (Amazon, iTunes), or cutting out marketing costs through utilizing social networking sites (major artists and major record labels being regular contributors to 'community' websites). Again such developments have been driven by refocussing on certain aspects of value from the customer's point of view (convenience, interaction, choice) rather than cost reduction alone. And as with the airline industry, some of the costs which were stripped out by price competition are now being put back in. High street bookstores have recognized the value of personal, friendly advice from knowledgeable staff – something which Amazon's automated recommendations and star ratings cannot replicate. CDs include embedded games and videos or exclusive online interactive services in order to compete with ubiquitous free content. Cost innovations have eventually prompted a second wave of value innovations as producers and distributors are forced to re-evaluate the relationship between cost, price and perceived value.

If we were to do or sponsor a Master's or PhD thesis what would it be about?

If value innovation is essentially concerned with discovery and creation, cost innovation is focussed on rediscovery and re-creation. By stripping back the value chain to its essentials, we may find ways of creating new value by reducing costs without harming and maybe even improving the product.

The 3rd Degree of Strategic Innovation: Volume Innovation

The 3rd degree of innovation is about discovering and creating ways to produce, provide, sell and move products and services in far greater quantities than previously thought possible. What makes these innovations strategic (as with any of the six degrees) is their awareness of and systemic linkages to other elements in the value chain as well as to other forms of innovation: cost innovations often lead to steep increases in demand, so they must be matched with volume innovations to meet these new demands.

Nike's cost innovations were matched by the realization that higher volumes could be met by sub-contracting manufacture rather than growing and owning plants 'in-house'. Ford's cost innovations with the Model-T led to an exponential growth in demand. This demand could only be sated by employing volume innovations. Ford introduced a production 'line' where the work moved and the worker stood still (the opposite had always been the case) and a '$5 dollar day', which doubled the standard wage for autoworkers. This ensured that there was a ready supply of workers willing to subject themselves to the Ford way, filling every shift that the Ford plants could run.

What would we give people that would encourage them to innovate more?

Google brings information to one's finger-tips quickly and cheaply, but it was the quantum increase in the volume of information that it connected people to which truly changed the context. Google's transformation from a search engine to a global information service demonstrates how dramatic increases in scale can effectively transform the value and definition of a service. According to 'Metcalfe's Law', the power of the network is related to the square of the number of its users. Following this logic, by increasing the number of its users Google has changed from being a channel for information to a channel for communication – from a service to a network.

What state is our 'customer network' in and how could we increase its power?

Similar mechanisms enabled eBay to increase the volume of sellers that could be accessed by potential buyers, and, going back the other way, the number of customers who might bid up a seller's price. iTunes contributes to the success of the iPod by linking customers to a volume of music beyond anything that could be held in a record store. This, in turn, changes the way iPod-owners purchase and listen to music (Metcalfe's Law in action again).

What if we got an order for three times our normal monthly sales tomorrow? What could we learn from meeting the order?

Less ethereal perhaps, but just as valuable, are the volume innovations embedded in Holland's Aalsmeer Flower Auction or VBA (Bloemenveiling Aalsmeer). If you have ever flown into Schipol airport you may have noticed the flat building nearby that spans an area of around 100 football fields. This is the VBA. The VBA maintains its place as the world hub for fresh flower distribution with the help of two interrelated volume innovations. The first is the 'Dutch auction' approach to selling the flowers. Instead of a conventional auction where it can take time to bid up the price, an electronic screen counts down the selling price of the batch of flowers on display in the 'ring' or arena. The first buyer to press 'buy' on his electronic bidding device gets the flowers. The second innovation involves the fleet of golf carts that move the flowers quickly. The flowers are brought into the ring on a cart (which hardly stops as the auctions happen so quickly). The cart then drives direct to the hub on the edge of the building for the particular courier company that distributes for the buyer.

Would our prices be higher or lower if we sold via a Dutch auction?

How could we distribute faster?

But there are other forms of volume innovation that are driven more by managing demand than increasing throughput. When Oral-B discovered that many people never noticed when their toothbrushes were worn beyond optimum effectiveness, they developed a patented blue dye and inserted it on the middle bristles so that it faded over time: signalling it was time for a new brush. Better volume for Oral-B was the result; but so too, they could argue, was better hygiene for customers.

How could we help people remember that they should buy another of our products?

Volume innovation can be achieved by changes in format. Online newspapers and blogs reach more people than their print equivalents, but usually have to sacrifice sales revenues in order to achieve higher exposure for advertisers or greater influence over readers. On the other hand, Australian cookbook author Donna Hay recognized that people buy more magazines than books and started producing monthly cook-magazines available on high-visibility magazine racks.

Could different media or packaging formats help us sell more?

Could we reduce durability below the industry norm and sell more?

American King Gillette's fortunes were nearly destroyed in the Chicago fire of 1871. But while working as a travelling salesman to keep his family going, he hit upon two interrelated ideas for shaving. The first was that having only a thin sliver of the blade protruding from a case would improve safety. The second was that the support of a case would mean that a much thinner blade could be used. When he set out to make a thinner, cheaper blade, industry experts said it couldn't be done. And it couldn't, to the quality standards that experts applied. They claimed that such a blade wouldn't last very long – without realizing that the disposable nature of the new thinner blade (and subsequent increase of the number of shavers that an individual would buy) was to be Gillette's greatest innovation. Reputedly Gillette's volume innovation was inspired by William Painter, inventor of the crown seal bottle-cap, who told Gillette that a successful invention was one that would be bought over and over again by a satisfied customer. But like Perkin's discovery, it was also a result of experimental failure.

Rather than disposable, could we make what we do biodegradable?

Swatch changed the context for watches in a related way. People used to only have one watch. The notion that they might own as many watches as pairs of shoes increased volumes beyond anything previously considered plausible. Patek Phillipe increased their volume by promoting the idea that their expensive watches were as much for their owner's children and grandchildren as for the original purchaser. Throx sell more socks by selling them in threes rather than pairs (you know you always lose one!).

Can we change perceptions of how many of our products customers need or who they are really buying them for?

The advent of frequent flyer programmes in the 1990s was a volume innovation of a further kind. Here airlines were able to fill what we might call marginal volume (seats that were going empty anyway and carried very little marginal cost). This marginal volume held greater value to the airline when 'given away' to good customers. And, subsequently, what the airline gained was increasing volume as the 'sunk cost' (accumulated points) from having flown with that airline made people more likely to choose that airline again; and again. This was crucial in an industry where it was hard to differentiate the product in other ways – apart from price. The success of frequent flyer logic has fuelled wallets full of cards offering goodies in exchange for frequent purchases.

How would our 'frequent flyer' programme operate?

The 4th Degree of Strategic Innovation: Market Innovation

The 4th degree of innovation is market innovation. Here the focus moves further along the value chain, from reconfiguring products and processes, to redefining markets in order to change the way people think about or use the product.

How does our stuff really look 'on the shelf'?

Francis Bacon, whom we encountered in the first paragraph of this part of the book, might have been saved by the market innovations of Clarence Birdseye. Bacon reputedly died in 1626 from a chill caught while stuffing a chicken with snow as an experiment in food preservation. By 1930, Birdseye had perfected a range of frozen food. But retail sales were slow. Stores displayed the food ad hoc in ways that did not inspire interest or confidence in potential consumers. Birdseye got around the problem by 'gifting' retailers standard freezer cabinets designed to show his products in the best possible light and his company took off from there.

What 'gift' would help our partners sell more for us?

This 4th degree of innovation involves discovering new and valuable ways of selling to, relating to, or involving, the market. This may mean innovative approaches to who pays for things, being quick or slow to market, involving customers inside the value creation process, or enlisting unusual forms of marketing, or packaging products and experiences in interesting ways.

What if our main distribution channel fell over – how would we sell?

It is well known that Apple did not invent MP3 players, and that Amazon didn't invent online shopping, and that Sony didn't invent games consoles. What made these companies successful in these instances wasn't value innovation, it was market innovation.

For example, it was Elias Howe who invented the value innovation that was the sewing machine and who won the court battle over patent rights against the upstart Isaac Singer. But he was quickly overtaken, and has been long since forgotten, as Singer added a few refinements to the design and introduced a clever instalment plan that 'loaned' machines to customers still unsure of how the machines would come to revolutionize their businesses.

What if we just loaned products rather than sold them?

And there are many other examples of changing norms about payment. Google is only the most visible example of a business model based upon giving consumers products for free and utilizing the volume and value of those customers to advertisers. A host of online music services, from Spiral Frog to Spotify, use a similar model, offering free music in exchange for exposure to targeted advertising. And like many innovations, advertiser-funded free music is of course itself a recasting of a previous innovation: free-to-air commercial music radio!

What would happen if we asked people to just pay what they felt our product/service was worth?

What Radiohead lost in direct revenue from launching its *In Rainbows* album online with an 'honesty box' system whereby people could download it for whatever price they thought it was worth (or no price at all) was easily offset by the publicity it generated. The band sold out their live shows and when they later released the album as a conventional CD it topped the charts. At around the same time as Radiohead were offering fans a free album online, Prince was giving away his album *Planet Earth* with a British Sunday newspaper. Two months later he sold out 21 successive live shows at London's O2 Centre, one of the largest venues in Europe, as well as enjoying increased sales of his back catalogue. Whereas live music was once used to promote recorded music, today that relationship has been reversed. Consumers, who are often unwilling to pay for music downloads are sufficiently excited by the live, one-off, shared experience of the gig or music festival to pay for it.

How could we make money if we sold what we do for free?

Recorded music, instead of attempting to compete against free content and illegal copying, is now often a promotional channel for live music or other related services (merchandising, ringtones, movies, magazines). Similarly, many Bollywood movie production houses simultaneously release films at movie houses, on DVD and online, unlike the traditional drip-feed of formats. They've realized these markets and experiences have become different enough (seeing a Bollywood movie in a cinema is quite another level of experience from downloading it to watch at home) to ensure that any lost revenue would be less than the cost of pursuing pirates. These market innovations are sending shock waves through the recording industry that are still redefining its context.

What if we mixed up our normal product/ service release format?

A similar new business model is sweeping the gaming community in East Asia. Massive multiplayer online games such as MapleStory and Legend of Mir are given away as free downloads, but avid players buy extras for their in-game characters: anything from new weapons to haircuts.

How would selling convenience or speed of transaction rather than what we now consider as our product/service change how we do things?

For other companies, market innovation means that speed is the critical factor. Peter Lewis, CEO of Progressive, completely reorganized its business around a revised view of what they could do for customers: save them time getting insured: 'we don't sell insurance any more', said Lewis, 'We sell speed.' On the flip side, Ferrari builds desire by maintaining a waiting list for its cars and many companies have tapped into the 'slow-food' movement which encourages people to take time and relax over food. Indeed, market innovation often requires thinking beyond the conventional economics of value.

How could we help our customers relax?

It can also be about thinking about how environmental changes can create new opportunities for marketing and product and value chain design. Sales of Johnson and Johnson's most famous product, the Band-aid, were slow until J&J hit on the idea of giving away free samples to the Boy Scouts organization which, at that point in time, were becoming a part of life for families all across America.

If we had 1000 'freebies' who would we give them to and what might the effect be?

Michael Dell's company was built on a market innovation hypothesis, predicting that the value/cost ratio of Internet sales and an after-sales service would be superior to that of distributing computers through traditional channels. Dell's reading of this equation was new because he factored in how the spread of the Internet and the ubiquity of credit cards would alter buyer behaviour to the point where a growing proportion of customers would have the confidence to make a large purchase without physically touching it – if the price and sales support were right.

Just as Apple's market innovations are related to the fact that people like the feel or tactile nature of their MP3 players more than other brands, Evian increased demand for their personal bottled water in France threefold by devising a bottle cap with a loop that made it more fun to carry. This market innovation coincided with growing trends toward carrying bottled water not just while at the gym, but while on a bike, or walking, or at work. Evian's bottle is one that's fun to twirl. And, just as Apple and Evian recognize the market sensuality of touch, Crayola and Harley-Davidson have recently taken steps to market and protect the distinctive smell of their crayons and the sound of their bikes.

Market innovation recasts the meaning of the product by redefining how consumers understand or use it. This 4th degree flips the value chain, inviting consumers to create or discover new sources of value in products through innovative approaches to marketing and mediation.

How does what we do look? Feel? Smell? Sound?

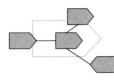

The 5th Degree of Strategic Innovation: Boundary Innovation

The 5th degree of innovation takes this reinvention further, mixing up different stages along the value chain, from production to consumption, in order to discover or create what are in effect entirely new products and experiences in the mind's eye of the consumer. As we outlined in Chapter 1, this degree of innovation might involve a 'postmodern' mixing, matching or juxtaposing of things that might not normally have been blended; crossing or disregarding conventional borders; and, subsequently, embracing the paradoxes that the modernist era sought to resolve in its quest for essential logical truths.

This degree of strategic innovation is not as avant garde as it might at first sound. As far back as 1992, an article in the *Harvard Business Review*, called 'From Value Chain to Value Constellation', predicted the crumbling of the rigid in-house value chain as firms sought to specialize in what they did best and made that the hub of a system of contracting arrangements that added up to a web of value creation. And in 1999, Philip Evans and Thomas Wurster's book *Blown to Bits: How the New Economics of Information Transforms Strategy* dramatically drove home an argument that a chain in a box would not be the shape of value creation in the future.

Which bits would we look to salvage first if our value chain was 'blown to bits'? Which bits wouldn't matter so much?

But, as the quotation from Plutarch at the head of this chapter suggests, a simple model like the value chain is still a good place to start (even if not a good place to finish); a springboard from which to explore how the crossing and blurring of conventional value adding boundaries can lead to strategic innovation. The 5th degree of strategic innovation may involve the removal and/or bundling of aspects from other pre-existing value chains or industries to uncover unique new forms of value; or it may derive from leading into the value chain elements traditionally seen as outside it in order to create new value. Let's look at some examples of both.

The most obvious expression of the former type of boundary innovation is the dispersal of part of a chain once thought vital, often achieved by an unexpected combination with a new channel or medium. For example, Amazon embraced the Internet and shed the necessity for a bookseller to have stores. This allowed it to focus on what it does best – being a branded, and thus trusted, marketplace. Online or telephone banks have increased security and decreased costs by working without physical branches. But there are many more intriguing varieties of innovative chain 'combos'.

Nintendo's Wii is a boundary crossing blend of nostalgia and novelty as diverse as the company's background. Nintendo started life as a producer of playing cards in the late 19th century. After failed diversifications into taxis, hotels and instant rice, the company settled on toy-making, its first real hit being a fake extending arm called the Ultra Hand. The Wii's player's cartoons draw on traditional Kokeshi, or Japanese wooden dolls. Its novelty is that its bats, racquets, balls, poles and swords play like an extension of the body. Its

How could we link with others to enable our customers to build something interesting?

remote is packed with old, off the shelf technology, while the graphics are state of the art. Even the name 'Wii' combines a contemporary signal of the console's unique appeal ('we' indicating a shared, social gaming experience) and a historical allusion to the console's competitors ('wii' in ancient Japanese translates as 'over-turning the traditional Gods' – perhaps a reference to Sony and Microsoft and the traditions they represent). Rather than competing head-to-head against Sony and Microsoft with a cutting-edge, high-tech console like the PSP or Xbox, this blending of old and new technologies has allowed the Wii to appeal to non-traditional gamers as a family friendly, multiplayer experience whilst also attracting older gamers with its retro look and feel.

Facebook and YouTube haven't really invented any new technology, they've just networked together emerging technological capabilities and effective market innovation to take advantage of growing trends toward self-expression. Ponoko.com is a website and network which invites people to add their own values to design, and so make their own unique products (a chair, for example). It allows people who would like to build something unique to them, but who may lack some (or almost all) of the necessary skills, to connect with designers, woodworkers, upholsterers and so on. It also lets participants customize or 'mash up' other people's designs. In this case, boundary innovation is becoming harder to distinguish from some value innovations. But there are more advanced forms.

What companies from industries other than our own do we like and why?

For some, the boundary innovation may go beyond simply combining pre-existing elements into a service: it may be about crossing borders and networking products and whole industries in addition to emerging technologies. The battle between the HD DVD and Blu-Ray formats seems to bear many similarities to a contest thirty years ago between video-recording formats: Betamax and VHS. Then Sony's Betamax was soundly defeated. This time around it looks likes Sony's Blu-Ray will prevail. The reasons behind victory are not necessarily about the quality of invention (many considered Betamax to be superior to VHS). They may be more about the quality of the 'value system'.

With Blu-Ray, Sony had more than a good format: it had connections that would channel more customers to it than to the competitor. Sony owned two major Hollywood studios, suppliers of DVD content (who would, obviously, package this content in Blu-Ray format). And it produced the PlayStation. The decision to fit the PlayStation 3 with a Blu-Ray player, although expensive, was clever (if you owned a PlayStation you didn't need to buy a DVD player, you already had one: a Blu-Ray one). Toshiba and Microsoft, HD's backers, didn't have a movie studio and they didn't have a games console. Sony's value system, crossing many traditional boundaries, stacked the odds.

Other boundaries are ripe for plundering by boundary innovators. In theory, products are supposed to peak, mature and decline. But there are many examples of innovations involving resuscitation of industries or products once thought dead. Condoms are an obvious example. Once deemed redundant after the invention of the Pill, the spread of AIDS and a focus on sex for recreation rather than procreation changed the landscape and thus the shape (and colours) of branded prophylactics.

What's the most mature product in our industry and how would we revitalize it?

It may not have seemed so a few years ago, but it could be that the second music format that survives into the 21st century alongside downloading is the vinyl record album. The CD was thought to have led to the maturity and decline of vinyl, but vinyl has made a comeback through the noughties. Despite its convenience, the CD never rivalled the affection and the mystique associated by many with the vinyl album. This is partly because of the album's material and tactile qualities (which may also be behind the resurgence of wood as a material for all things from cellphones to computer mice), and also because of a nostalgia for things past. Radiohead's *In Rainbows* free-to-download album described earlier in this chapter, was also offered as a premium priced box set, including limited edition art work, a book of lyrics, a bonus CD and the *In Rainbows* album – on both CD and vinyl formats. The emphasis on special editions and personalized content in the music industry, like the growth in live music, is partly a reaction against the availability of free content, but also reconnects the music fan back to the mentality of the record collector and nostalgia for the tactile, sensual qualities of the vinyl era.

Could we make our product in another medium or sell our services through other media?

The resurgence of vinyl may be linked to what American film director and commentator John Carpenter calls a 'nostalgia cycle', which disturbs, blurs and complicates conventions about values ascribed to new versus old products. 'My theory', Carpenter explains, 'is that there's a 20 to 30 year nostalgia cycle in pop culture.' This nostalgia cycle can be seen equally in the 'creative' and 'conventional' industries: from cars, to furniture, to clothing, to cosmetics, to packaging, to music, to film, and to dance. But good, or strategic, innovations cannot simply be dredged up and reproduced from a back catalogue. As with the value of a movie sequel discussed in the previous chapter, a nostalgic discovery can drive value innovation, but only when it is successfully re-created. Hip hop artists take an old riff or song and combine it with their own sound and production values to create something new. Likewise retro clothing, now a staple of the fashion industry, never quite repeats the old model, offering instead a restyled, re-imagined and stripped down version of a previous decade. As every fashionista knows, retro means 'classic' – not just old. Something old and something borrowed get remixed into something new.

What did people like about our industry 20 years ago and how could we bring it back?

So, boundary innovation can come from disturbing the conventions associated with the product life cycle. But this is just one common framework. Think of any management structure or mantra that your organization submits itself to (the customer is always right; the best form of advertising is word of mouth; there is no substitute for good service . . .). Boundary innovation can stem from thinking the opposite (challenge the customer; advertise through exclusivity; cut service costs).

Blue Oceans may be the opposite of red oceans, but what other coloured oceans are there and what should we do about them?

And then there is another kind of boundary innovation, based upon bringing what would once have been seen as unusual bedfellows 'inside the value tent' so to speak. Many have advocated closer relations with those suppliers that were once seen to exist outside of and to the left of (if one looks at the conventional drawing of the chain) an organization's operations. In the creative industries, major actors who 'minor' in directing, artists who curate exhibitions, even bands who sell their own records, bring new insights as intermediaries. Many of the marketing innovations in the music industry described in this chapter have come from the artists, often against the advice of their record labels. Trent Reznor of the band Nine Inch Nails has been one of the most radical advocates of free content and promotional add-ons to personalize or customize music. Yet his label seemed more concerned at the loss of revenue and it was only when he struck out on his own that Reznor could build his repertoire of 'special features' which accompany each of NiN's releases.

Another musician/businessman, Peter Gabriel, incurred the wrath of many musicians with his OD2 project which encouraged the customer (he provocatively terms music customers 'curators') to become a blender or creator of unique musical combinations. His operation lacked scale, but its innovations paved a way for others such as iTunes to fundamentally alter the music industry, and perhaps time will vindicate Gabriel as an innovator for good in this regard. 'All sorts of new life forms are emerging out of the corpse of the music industry', he said in 2008. 'Anything the old music business was looking at, they had to feel like there was going to be $100,000 in sales before they put their hand in their pocket [the changed value landscape is actually enabling a lot more] experimental projects.'

Which customers would we want as co-designers? Which suppliers?

Moving to the other end of the conventional value chain there are the stories of firms who have made the customer (formerly somewhere out to the right of the point of a value chain) an 'insider'. Several clothing brands encourage customers to become co-designers, building their own customized products, from Levis to Nike. Threadless.com allows participants to design and sell their own T-shirts, rate other people's designs and compete against each other. Wikipedia turns encyclopedia users (and many who never looked at an encyclopedia) into encyclopedia producers.

What might our customers be interested in talking about?

Many of these boundary innovations gain added value by connecting an organization's customers, or potential customers, to one another as well as to the product. Customer camaraderie or shared experiences can encourage brand loyalty. Dove's multi-media, cross-platform endeavour 'The Campaign for Real Beauty' sought not to shift product to consumers directly, but rather to promote an inter-consumer debate about an interesting issue for many women.

Radiohead's strategic innovations (mentioned in the 4th degree above) also include a recent online competition that invited fans to make a mini animated video to accompany any song from *In Rainbows*. Online voters selected finalists, with the winners receiving funding to produce a full-length music video. They also made available the original 'stems' to some of the songs from the album via iTunes and invited fans to remix them in a competition which drew six million unique visitors to the band's website. In this instance, blended value production resulted in valuable market innovation.

How could we help people remix our products/services? What could we learn from their remixes?

Sellaband.com connects two ends of the music industry value chain usually poles apart – investment in new talent, and fans. Members of the site's community are invited to invest in unsigned artists. Once a band has raised $50,000, they record an album which is made available to their 'investors' – and released to the public. The future revenues are split three ways between the artists, the fan-investors, and the users. Artists tap into a new source of finance, cutting out the need for a record deal. Consumers are implicated as co-producers and their involvement also builds a loyal fan-base for the featured bands. The concept is similar to Korea's 'netizen' funds which allow ordinary film fans to invest in film production. The 2008 film *Faintheart* took this a step further, allowing users of the MySpace social networking site to contribute to the script and to choose a director and some of the cast.

List the ways in which people could actively invest in our organization (beyond buying shares)?

Sellaband (and related sites like Slicethepie.com) reverse the traditional relationships between producers, consumers and distributors. Sites like YouTube facilitate user-generated content as well as user-distributed content. Authonomy.com is a website which allows readers and writers to become editors. The website acts as a virtual 'slush-pile', with users voting on which authors deserve a publishing deal. Mainstream publishers, including Harper Collins, have used this as a source of new writing and new authors, cutting out the laborious process of wading through unsolicited manuscripts themselves. Even if these innovations don't always generate better products, they help to redefine relationships between consumers and producers. It is doubtful whether the Royal Opera House's 2009 experimental 'twitter' opera, in which composer Helen Porter set to music lines of text message contributed by members of the 'twitter' social network, will produce a great libretto. But it will certainly help the opera house to involve a different type of audience. The same might be said of films developed through social networking sites – the value of such innovations may be realized not in the product itself but in other types of productive relationship between and among producers and consumers.

What's our slush-pile? Could we develop a cheaper or better one?

Boundary innovation is similar to the 'creative rediscovery' of market innovation. In this case by drawing in different ways of thinking about and valuing the product from outside the traditional value chain, by switching value chain positions or by connecting these perspectives in unexpected ways, boundary innovation allows a further reinvention of familiar products and experiences.

The 6th Degree of Strategic Innovation: Learning Innovation

The final degree of strategic innovation is about learning during the process of developing an innovation and bringing it to market in order to develop further innovations. There are three main types: pre-market learning; learning after market success; and learning after market 'failure'. All of these forms occur as the result of people interacting with new products and services, or even just stimulating interactions between potential customers and the organization itself.

Pre-market learning may require an innovative approach to understanding the target market. For example, New Zealand's Industrial Research Limited, a research consultancy, developed a competition called 'What's Your Problem New Zealand?' and offered $1 million of free research to the company with the most interesting business problem. This would cost the IRL significantly less than the charge out value of $1million, but, more importantly, the entries to the competition (to be filled out on a form provided by IRL) would provide an easily coded database of common problem areas, potential clients to build relationships with, and reasons why potential customers may not have sought out IRL previously.

How could we engage in 'problem-sourcing' or create a database of our customers' problems?

IBM's move into consultancy services in the late 1990s under Lou Gerstner has been seen as making good business sense because services offered better margins (and a faster growing market) than IBM's traditional domain of computer hardware. A presence here would also enable cross-selling of hardware products. But the firm's consultancy arm also provided a source of pre-market learning. IBM became more able to see how people used their products, or why they didn't use them and incorporated this into their new product development.

What services could we provide (if you're a product company)? What products would we make (if you're a service company)?

The film *My Big Fat Greek Wedding* used a targeted release amongst America's Greek community to build a pre-market word of mouth 'buzz' about the movie. Reversing the normal release strategy, the film was shown as in-flight entertainment *before* the film's release and in special screenings for Greek organizations and church groups. The approach not only built a strong pre-release buzz around the film, it also allowed the film's marketers and distributors to learn more about their audience and tap into audiences who were less susceptible to more traditional media channels.

What might we learn if we showed our new products/services to people on a plane (or a train or some other confined space)?

Learning innovation can also develop after a product has been successfully launched. Fisher & Paykel's DishDrawer, a double-drawer dishwasher where dishes can be washed in one drawer while new dirty dishes are placed in the other, is a great value innovation. But it has gone even further as a result of the company's ability to learn from and adapt to its initial success. The company discovered that in Japan, where space in many homes was limited, customers liked the fact that they could rotate their dishes within the DishDrawer, and were using one drawer for storage to save valuable cupboard space. In the United States the DishDrawer was becoming popular among some Jewish families who saw its two drawers offering the possibility of providing a meat and a dairy drawer and hence being 'kosher'. Learning from these adaptations or re-interpretations of the original value innovation, Fisher and Paykel were able to redirect their marketing efforts in these locations.

Define an alternative use for one of your products/services?

3Ms famous Post-It Notes may be an example of both learning from product development and market success. As described in Chapter 3, Post-It Notes emerged from a failed experiment in adhesives carried out by a lower-level researcher during the 15% of time that 3M encouraged employees to use for working on their own ideas. The idea wandered around the lower echelons of the company until a small number of internal sponsors realized its potential and sought to develop it into a product for whom poor, or temporary, adhesivity was actually a virtue. Beyond the initial market success of Post-Its, 3M showed incredible awareness of how people were using and customizing their notes and used this to develop a whole raft of related products.

If you had one day a week to work on a project of your own choosing what would it be and why?

In 2007 Cadbury launched an advertising campaign for Cadbury Dairy Milk chocolate featuring a gorilla playing the drums, in time to a Phil Collins track – 'In the Air Tonight'. Shortly after the campaign appeared on British TV, it was posted on the video sharing site YouTube from where it became a popular viral download, with an estimated six million views in six months, at zero cost to Cadbury. One viewer remixed the gorilla footage to the music of Bonnie Tyler's 'Total Eclipse of the Heart'. Cadbury returned the compliment, broadcasting this 'unofficial' remixed version on British television in 2008. Through viral campaigns, companies not only benefit from free advertising (4th degree innovation) as consumers do their advertising for them (5th degree), they also tap into consumer creativity to learn more about how their product is perceived and how this view can be exploited (6th degree).

One of the most successful examples of a company both feeding and being fed by consumer creativity is LEGO. LEGO action figures are a staple of user-generated content on YouTube – conversely the LEGO console games based on Star Wars, Batman and Indiana Jones play with the same DIY aesthetic as their fans. Instead of attempting to close down unlicensed imitators, LEGO has used its fan-base to promote, learn about and develop its own products. This is a form of boundary innovation (5th degree) in which the product is reconfigured through user involvement, but it is also a learning innovation which adapts to changing customer behaviour and emerging markets.

LEGO's decision to learn from customers rather than insisting on the integrity of its product is comparable to the open source model for software development, pioneered by Linux in the 1990s. By releasing a beta (prototype) version of the Linux operating system and the source code that lay behind it, Linus Torvalds invited users to do his R&D and beta-testing. The Linux operating system was consequently developed as a user-friendly, glitch-free system capable of competing with the likes of Microsoft. Open source has become a popular method for adapting and learning from customers in many parts of the music and games industries too.

How would our organization be different if it was run on an 'open source' basis?

But learning innovation is not just about learning from success. It can also come from learning from and quickly responding to failure. 'If Microsoft is good at anything', claims Seth Godin in the book *Survival Is Not Enough*, 'it's avoiding the trap of worrying about criticism. Microsoft fails con-

How does customer feedback change our products/services?

stantly. They're eviscerated in public for lousy products. Yet they persist, through version after version [learning continuously].' And use the feedback to finish the product.

Learning from failure has recently given rise to popular new management mantras like 'Fast failing' and being at the 'Bleeding Edge'. Jeff Bezos of Amazon claims to encourage people to go faster in order to get products out, even if it may mean a worse initial product and result in a few 'nose bleeds'. 'The cost of trying to avoid mistakes is huge in terms of speed [and] I want us to start learning.'

What was our last failure and what did we learn from it?

Herein we can see the importance of prototyping for any form of learning innovation: it is only through the attempt to make something and operate it that one can fully learn about it. In the words of Michael Schrage, co-director of MIT's Media Lab and author of the book *Serious Play*, 'Effective prototyping may be the most valuable core competence an innovative organization can hope to have.' 'Innovation equals the reaction to the prototype', claims Schrage.

Clearly there is much to learn and many more innovations waiting to be discovered once people start interacting with a product. And this, combined with the 4th and 5th degrees of strategic innovation, makes customers not just consumers of innovation but very much a part of the strategic innovation system.

It is interesting that many of the best examples and proponents of learning innovation are American. While its recent economic troubles have been widely reported, Amar Bhide points to something that should give hope, in the book *The Venturesome Economy*. Bhide argues that America has an integral advantage when it comes to innovation: 'venturesome consumption', or, an extraordinary willingness among American consumers to try new, sometimes imperfect, things, and to say what they think about them.

How would we rate our customers on a scale of venturesome-ness? Do we need to find better customers?

Learning innovation requires another twist on the value chain, with innovation coming at the point of consumption and feeding back into product development. The process connects consumer creation and discovery back into the re-creation and re-discovery of the product.

The figure overleaf provides a summary, or a refresher, of what each lens or degree of innovation magnifies or reconfigures on a conventional value chain and lists the examples used as illustrations.

The outcomes of strategic innovation considered in this chapter show innovation taking effect, not only at the point of conception, but in reconfigurations and reinventions up and down the value chain. We have also considered how discovery (the revelation of a potentially valuable innovation) requires creation (imaginative reworking) if it is to be truly innovative. The first two degrees of innovation – value innovation and cost innovation – depend primarily on 'discovery' unlocking a

Degree of innovation	How it changes the chain	Examples
1st Value: 	*Inventing* **the chain** *Extending* **the chain**	Perkin's mauve, FedEx, Walkman, Dyson, Alessi, instant noodles, Toyota and the Prius.
2nd Cost: 	*Shortening* **the chain**	Frozen airfreight, 1 Laptop Per Child, General Motors, Southwest and Ryanair, Tata's Nano, Nike, Amazon, barcodes.
3rd Volume: 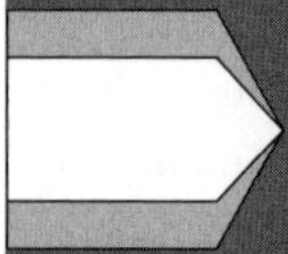	*Widening* **the chain**	The Model-T and $5 day, Google, eBay, iTunes, Aalsmeer Flower Auction, Oral B, Gillette, Swatch, freq. flyer programmes.
4th Market(ing): 	*Broadcasting or recasting* **the chain to the market**	Birdseye's chillers, Singer, Spotify, Radiohead, Prince, Bollywood, slow food, Harley, Band-aid, Dell, Evian
5th Boundary: 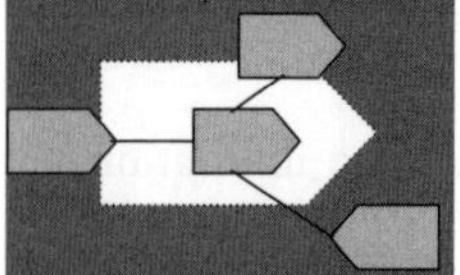	*Scattering* **the chain** *Sharing* **the chain**	Blu-Ray, vinyl albums, condoms, BMW's Mini, retro, Threadless.com, Wikipedia, NiN, Dove, Sellaband, Authonomy, Gabriel's OD2.
6th Learning: 	*Adapting* **the chain**	Post-its, Industrial Research Limited, IBM, *My Big Fat Greek Wedding*, Fisher and Paykel, Cadbury, LEGO, Linux, Microsoft.

Figure 7.2 Six degrees of innovation

new product, idea or process; the remaining four (volume innovation, market innovation, blend innovation and learning innovation) contain a stronger element of 'creation', reworking our own and other people's discoveries in order to reinvent them.

The previous two chapters have taken us a long way from thinking that innovation comes from a solitary genius inventing something out of nothing. But if innovation derives from a system rather than a genius, how might we intervene in this system to actively spur on a strategic innovation process that could lead to outcomes like these?

CHAPTER 8

Sparking Strategic Innovation

'There's no use trying', said Alice. 'One can't believe impossible things.' 'I daresay you haven't had much practice,' said the Queen. 'When I was your age, I always did it for half an hour a day. Why, sometimes I've believed as many as six impossible things before breakfast.'

Lewis Carroll, *Alice in Wonderland*

The previous chapter outlined six degrees of strategic innovation and provided examples of outcomes which might spur on the development of strategic innovation in any organization or field of endeavour. In this chapter we describe five perspectives which, when combined, can contribute to a process that can spark the bisociative thinking loops described in Chapter 6 and give rise to outcomes in each of the six degree categories, before breakfast or any time after that. The five perspectives which characterize this process of strategic innovation are: diversity, naivety, curiosity, urgency and thinking beyond best practice. The first two attributes, diversity and naivety, describe an openness to new ideas and experiences which relates to the *discovery* of strategic innovations; the other two traits, curiosity and urgency, describe a more active orientation needed to drive the process of strategic innovation, which relates to our category of *creation*. The last, thinking beyond best practice, will lead us to a framework for generating strategic innovation that will combine both creation and discovery.

Diversity

The importance of diversity has already been expressed a number of times in this book. But it is worth reiterating, briefly, the link between being able to look at a situation from a number of different perspectives and the *discovery* of strategic innovations. Examples of diversity influencing scientific discovery include Aristotle's and Leonardo's polymathy, Galileo's understanding of physics being informed by his watching dockmen at work, Einstein's greatest discoveries being shaped while he was a Swiss patent officer because he couldn't secure a university position and Edison's bringing a range of personalities together at Menlo Park (perhaps the first modern research lab) to complement the peculiarities of his own. Diversity is also linked to discovery in the arts, politics and research, from J.R.R. Tolkien and C.S. Lewis composing their epic novels in concert with their social groups to the American Constitution being born out of the conflicts between the men from different backgrounds who were charged with its conception, and the recent study in the journal *Science*, mentioned in Chapter 3, that linked a narrowing range of sources to a potential decline in innovation.

This link between diversity and innovation has recently been given a catchy name by Frans Johansson: the 'Medici effect'. Johansson argues, and we would agree with him, that innovation is created at 'intersections': intersections that are found when individuals see beyond their particular expertise and actively seek to link with others with different perspectives. Johansson calls this the Medici effect in honour of the Medici family, who played a large part in stimulating the innovative culture of the European Renaissance by acting as a junction for art, commerce and the sciences.

With hindsight we can see the Medici effect at work in forming the American state. Joseph Ellis' recent book, *American Creation*, argues that the ideological and temperamental diversity of the founders who came together at that crucial juncture was a crucial element in their success. Their different beliefs about what the American Revolution meant created an atmosphere or ferment that enhanced creativity and 'replicated the checks and balances of the Constitution with a human version of the same principle'.

In more recent times this linking perspective has been behind the World Wide Web, both in its operation (as a global exchange of knowledge and ideas) and in its history (as the unexpected outcome of a group project). At the time he developed the World Wide Web, Tim Berners-Lee was working on the CERN European particle accelerator, an international scientific group project in Switzerland. The discovery grew out of a kind of side-project. And his managers, like the Medicis, simply let him do it – in Berners-Lee's recollection, 'they didn't say yes, they didn't say no'. In this context, diversity relates to the 'tolerance for contradictions' which we highlighted in the first part of this book as an essential component in the bisociative process of creativity. Only by opening up to unexpected and unfamiliar ideas and people will we be able to discover novel and valuable connections between them.

Naivety

The Medici effect leads us to a second perspective needed for the process of strategic innovation: naivety. If we want to discover something new, sometimes it helps not to be an expert; or, at least, not to consider oneself an expert. Experts can fall into two traps: some can be complacent, breaking problems down into conventional categories and offering off-the-shelf solutions that they feel comfortable with because they have seen them work before; others find making a decision difficult because they can see all the possible pitfalls in advance.

Novices, on the other hand, are not expert enough to fully understand the potential consequences, and are subsequently not put off by them. And, they think about their answers in new ways and apply whatever knowledge they may have from other spheres to the problem at hand. In the previous chapter, the examples of Perkin's mauve dye and Gillette's disposable razor both illustrate the benefits of a naive attitude towards expert opinion and expectations. A lack of complacency may explain why a number of experiments have shown novices to make fewer mistakes when compared to people who are expert in that area. Focused naivety may also translate to a loss of self-doubt or self-consciousness, allowing the novice to become wholly absorbed in the creative moment, a euphoric state of heightened creativity described by the psychologist Mihaly Csikszentmihalyi as 'flow', during which the artist or performer seems to achieve perfect results without consciously striving towards them.

Mark Twain described the novice's ability to innovate when he wrote that: 'The best swordsman doesn't need to fear the second best; no, the person for him to be afraid of is some ignorant antagonist [who] does the thing he ought not to do.' Michael Stedman, CEO of the world's second largest producer of nature films, Natural History New Zealand, claims for this reason that he tries to hire people whom he identifies as having 'an inquisitive naivety, but with brains'.

This is an approach that can be engendered, simply, for example, by creating a little more mess in your operations. In the book *A Perfect Mess: The Hidden Benefits of Disorder*, Eric Abramson and David Freedman argue that one of the virtues of a certain level of disorder is that it can lead people to encounter (or find) forgotten objects which can put a new spin on problem solving or to find (eventually) familiar objects in unusual contexts or juxtaposed against other interesting items. Hence, messier people, like inquisitive but naive people, may look at things from different angles and in different combinations and thus be more serendipitous and, consequently, more innovative.

Curiosity

Michael Stedman's focus on 'inquisitive naivety' brings us to a third perspective that can promote strategic innovation. To be constructively innovative it is not enough to bring diverse approaches to bear and to be naive (or not think oneself an expert). This might open up possibilities and allow us to discover new ways of seeing or thinking, but we also need to animate our new ideas and perceptions. We need to build upon our discoveries with active *creation*. An individual or a group must also be curious, or interested enough in the problems at hand to inquire further and look deeper.

Curiosity has often been seen as an important characteristic of the creative mind. A British art historian summed up Leonardo da Vinci as 'the most relentlessly curious man in history' and Newton would write of being 'excited beyond an ordinary curiosity' when he could sense he was closing in on a significant discovery. But the word was tainted in many circles through its association with the word 'idle' and, indeed, it was often used in furthering the divide between those who saw themselves as industrious and those creative types who might be branded the 'idle curious'. Curiosity and innovation did, subsequently, lose touch with one another.

But, the word curious has made something of a comeback in recent times as a positive trait broadly associated with leadership and innovation. This may be in no small part due to former President George W. Bush being dubbed 'incurious George'. In 2001, influential Princeton University political scientist Fred Greenstein observed that Bush 'lack[ed] intellectual curiosity and is impatient with the play of ideas'. This line of thinking struck a chord, resurrecting the word 'incurious' from the lexicographical graveyard, and pushing it toward the top of indexes that monitor words and phrases that appear in the news media. In parallel, many influential commentators identified curiosity as an important trait of a President or indeed any progressive leader of substance.

Given this context, it may be no surprise that 'curiosity' made an appearance in Barrack Obama's Presidential inaugural address. Toward the end of his address, Obama stated: 'Our challenges may be new. The instruments with which we meet them may be new. But those values upon which our success depends – hard work and honesty, courage and fair play, tolerance and *curiosity*, loyalty and patriotism – these things are old. These things are true. They have been the quiet force of progress throughout our history.'

However, while most of these 'old and true values' driving 'progress' (a word used in almost every inaugural address) are old and true inaugural address terms ('hard work' or a variation has been cited eight times; honesty, six times; courage, 10 times; 'fair play' or a variation, four times; tolerance, five times; loyalty, four times; and patriotism, twenty-one times), curiosity is a new 'old and true' expression here. The word had been used only once before in an inaugural address, by William Henry Harrison in March 1841. And Harrison referred pejoratively to 'the gratification of the curiosity of speculative statesmen'.

So, curiosity is back. Installed in what we would say as its rightful place at the centre of an innovative process, alongside diversity and naivety. And where past generations might have associated curiosity with idleness, here it is conceived as a progressive, driving energy – a form of active *creation* to animate *discovery*, and so a crucial link in the bisociative process of strategic innovation

Urgency

But diversity, naivety and curiosity need to be directed. They must be given a point or purpose for them to lead to strategic innovation. To build on the Mark Twain quotation above, the relative novice is only effective if he gets angry enough to direct his energies and attack. Like curiosity, urgency is an active, animating force which we associate with *creation*. Where curiosity added energy to inquisitive naivety, urgency adds focus and direction to that energetic curiosity. Urgency, then, is the fourth driver of the strategic innovation process.

Urgency is often at the core of innovation. From the folk wisdom of Plato's statement in the Republic that 'Necessity is the mother of invention', to 'deadline magic' in the rehearsal room, urgency speeds up the decision-making process needed to turn potential solutions into purposeful innovation. IKEA has defined its progress in terms of the crises that it has turned into opportunities. It started to develop showrooms as a response to being overwhelmed by the competition with other mail-order firms; supplier boycotts led it to design and build its own furniture; increases in transportation cost provoked research into flat-packing; insufficient sales people turning up for a showroom launch led to IKEA's self service concept, and so on.

But organizations need not wait for crises to occur, they can help engender a sense of impending crisis and use this as a stimulus for innovation. Samsung, for example, promotes a sense of 'perpetual crisis' as part of its organizational culture and links this to its achievement of over 1600 patents each year.

In 1995 John P. Kotter published what has become the seminal framework for thinking about managing change initiatives in the *Harvard Business Review*. This has come to be known as Kotter's eight steps for managing change. The last seven steps are: forming a powerful guiding coalition; creating a vision; communicating the vision; empowering others to act on the vision; planning for and creating short-term wins; consolidating improvements and producing more change; and institutionalizing new approaches. The first is 'establishing a sense of urgency'. In more recent times, having been struck by just how much everything else stands or falls on achieving this first step, Kotter has returned to focus on just how urgency can be encouraged. In his recent book, *A Sense of Urgency*, he describes a range of urgency spurring tactics such as sending employees out of the organization and bringing other stakeholders in, looking for opportunities in crises, using unusual media (if your people are used to PowerPoint presentations, then unplug the computers and tell them a story), and disseminating surprising or dramatic data.

To summarize, the process of innovation will start from *diversity*, creating the conditions in which new connections can be discovered or created. *Naivety* instils an attitude of engagement and openness towards the discovered material rather than falling back on established routines and mindsets. *Curiosity* contributes an attitude of active *creation*, animating the cycle of *discovery* and *rediscovery*, opening up new angles and continually reorienting the process. Finally *urgency* directs and drives the innovation process forward, forcing us to make decisions on which ideas to develop and implement, and which to reject or recycle. But how might you then move this diverse, naïve, curious, urgent group from neutral to in gear?

Beyond Best Practice

In Chapter 6 we noted that innovation is not a transferable commodity, it is rooted in a particular time and place. The Romans identified 'genius' with the spirit of a place (usually the home), and the neo-classical philosophers of the Renaissance period picked up this idea, locating genius in the 'character' of specific places or personalities. For innovation to take root, it needs to be embedded in our own specific identities, cultures and contexts – we must, in other words, make our own music.

Picking up on our earlier discussion on how copying best practice does not lead to strategic innovation, we have developed a matrix of alternative mindsets that can help to orient a diverse, and naïve, and curious, and urgent group of people to develop their own unique approach to strategic innovation. In time, such an approach can help to embed an innovative culture that is difficult for other organizations to replicate. This is important. In an age where products and simple business processes are easily copied, a culture of continual innovation is harder for others to copy or to outflank than a one-off innovation. Seth Godin in an article for *Fast Company* described the challenge this way: 'You can't be remarkable by following someone else who's remarkable... The thing that all great companies have in common is that they have nothing in common.' Or, as musician Jerry Garcia put it: 'You do not merely want to be the best of the best. You want to be considered the only ones who do what you do.'

The Innovation Generation Matrix arranges four alternatives to best practice: worst practices, good practices, promising practices, and next practice. These are defined in terms of orientations to innovation and orientations to learning. The two columns present our two orientations to innovation: creation and discovery. As we saw in Chapter 6, discovery and creation represent two halves of the bisociative innovation loop, but one may choose to start from either side of this loop as an entry point to the innovative process.

The two rows present two approaches to learning. The first row describes an external or empirical orientation, like that associated with Edison in Chapter 6, an approach to learning where one believes that knowledge exists 'out there' in the world. We just have to look for it. The second row describes an internal or intuitive approach, which instead believes that our own mind, or imagination, is a better place to begin.

The ensuing two-by-two matrix results in four alternatives to copying best practice and the de-animation or strategic 'dumbing down' that this can breed. Its approach aims to spark strategic innovation through a focus on:

- *worst* practices and products, based on an active/critical reaction to experience (especially to experiences of failure);

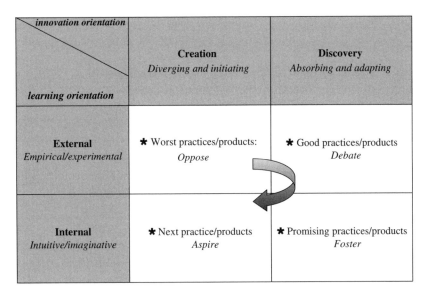

Figure 8.1 Beyond best practice: a strategic innovation generation matrix

- discovering current *good* practices and products from across the industry, based on accommodating and debating alternative ideas and perspectives;
- shifting attention back inside the firm to discover *promising* practices that could be sponsored and advanced; and
- focussing on creating advances beyond what is currently regarded as best practice in an industry and which is distinctive to the organization in question, an approach that focusses on creating *'next* practice' from within.

The matrix is presented in Figure 8.1, and the following paragraphs describe each of the approaches and how they might spur the innovation process in more detail.

*Worst Practice

It is certainly not new to suggest that much can be learnt from failure. That you can learn more from a defeat than you can from victory is a well-established coaching mantra. However, as we've already expressed in this book, the field of management often shies away from failure.

It is difficult to know when worst practice as an alternative learning tool to best practice first emerged, but David Snowden of the think-tank Cynefin has been espousing the benefits of focussing on understanding and discussing worst practices since the late 1990s, claiming that 'striving to avoid failure is more compelling than imitating success'.

Since that point, others, such as management guru Tom Peters, have promoted related approaches like 'fast-failing' (having the courage to try things quickly and then adjusting quickly as one learns by doing). In 2008, Richard Watson in the business magazine *Fast Company* wrote an article on how to 'Celebrate Failure' and outlined 'five tips for failing with greater frequency and style':

- Try to fail as often as possible but never make the same mistake twice.
- Set a failure target as part of each employee's annual review.
- If projects are a failure, kill them quickly and move on.
- Create a failure database as part of knowledge management.
- Set up annual failure awards.

However, on this last point Watson wryly notes that if the 'failure awards' become too competitive, a badge of honour rather than an opportunity to have a bit of a laugh and feel that it is okay to try and fail, then it might be time to stop them!

Creating views about worst practice can focus on worst examples from within the company, and how they might be best avoided or *opposed* in the future, or on examples from further afield. For example, despite one being seen as a creative enterprise and the other industrial, a good illustration of how worst practice can be learned from is to explore 'bad band names' and 'bad brand names' to see if there are common elements that could be discussed and subsequently opposed in marketing innovation development in an organization. The table below outlines five lessons that could be learned from worst practice band names and brand names.

The learning orientation to worst practice is externally oriented and empirical, opening out to experiences of failure rather than keeping them to ourselves. The innovative orientation is to use these experiences as a stimulus to actively create something new and different. We summarize these orientations as 'opposing' worst practice.

Worst Band Names (sourced from spinner.com)	Worst Brand Names	Worst Practice Lesson
Dysfunkshun Junkshun	*Blosxom, Sxoup, Fauxto*	Overly clever spellings can confuse and irritate
If your hands were metal that would mean something	*Intel @ dual socket extreme desktop platform*	Trying to capture detail can lead to a name so long that the reader is bored before he gets to the end of it
Juzt Nutz	*Duz*	Avoid appearing juvenile
The house that Gloria Vanderbilt Harmonica Lewinsky	*Slanket* (a blanket with sleeves)	Beware of trying too hard to create clever concept combinations
Buttstomach	*Publishit.com* (online publishers) *Poolife* (pool cleaning company)	Beware of scatological references, intended or otherwise

Figure 8.2

* Good Practices

Our second alternative to best practice begins by scanning the environment to discover examples of good practices. The advantage of a focus on good practices as opposed to best practice is that the former allows for more than one form, and innovation can stem from a *debate* between diverse, naïve, curious and urgent individuals as to which good practice, or combination or adaptation of good practices, might be most appropriate for the group's organization to adopt at that point in time.

This notion of promoting discussion about good practices has recently been advanced by IBM. IBM has discouraged staff from talking of 'best practice' for the reason that it implies that there is only one best way that cannot be surpassed, and this encourages complacency rather than debate and innovation.

The learning orientation is again open-minded and outward looking. This time, rather than actively creating alternatives to worst practice, our innovation orientation is to discover alternatives and options. This provides the springboard for our own innovative processes.

* Promising Practices

Moving from an empirical orientation on to one that requires exercising collective minds to imagine what the future might be can lead a group to debate what emerging practices might be identified as 'promising' practices. These practices might be bubbling up in an organization or in the wider environment, which, if *fostered* correctly, could become tomorrow's good practices.

The notion of promising practices has been promoted in recent years by the Advanced Institute of Management (AIM) research network in the United Kingdom which has developed a particular interest in identifying how companies sponsor and bring through emergent new approaches.

Many of the positive examples already related in this book can be seen, in hindsight, to have stemmed from sponsoring promising practices, from 3M's development of Post-It Notes, to Google's granting of 20% of staff time to working on their own group projects, to Peter Gabriel's OD2 platform.

Recognizing the value of sponsoring promising practices should, by association, help organizations recognize the value of good middle managers. Much maligned in recent decades, and often 'let go' through the short-sighted application of techniques like Business Process Reengineering and an inability to quantify what middle managers did, good middle managers are making a comeback. (Given the stigma attached to the title, however, they now have other names such as team-leader, information manager or quality manager.) A good middle manager, in a strategic innovation context, is one who can articulate how people in an organization can best contribute to an organization's strategy and recognize, select and sponsor promising practices in this regard. (Related to this, we will have more to say about leading from the middle rather than the top in Part 3). Simply encouraging people to look for, present, discuss and develop promising practices, as opposed to copying brought in best practice, can promote a good deal of creative energy in an organization.

The focus of learning from promising practice is more internalized to the firm or industry rather than scanning the wider environment and requires an imaginative mindset rather than a pursuit of evidence. The innovation orientation is based on adapting and accommodating ideas and knowledge, based on an awareness of our own resources and abilities, rather than initiating. This supportive approach to innovation is undervalued but is crucial if we are to capture the value of smaller, incremental innovations and build upon them.

Next Practice

In the book *Disruption*, Jean-Marie Dru describes Sony as: 'the epitome of discontinuity. It sees all its competitors' accomplishments merely as conventions to be overturned.'

The final square on the Innovation Generation Matrix combines an imaginative orientation towards the future with an active orientation to innovation (creating new practices not discovering and reconfiguring old ones). This is an approach that the book *Recreating Strategy* terms 'next practice'. The approach encourages us to ask, not who is doing the best now and how might we copy that, but 'given what we know about what is regarded as best practice, and what we've identified as worst practice, good practice, promising practices, and our own unique capabilities, what are we going to do next?' Or, 'what are we going to do in advance of other organizations' conventions?'

Whereas copying best practice can, over time, dull the minds of an organization's employees, encouraging them to create innovative next practices can enliven them. The 'internal' learning orientation means they are rummaging in their own imaginations while the 'creation' orientation to innovation invites them to take the initiative and develop their own approach to strategic innovation.

We began Part I of this book by warning against a 'best practice' approach to innovation, and have finished by presenting an alternative framework whereby organizations can develop their own cultures of innovation. The Innovation Generation Matrix described four ways of analysing and building upon our own and other people's innovative practices, based on a combination of internal and external orientations to learning and of active (creation) and adaptive (discovery) modes of innovation. If innovation is the heart of creative strategy it should also be 'personal', based on our own particular skills, perspectives and attitudes.

The Innovation Generation Matrix allows us to combine different thinking styles and business models in order to initiate the double loop of discovery and creation, newness and originality, as described in Chapter 6. And it can be fruitfully combined with the sense of purpose provided by the six degrees of innovation described in Chapter 7. We have found it to be extremely useful to brainstorm Market Innovation, for example, by working through what a group sees as worst practice, good practices, promising practices and, consequently, debate and decide what to do next.

However, as with all of the frameworks in this book, the Innovation Generation Matrix is best thought of as a starting point rather than an end in itself. For the very reasons we have presented here in Part I of *Creative Strategy*, it is important that the actual strategic innovations that they spur you towards are unique to you. The models and cases we have presented in Part I are designed to stimulate us to innovate on our own terms, not other people's.

Part I, Strategic Innovation, has argued that for an innovation to be strategic it should be not just new but transformative in its outcomes, providing a point of origin for further innovations. In Chapter 6 we explained why innovation has become increasingly important from a strategic perspective and we have defined the content of strategic innovation thinking in terms of a double loop which combines discovery and creation and which generates something new and original that has value.

In Chapter 7 we attempted to give purpose to strategic innovation by outlining its six generic outcomes (summarized in the graphic at the end of the chapter), outlining how different 'degrees' of innovation can result in different types of value and take place through different points on the value chain. Finally in this chapter we have summarized an approach and framework for the *process* of strategic innovation. The process of strategic innovation leads to a bisociative combination of discovery and creation, summarized in the innovation loop in Chapter 6. But to activate this process, we also need to have an innovation system which can animate and orient acts of discovery and creation. We argued that this required a combination of five perspectives: diversity, naivety, curiosity and urgency and thinking beyond best practice, which together allow organizations to develop their own unique cultures of innovation.

We have described strategic innovation as the heart of creative strategy. Recognizing that even the most impressive strategic innovation still requires further impetus to reach the market, the next part of the book describes how strategic entrepreneurship is needed to give this heart some 'legs'. But first, to reinforce the ideas covered so far we provide two examples, concerning two of the most successful strategic innovations of the 20th and 21st centuries, where many of the definitions and frameworks described in Part I come together. We then revisit the Royal Shakespeare Company to look at how strategic innovation works for them.

MODEL-Ts AND iPODS – STRATEGIC INNOVATIONS THAT COVER ALL THE BASES

Perhaps the world's most significant new products at the beginning of the 20th and the 21st centuries cover all of the strategic innovation bases described in this part of *Creative Strategy* at once. While describing these strategic innovation 'bases loaded home runs' here is not to suggest that this is what you should be seeking (far better to get on base with one

(Continued)

or two incremental bunts than spend months swinging wildly for no result), it is interesting to reflect on why Ford's Model-T and Apple's iPod represent such revolutionary keystones by viewing them through the lenses developed in the last few chapters.

Henry Ford's Model-T was clearly a value innovation. It was quite simply better than its competition in terms of durability, reliability, manoeuvrability, flexibility, simplicity and 'fixability' (i.e., one didn't need to be a master mechanic to keep it on the road). Ford recognized that these value adding attributes were very important given the state of the roads in the USA at the time, particularly outside the cities on the frontiers where America was growing quickly. But, the T also ticks off all of the other five degrees of innovation. Through design innovation Henry Ford simplified parts and reduced their number making his revolutionary production line concept workable. This, and limiting consumer choice as to variations, significantly reduced production costs. Offering new value that a new breed of car consumer wanted, at a lower price, opened up huge new markets for the T. It made owning a car not just the preserve of the wealthy, but of the farmer and the middle manager too. But it would have been no use to create this demand and not be able to match it with the sort of volume innovations that we attributed to Ford in Chapter 7. Cost innovations and volume innovations combined led to a drop in the time needed to produce a T from 12 hours 8 minutes to 1 hour 33 minutes a year later in 1913. The price went from $900 in 1912 to $440 by 1919.

Ford was also a marketing pioneer, arranging races where he would drive a 'souped up' Ford against more expensive cars and better drivers, attracting unprecedented publicity. But perhaps Ford's most significant market innovation was the rigorous selection of dealers. The dealers were imbued with a sense that it was their responsibility to keep in close and regular contact with customers and prospective customers alike, and acted as a valuable 'information system' for Ford. Because of the T, there was no shortage of capable dealers wishing to 'buy into' Ford. This made it a seller's market for the company who only accepted those dealers who would agree to pay cash, up front, for factory deliveries. This unheard of practice also acted as a great motivation to dealers to get out and sell cars quickly in order to recoup their outlay.

This blurring of the line of the border of the company may also be seen as a boundary innovation, but on the 5th degree of innovation Ford was also actively looking for ways to combine insights from a burgeoning electrical industry with his mechanical knowledge in order to add new value to an automobile. Furthermore, Ford was an active learner. As the letter T designation indicates, a great deal of prototyping and responding to the market happened between 1903, when the company was incorporated, and 1908 when the first Model-T was being rolled out.

This would suggest that Ford was able to create innovations through learning from *worst practice*. Indeed, one of his more famous aphorisms was that 'Failure is the opportunity to

(Continued)

(*Continued*)

begin again, more intelligently.' But he also kept abreast of *good practice* throughout the industry of which he had been a part since the late 1800s (he paid particular attention to Henry Leland's development of precise machine tooling and interchangeable parts – which would make Ford's own cost and volume innovations possible), and he was a great stimulator of *promising practices*. As a manager he was fond of claiming that 'I don't do so much, I just go around lighting fires under other people.' Or, as one shop worker put it 'He'd never say, "I want this done!" He'd say "I wonder if we can do it, I wonder." Well, the men would just break their necks to see if they could do it. They knew [broadly] what he wanted [and] they figured it was a coming thing.' And what came *next*, which nobody else but the Ford Motor Company at that point of time could have brought home, was the Tin Lizzie.

Ford's innovations also point to the importance of other aspects of creative strategy – Ford's leadership on the shopfloor connects with the kind of 'leadership from the middle' we discuss in Part IV of this book. The organisation was tightly run but there was also an openness to new ideas, at least at the design concept stage or production. And Ford was an entrepreneur who applied himself diligently to improving the process of production but who was enough of a dilettante to pick up other people's innovations as well as implement his own.

Unlike the Model-T, the iPod is available not only in black, but like it the iPod covers all the bases.

Before the iPod, MP3 players competed on the basis of technology, in particular on data capacity. Apple recognized that the majority of consumers did not need several thousand songs on the move, and that attractive design and consumer interface were more important than data capacity or even sound quality. This moved Apple from red ocean competition (competing on technology) into a market of one (competing on design), where the best-selling alternative to an iPod is another form of iPod. This was the first degree of the iPod's innovation – a value innovation or discovery which redefined the product and the market in which it operates.

Another key innovation was Apple's coupling of the iPod with iTunes, the music download service which uses a proprietary format uniquely compatible with the iPod. Consumers were thus locked into a hardware-software package which allowed Apple to cross-subsidize iTunes while increasing sales of iPods. Here Apple used second and third degree innovation (increasing volume and reducing costs of its music downloads) in order to achieve market dominance, and thereby outflanking the record labels' belated attempts to develop their own music download services.

(*Continued*)

The iTunes innovations on inventory and price thus complemented the iPod's value innovation, allowing the iPod to command a premium price for a desirable product even as iTunes cut the cost and increased the total market. The decision to base the business model on hardware (sales of iPods) rather than software (sales of music through iTunes) was later borne out by the discovery that only around 2% of the music on iPods has been purchased online – consumers were using their iPods to copy, store or organize music collections, not to purchase new music.

Apple used its own good and worst practices to develop the iPod, and had succeeded in the personal computer market by prioritizing elegant design and user-friendly customer interface over technical specifications; this 'good practice' was re-applied to the iPod (and subsequently the iPhone). Indeed, the creation of the iPod and iPhone helped Apple to rediscover its core strengths and reinvigorate its other computing products – so the cycle of discovery and creation continued to fuel innovation across the company's range.

Apple also learned from its own mistakes – an example of 'learning innovation' (6th degree) – and from the mistakes of its competitors ('worst practice'). Apple's first entry into the mobile phone market was the Rokr, a mobile phone produced by Motorola which was compatible with iTunes. The device was expensive: most mobile phone companies subsidize the cost of the phone through service charges, and customers are often given the phone for free in return for signing the service contract. The Rokr did not benefit from this cross-subsidy, because iTunes had to be purchased separately from the service contract and mobile networks were consequently unwilling to subsidize a product where a large part of the revenues were flowing back to a separate organization. And the collaboration with Motorola meant that Apple's distinctive 'look and feel' were missing, thereby alienating Apple's loyal customer base who might have adopted the product at a premium price and drawn in other customers.

The iPhone reversed these mistakes – it was a distinctive, branded Apple product, marketed to iPod users and Apple loyalists first before diffusing to later adopters. Apple can now afford to diversify its market, offering other types of iPhone just as it has developed new formats of iPod (Shuffle, Nano, Mini, Classic) and opening up to new partners and customers.

Finally, the iPod/iPhone exemplifies 'boundary' innovation (5th degree) connecting together different competences and attributes and bridging several markets (personal computer, phone, MP3 player, portable video) within a single product. The vision to move sideways from Apple's core expertise (computers) into the music download market is another boundary-crossing innovation, reconfiguring and redefining its new and existing markets. This required an imaginative recasting of the existing market based on 'next practice' – recognizing that what had been a piece of technology, appealing to a few enthusiasts, was now a lifestyle accessory, customized to a variety of users. In doing so, the iPod has joined that exclusive family of products (Biro, Hoover, Google) where a brand name becomes a generic term for the entire market.

THE ROYAL SHAKESPEARE COMPANY
ACT I: THE INNOVATIVE ACT

Where do new ideas come from? In November 2006, we observed the Royal Shakespeare Company (RSC) rehearsing a new production of *Richard III* under the direction of Michael Boyd, the company's Artistic Director. The play formed part of Boyd's ambitious plan to stage eight of Shakespeare's history plays, working with the same ensemble of actors over two and a half years.

Based on our observations, the idea generation process in rehearsals follows two dynamics. First of all innovation operates through the discovery of ideas and meaning in the text, but new meanings are also actively created by the actors improvising and experimenting. Secondly, individual moments of discovery and creation are embedded in a collective consensus. These two sets of dynamics feed off each other.

Creation in rehearsal occurs when an individual tries a new way of delivering a line, or a scene suddenly 'clicks' to reveal a new meaning or a new relationship. On one occasion, the actor playing Richard picked up a handful of strawberries he was eating and hurled them at the actor playing Hastings. The effect was vivid and unexpected, exploding the tensions within the court and Richard's underlying threat of violence. Most creative artists will have experienced these moments of breakthrough thinking. Mihaly Csikszentmihalyi describes a 'flow' state where performers find themselves operating at a pitch of unfettered and heightened creativity. Athletes will likewise occasionally find themselves 'in the zone'. Such moments are rare, compensating for long periods of underachievement or frustration, resulting in feelings of euphoria and self-fulfilment.

Discovery in the rehearsal room is less spectacular but equally important in generating new ideas. Most of the rehearsal process passes in a laborious process of investigation and analysis. The RSC is unusual in having a strong focus on textual analysis and Boyd's ensemble adopted a literary, 'academic' approach, especially in the early stages of rehearsal, reading and paraphrasing the lines, often referring to footnotes or to variant readings from the Folio edition of the plays and scouring the text for nuances of meaning. It was not until two weeks into rehearsals that the actors were ready to 'stand the scene up', translating language into action. This approach, especially in the early rehearsals, fits with the 'discovery' paradigm, requiring a deliberate, 'forensic' exploration of the text. Insights emerge incrementally through collective effort, accumulated understanding and specialized knowledge. The attitude of 'inquisitive naivety', which we have related to the discovery process, was palpable in the rehearsal room.

Of course these two dynamics reinforce each other. Breakthrough thinking is usually framed by a steady accumulation of understanding – what appears in rehearsal to be spontaneous has often emerged from a process of preparation and planning. The 'strawberries' incident drew upon an ongoing discussion of relationships within the court and some ideas about Richard's association of violence with eating, developed through conversations and rehearsals with the assistant director. Rehearsals are most of the time rather boring to watch – the downbeat, workmanlike process of discovery (like watching a mathematical equation or an archaeological dig) makes possible the occasional flights of invention and beds them into a gradual accumulation of clarity and meaning. Similarly, discovered meanings are made vivid and expressive through deliberate acts of creation.

The dynamics of discovery and creation reflect a relationship between *collective* and *individual* processes in rehearsal. Rehearsal is a collaborative process, but the shared understanding of the play is continually being animated, elaborated and disrupted by individual acts of creation and discovery. Boyd's ensemble approach to acting provides a collective context within which individual moments of creation and discovery can take flight and take root. As noted in Chapter 8, a collective culture of innovation becomes more significant than any single breakthrough. Diversity, naivety and curiosity animate this innovation culture. Urgency comes not just in the looming deadline but in a sense of collective purpose, providing focus and direction.

These dynamics of innovation play off each other in interesting ways. Firstly, the 'breakthrough' moments of creation reanimate or reorient previous discoveries, and what has been discovered through collective effort in turn lays the groundwork for individual acts of creation. Secondly, the processes are self-correcting. Too much creation results in a superficially flashy but ultimately incoherent performance; too much discovery results in a worthy but dull exercise in literary criticism. Thirdly, as rehearsals progress from page to stage, there is a shift in rehearsal style from collective discovery through the text to individual creation through performance. The early rehearsals are concerned primarily with discovering meaning in the text; in the later rehearsals, active creation brings that meaning alive for an audience.

Two further aspects of innovation were observed in rehearsals. First, the switching between creation and discovery modes requires a dual focus from the actors. Within the logic of the scene and the character the actors are creators, bouncing ideas off each other and initiating and responding to new ideas. Actors switch into discovery mode both at the end of the scene, when they step back to analyse what they have been doing, and during it, as they half-observe and control their own performance. This dual focus leads to a stop-go cycle of the rehearsal with restarts and repetitions, running through successive 'drafts' of a scene, but it also requires of the actors (and the director) a measure of reflexivity and an ability to switch in and out of the immediacy of rehearsal. This switching of focus between creation and discovery reflects a similar switching between individual and collective perspectives. Individual experiments and initiatives refer outwards to a shared understanding and mutual trust accumulated through many months of working together. We will say more about this switching between perspectives and approaches in the next 'act' of the case in relation to entrepreneurship.

Secondly, the innovative process of rehearsal is iterative – ideas are continually being tested, refined, discarded or recycled. Rehearsal is a continual debate between 'good practices' rather than a pursuit of one 'best' practice. Actors and directors have to be prepared to discard an idea which required considerable effort and start again. This can be painful as well as frustrating – a television producer uses the phrase 'killing your babies' to describe the evolving process of script development. It also becomes difficult for the outside observer to track progress or completion.

The business with the strawberries did find its way into performance, but some directors question the value of such breakthroughs in the rehearsal room, when something is 'suddenly right'. Partly because it is exciting, the breakthrough moment of creation can defy analysis and create its own logic which is at odds with the rest of the play. Sometimes actors discover or create something in spite of themselves, or the breakthrough moment distracts attention away from a more important but less spectacular act of creation or discovery. So the director must filter and nudge the innovation process, following Polonius's advice that we 'by indirections find directions out.' The ability of the director to change the way the actors see themselves and the meaning of a scene will be picked up in our later discussion of leadership.

Ideally this iterative cycle of discovery and creation continues into performance – as another director commented to us, 'in theatre there is no cut off point'. One of the paradoxes of innovation, especially successful innovation, is that it can discourage future change. Having marked out a strategic advantage by identifying a new market, product or process, businesses can become locked into a successful formula. In theatre, actors must find ways of making a play feel newly created, not only to successive audiences but to themselves. The attitude for innovation – diversity, naivety, urgency, curiosity – means that actors are continually seeking improvements or further innovations rather than closure. The meaning is never fixed and the 'product' is continually modified. Actors continue to reinvent and reanimate the performance night after night – and the best performances should perhaps be imbued in the innovative culture of rehearsal.

'SPARK-NOTES'

- The RSC ensemble has developed a '**culture of innovation**' in rehearsals, framed by perspectives of **diversity**, **naivety**, **curiosity** and **urgency** and a sifting of '**good practices**' rather than a pursuit of 'best practice'. These perspectives **orient** and **animate** the innovation process.
- Innovation in the rehearsal room proceeds through a combination of **discovery** and **creation** and through **individual** and **collective** processes:
  - in the early rehearsals, **discovery** of meanings in the text accumulates a shared understanding of the play.
  - in later rehearsals, **individual acts of creation** are embedded in **collective discovery** which gives these acts meaning and context.
  - the actors are able to **switch** perspectives from discovery to creation, stepping in and out of the role. This dual focus speeds up the process of innovation and is guided by the director.
- Innovation in rehearsal is an **iterative, circular process** which continues up to and into performance – new ideas are continually being rejected, recycled and refined and there is a deliberate avoidance of 'fixing' on a single interpretation.
- Strategic innovation connects with other dimensions of creative strategy – **entrepreneurial** attitudes give the innovation process energy and drive, **leadership** frames and guides innovative practices, and **organization** supports a culture of innovation which can reignite a new cycle of innovation. The next acts of the *Royal Shakespeare Company* will explore these other elements of creative strategy further.

PART II

STRATEGIC ENTREPRENEURSHIP: DILETTANTES AND DILIGENCE

CHAPTER 9

The Five Angles of Strategic Entrepreneurship

The problem with the French is that they don't have a word for entrepreneur.
  George W. Bush (allegedly, to Prime Minister Tony Blair after an economic summit in France)

Of course, the word entrepreneur is French. According to the *Complete Oxford Dictionary*, it was first used to denote a director or manager of a public musical institution: 'One who "gets up" entertainments, *esp.* musical performances.' The origin is apt. Entrepreneurship, even in its now broader business sense, is the bridge between the art of innovation and a viable market. This chapter focusses on the seemingly contradictory entrepreneurial traits and capabilities which take innovation over this bridge.

In previous chapters, we have noted how creativity and innovation draw upon quite different, seemingly paradoxical, capabilities. The same is true of entrepreneurship. The two words that we believe best represent the essential dichotomy of the entrepreneurial challenge are also French in origin. They sit side by side in English and French dictionaries and, indeed, there are probably no more incongruous neighbours in our languages. We argue that the strategic entrepreneur (or entrepreneurial group) must be equally *dilettante* (pursuing something for its own sake and without serious study, amateur, non-expert, dabbling), and *diligent* (constant in application, persevering in endeavour, industrious, not idle, not negligent, not lazy).

As in other parts of this book, we refer to one of our four key dimensions of strategy (innovation, entrepreneurship, leadership, organization) as 'strategic' when they are being enacted while mindful of their interrelations with the other three. Often entrepreneurship fails to be strategic, and hence does not contribute as well as it might to creative strategy, because it is viewed in isolation – as if entrepreneurship occurs independently, miraculously.

We begin this chapter by describing how entrepreneurship connects with innovation within the overall framework of creative strategy. We then introduce our model of strategic entrepreneurship based on five 'angles'. These angles emphasize two important aspects of entrepreneurship, firstly the paradoxical combination of different entrepreneurial roles and attributes, secondly the dynamic connections between them. The need to forge these connections takes us back to the paradox of the 'diligent dilettante'. Taken together, these seemingly opposing tendencies amount to a motivating entrepreneurial force that animates innovation and moves the overall process of creative strategy to market.

In the next chapter we will consider how strategic entrepreneurship plays out in three individual journeys, animating and connecting innovative practices in the arts and in business. First, let's begin by considering the place of entrepreneurship within the overall framework of creative strategy.

The Force of a Creative Strategy

LAW II: The alteration of motion is ever proportional to the motive force impressed.

Isaac Newton

Part I of this book outlined what we might call the first law of creative strategy. Simply put, this is that without innovation at its core, creative strategy is a corpse. The second 'law', which we propose here in Part II, is not dissimilar to Newton's second law of motion quoted above. This is that:

> The force of a creative strategy = innovative mass × entrepreneurial acceleration.

This 'second law' of creative strategy often gets overlooked. There are now thousands of books written on innovation and nearly as many on entrepreneurship, but often what falls between these growing pillars of knowledge is the interdependency between the two.

One of the first examples we examined in our discussion of innovation, 'Perkin's Mauve', is a classic case of a great innovation that was coopted by people other than its inventor, people who went on to entrepreneurially connect Perkin's innovations to markets and who subsequently created a thriving industry.

A few years before Perkin's discovery and creation of his coal tar dye, the leading German scientist Justus Liebig had prophetically issued the following damning assessment to delegates at the British Association of Scientists meeting in Liverpool: 'England is not the land of science. There is only widespread dilettantism, their chemists are ashamed to be known by that name because it has been assumed by the apothecaries [what we might call dispensaries or pharmacies], who are despised.'

He had a point. While there where professorial chairs in chemistry at both Oxford and Cambridge, the idea that students would actually learn in a laboratory or 'practise' chemistry, let alone seek to think through how chemical innovations could be brought to market, was frowned upon by the upper echelons in Britain. It was different in Germany.

Perkin and England's progress duly followed Liebig's prophesy. Perkin, who was not an academic and a far more practical man than the vast majority of English scientists, turned his innovation into a business, 'Perkin & Sons'. From 1870 to 1873, the company had the world market for synthetic dye almost all to itself, increasing its production by 1000 per cent in that period. But five years later, a concerted effort by German government, industrial, university and scientific bodies had created a cluster of companies that were producing five times more dye than that being produced in England. The play *Square Rounds* by Tony Harrison put it in verse: 'Like many a physical or chemical invention, pioneered by British I could mention, Perkin's valuable synthetic dyes, which will always, for yours truly, symbolise, the magic of chemistry, Germans monopolise.'

Those entrepreneurial German companies staffed with hosts of trained chemists capable of recognizing good ideas and working them out in all their applications are still well known: AGFA, BASF, Bayer, Hoechst. Perkin & Sons folded less than ten years after its inception.

Indeed, the box below presenting a list of great entrepreneurs, when contrasted with the box that listed ninety-nine industry spurring innovations on page 66, illustrates a key point here. If we listed the names of the people behind those ninety-nine innovations, most readers would not be able to associate more than a few of them with their inventions. However, most readers will be able to associate the names of most of the fifty entrepreneurs below with their achievements. If you are at all interested in creating a legacy, you would be better to be an entrepreneur than an innovator. At the very least, you will need to explore how entrepreneurial activity can help an innovation go places.

THE 50 GREATEST (AMERICAN) ENTREPRENEURS

Industry *Ben Franklin* 1706–1790; *Henry Ford* 1863–1947; *John D. Rockefeller* 1839–1937; *Cyrus McCormick Sr.* 1809–1884; *Andrew Carnegie* 1835–1919

Finance *Charles Schwab* b. 1937; *Amadeo P. Giannini* 1870–1949; *J.P. Morgan* 1837–1913; *Charles Merrill* 1885–1956

Media *Martha Stewart* b. 1941; *David Sarnoff* 1891–1971; *Robert Johnson* b. 1946; *Oprah Winfrey* b. 1954

(Continued)

(Continued)

Technology *George Eastman* 1854–1932; *Steve Jobs* b. 1955; *Michael Dell* b. 1965; *Bill Gates* b. 1955; *Thomas Alva Edison* 1847–1931; *Ross Perot* b. 1930

Consumer Goods *Estee Lauder* 1908–2004; *Madam C.J. Walker* 1867–1919; *Asa Candler* 1851–1929; *W.K. Kellogg* 1860–1951; *Milton Hershey* 1857–1945; *Eberhard Anheuser* 1805–1880; *Adolphus Busch* 1839–1913

Franchising *Ray Kroc* 1902–1984; *Harland Sanders* 1890–1980; *Juan Trippe* 1899–1981

Transportation *Herb Kelleher* b. 1931; *Fred W. Smith* b. 1944; *William S. Harley* 1880–1943; *Arthur Davidson* 1881–1950

Retail *Aaron Mongomery Ward* 1843–1913; *Sam Walton* 1918–1992; *Richard Sears* 1863–1914; *Alvah Roebuck* 1864–1948

Fashion *Ralph Lauren* b. 1939; *Levi Strauss* 1829–1902; *Phil Knight* b. 1938

Entertainment *P.T. Barnum* 1810–1891; *Louis B. Mayer* 1885–1957; *Walt Disney* 1901–1966; *Berry Gordy Jr.* b. 1929; *George Lucas* b. 1944

Hospitality *William Becker* 1921–2007; *Paul Greene* 1914–1994; *J.W. Marriott Jr.* b. 1932; *Conrad Hilton Sr.* 1887–1979

Internet *Jeff Bezos* b. 1964; *Steve Case* b. 1958; *Pierre Omidyar* b. 1967; *Larry Page* b. 1973; *Sergey Brin* b. 1973

Source: Success magazine 2008

To return to our second law and to paraphrase another physicist (Lucretius) 'nothing will come from nothing': nothing will result if there is no innovative mass and nothing will come without entrepreneurialism. If innovation is the heart of creative strategy, then entrepreneurship is the legs. So how do they work together? The entrepreneurial challenge is both conceptual and practical. To help conceptualize what strategic entrepreneurship requires we shall introduce a number of graphical aids in this chapter:

- Angles and leaps and bell curves show how entrepreneurship moves innovation forward;
- Cycles and stars will illustrate how the elements of strategic entrepreneurship are interconnected;
- And headphones depict how it adds to and should surround some of our earlier notions of the dichotomies that drive creativity.

In Chapter 10 we shall look at how these concepts play out in practice.

The Five Angles of Strategic Entrepreneurship

The tendency to see entrepreneurship in isolation, as something separate from other strategic dimensions of innovation, leadership and organization, means we often ignore its strategic

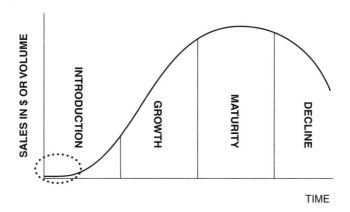

Figure 9.1 The product life cycle

significance. All too often entrepreneurship is left out of the picture in discussions of strategy, or even regarded as inherently 'unstrategic'; according to this logic, entrepreneurs do not think strategically and strategists are not entrepreneurial.

To illustrate, think about the general depiction of a product life cycle, one of the most ubiquitous reference points in strategic management. It depicts a smooth curve of phases of development (which are often associated with the critical success factors required at each phase – e.g., finance for decline, marketing and distribution for maturity, operations and marketing for growth) with the first phase, introduction, rising from zero.

But there is something very important missing from this shape. We may assume that innovation is happening to the left of the 'zero'. But what then links an innovation to the market curve depicted here? Assuming that we cannot change the laws of physics, and that we are not talking about immaculate conceptions here, something substantial has to happen to create the momentum that gets the ball rolling up this slope. Recalling Lucretius, surely nothing will come from flat nothing. Creative strategists should be interested in what is happening within the dotted circle in the figure above; with the movements that transform a 'flatline' into a rewarding growth curve. What needs to happen is strategic entrepreneurship.[1] But what does this consist of?

In the 1977 volume of *The Academy of Management Review*, Frederick Webster argues for a greater awareness of different categories of entrepreneur and entrepreneurship and proposes five types of entrepreneur: the Independent; the Cantillion; the Industry-Maker; the Administrator; The Small Business Owner. For Webster, entrepreneurial behaviour adapts to changes in the business environment and to the evolving enterprise. For example, the 'rapacious' Independent will have to take a more calculating approach to risk as he evolves into an Industry-Maker and

---

[1] Sometimes entrepreneurship is referred to as intra-preneurship when it occurs within a company, but this semantic change is reflective only of a change of setting rather than a fundamental change in behaviour. Hence, when we refer to entrepreneurship, we are encompassing intra-preneurial activities.

then an Administrator. In a sense then, Webster's types map on to a cycle of evolution similar to the product life cycle shown above. As with many other models of entrepreneurial types, Webster's approach was based on a study of the academic literature on entrepreneurship – consequently these 'types' do not necessarily map onto specific roles in a business. Much of that literature was concerned with the broader economic effects of entrepreneurial activity on economic and industrial structures, and two of Webster's categories (the Cantillion Entrepreneur, the Industry-Maker) reflect this tendency to see entrepreneurship in terms of economics rather than strategy.

But we want to focus more closely on that transition point from zero to market entry and show how entrepreneurship connects with an overall strategy. To this end we want to outline some general characteristics of strategic entrepreneurs and relate these to actual behaviours, tasks or roles.

In this respect we have observed five different 'angles' that effective entrepreneurs or entrepreneurial organizations generally take to get good innovations off the ground and into a community or market. And these seem to apply equally in what we might term the most creative pursuits (writing, music, theatre, fashion), and in more 'mundane' business settings. They are:

- Recognition
- Development
- Evaluation
- Elaboration and
- Launch.

We have found it useful to graphically represent these five angles as a momentum-gathering 'rise' which looks something like a bell shaped curve (see the graphic below). Referring to the previous product life cycle diagram, these angles can be transposed over the flatline inside the dotted oval,

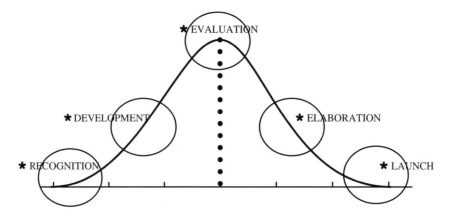

Figure 9.2   The five angles of strategic entrepreneurship

as the starting point of the overall enterprise. We explore each of these five angles in more detail below.

1st Angle of Entrepreneurship

The 1st angle is the RECOGNITION phase. This may be associated with a so-called 'aha' or eureka moment ('Eureka' means 'I have found it' in ancient Greek) or a milder moment of insight whereby sifting through ideas and events leads to something recognized as having potential. This potential is seized upon and lifted up for further inspection, thereby creating an 'angle' leading away from the flatline.

Unlike the sort of creations and discoveries we wrote about in the previous part of the book, these entrepreneurial moments of recognition are different in a crucial aspect. Here the 'aha' is in recognition of a potential *connection between* an innovation and a market rather than just in recognition of an interesting innovation. But, as with innovation, such breakthrough thinking typically occurs on the fringes of deliberate, conscious thought, where the mind wanders into unfamiliar territory and forges unexpected connections.

2nd Angle of Entrepreneurship

The DEVELOPMENT of that connection with potential that has emerged from the 1st angle will require a more deliberate process of applied thinking, but this angle still draws on eclectic sources to ramp up the complexity and depth to the original insight. At this stage, ideas and processes are still emerging through risk, experiment and drawing from a wide range of experiences or fields of expertise, but the idea is beginning to move closer to a marketable form. Development, like recognition, requires a dilettante's willingness to try out unfamiliar ideas and experiences.

In this phase it is useful to begin to consider how the development in prospect may be translated into a market advantage that can be protected. This might mean exploring whether this idea or project can give rise to, or be connected to, some form of intellectual property (or IP), or examining whether the idea is in keeping with and thus attributable to a certain style or character of the organization or individual – thereby making it harder for others to copy because they lack the resources or credibility to do so.

It may be useful here to use a checklist that assesses whether a strategic innovation will have a sustainable strategic advantage, like CASIS (which asks whether or not it is Congruent with things that are seen as important by customers; is not Appropriable by competitors; can not be Substituted for by customers, is Inimitable; and its development can be Supported by the organization).

> ☑ Congruent
> ☑ Not appropriable
> ☑ Not substitutable
> ☑ Inimitable
> ☑ Supportable
>   organizationally

3rd Angle of Entrepreneurship

EVALUATION is the point at which a decision is made to persevere and take the innovation to market, or, to cut one's losses and return to sifting for other ideas to pursue. Here the development ceases and is tested against the practical demands of implementation. Effective strategic entrepreneurs seem to be able to draw upon two important sources here. First, they seem to have good instincts and to know when not to trust those instincts. Second, they have a good set of people upon whom they can draw to provide a wide spectrum of feedback and whose opinions they can trust.

Sometimes organizations will draw upon individuals or groups whose sole purpose is to act as evaluators. The good ones can see both ways: working well with and providing useful feedback to the recognizers and developers coming up with innovations, while keeping one foot in the real worlds of applications and markets.

Two particularly important dimensions for the individual or corporate entrepreneur to consider here are scale and return. Firstly, will this idea be 'scalable', that is, can it be produced in sufficient quantities (and quality) to make market entry pay off? This is obviously necessary when one is thinking about a commercial product. But it is also the case when thinking about more artistic pursuits. In fashion, for example, it is one thing to have developed an innovative pleated feature that your pattern cutter and sample machinist can execute, but if you don't think your contract supplier can produce this at a high enough standard then it may be time to go back to the drawing board. In writing, one might have developed an interesting scenario but is there enough potential here to build this scenario into a screenplay or a novel? Secondly, can the idea be produced at an economic or personal cost that is less than what the market will reward?

The evaluation angle represents a crucial tipping point for the overall process of entrepreneurship. We might consider the angle or perspective taken by the evaluator (or the individual in the evaluation phase) as like that at the high point of a back-flip in the Brazilian art of capoeira (see Figure 9.3). At the top of the entrepreneurial leap that provides the elevated perspective necessary to evaluate an idea (a 360 degree view) one must make the call as to whether to just make a safe landing and start again, or, if one feels confident, to continue and follow through with the momentum developed up into the next move (continuing through to the product life cycle shown in Figure 9.1 above). The high point of the backflip allows a tiny readjustment without breaking the flow of the movement – evaluation, and readjustment, are thus a crucial part of the entrepreneurial process rather than standing outside it.

capoeira **noun**. *A Brazilian physical discipline involving an interplay between two people of improvised feinting and acrobatic manoeuvres (esp. using the legs and feet), resembling unarmed single combat but with little or no physical contact, and traditionally performed in a circle formed by onlookers with accompanying music.*

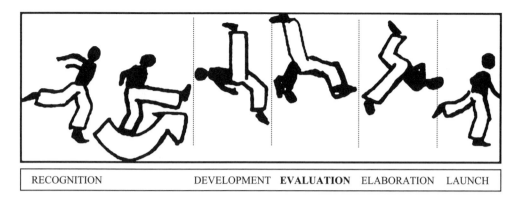

| RECOGNITION | | DEVELOPMENT **EVALUATION** ELABORATION LAUNCH |

Figure 9.3   The five angles of entrepreneurship, capoeira style

4th Angle of Entrepreneurship

Once the idea has been evaluated and deemed worth taking to market, the 4th angle or ELABORA-TION 'works out' the idea, drawing out the separate threads of thought that emerged during the evaluation process and hooking them to a stable point, gradually weaving them into the completed pattern necessary to land the idea into the market effectively and efficiently.

Elaboration is laborious work, requiring all of the *diligent* characteristics of assiduousness, perse-verance, planning and attention to detail. Whereas the earlier angles, recognition and development may be fluid and organic, elaboration is more mechanical: the work of an engineer. Like engineers, entrepreneurs must use diagramming, testing, fine-tuning and retesting to ensure their idea is ready for the market.

Elaboration also makes a transition from inspiration to implementation. Writers have to work out the details of their ideas, setting up routines and schedules for the more painstaking, elaborative process which translates a promising idea into a structured whole. The author Philip Pullman has written of the unromantic day job of writing in his garden shed. As we will see, this emphasis on the writer's craft, routine and perseverance connects with the diligence of the entrepreneur.

5th Angle of Entrepreneurship

Having created some angles that have enabled us to both see ideas in the round and build up a momentum that can see those ideas into a market, we are well set up for 'take-off', the final angle. This is the angle that brings us back into line with the product life cycle: the *LAUNCH*. At this point, what was some time ago recognized as an idea with potential is ready to be released, either as a fully fledged enterprise or as a new phase in the development of an organization or, indeed,

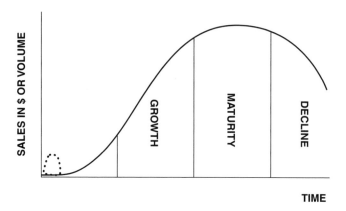

Figure 9.4   The product life cycle with a conception of the angles of strategic entrepreneurship superimposed

of an individual career. The launch completes the rising arc of the entrepreneurial journey (see Figure 9.4), replacing that barren flat line in the oval in Figure 9.1.

Like elaboration, the inflection leading to launch is an applied process requiring diligence, attention to detail and discipline. It is an angle that can be best guided by established expertise, particularly in marketing and public relations. If earlier stages on this journey (the sifting, the crossing of boundaries and experiences to find something of potential interest, the intuition), were more art, launching is more of a science.

The launch should lead us on two journeys. One onwards into the market where we will then need to move from thinking about entrepreneurship into thinking about leadership and organization in order to turn a beachhead into something sustainable. This is the subject of the remaining parts of this book. But the angles of entrepreneurship should also lead us back to further entrepreneurial 'rises' beginning with new attempts to recognize potential – but this time with the benefit of experience developed through the previous journey. After the case box below, which relates the example of Richard Branson to the five angles, the next section looks at how the rise should also be a cycle.

BRANSON'S ENTREPRENEURIAL ANGLES

Many have attempted to capture the traits of an entrepreneur. In our experience, this is problematic, as for every list there are many entrepreneurial exceptions who simply don't fit that particular mould. And, at the same time, many who wrongly rule themselves out as entrepreneurs because they lack certain traits on a list.

(Continued)

However, such lists can be a useful starting point for discussion (as opposed to universal theories) and this one from *Entrepreneur* magazine, with its focus upon Englishman Richard Branson, provides an interesting counterpoint to the earlier list of fifty American entrepreneurs. The traits may be related to our 5-angle process in that the first three to four may be more closely associated with the upward angles and the last two with the downward.

At first glance, Richard Branson is an enigma. Look a little deeper, though, and he's somewhat decipherable. At his core are traits that are good predictors of entrepreneurial success. We asked experts in the fields of psychology and entrepreneurship to share their thoughts on what makes entrepreneurs succeed. Through their answers and our interview with Branson, we shed some light on what makes him such a notable individual.

1. **Risk Taker:** 'Bold, brave risk taking is a central feature of human progress, innovation, creativity and entrepreneurship', says Dr Frank Farley, a psychologist at Temple University in Philadelphia. 'Much of Branson's success has come from taking big risks.'
2. **Lifelong Learner:** This trait is key to Branson's ability to successfully compete in various industries. He started out aspiring to be a journalist, co-founding a magazine called *Student* in his teens. Says Branson, 'Being a journalist and being an entrepreneur is not that dissimilar. You're learning all the time.'
3. **Swift Action and Experimentation:** 'Making quick decisions and experimenting are good predictors of success', says J. Robert Baum, a Professor of Entrepreneurship at the University of Maryland. 'Branson hasn't wasted a moment of his life, and he isn't afraid to experiment.'
4. **Thrill Seeker:** Farley says Branson fits the Type T Personality, which is characterized by 'risk-taking, stimulation-seeking, and thrill-seeking; is motivated by novelty and change with a high tolerance for uncertainty; is self-confident and optimistic; believes he can control his fate and his destiny; is creative and innovative; shows independence of judgement and likes to make up his own mind; is a natural-born rule breaker; and thrives on challenges.'
5. **Self-Efficacy and Confidence:** 'Entrepreneurs face big barriers to entering new markets with new products', says Baum. 'You get knocked down all the time, so you have to be able to hang in there even when other people are telling you that you're wrong.' Branson's own levels of self-efficacy and confidence were crucial in finding funding.
6. **Venture and Industry Experience:** Baum says experience is a good predictor of your success. 'With businesses spanning multiple industries, Branson isn't always knowledgeable about each one, but he surrounds himself with people who are.'

Source: Adapted from *Entrepreneur Magazine*, November 2008.

The Cycle of Strategic Entrepreneurship

One of the things we wanted to do in this chapter was to relate the phases of entrepreneurial activity to actual work tasks in addition to the somewhat abstract theories that are used to describe entrepreneurialism. One way to do this is to relate our angles to a taxonomy associated with a particular profession. The profession we have chosen is one that is easy for most of us to relate to: writing/publishing.

We all write to some extent, even if only letters or lists. So we can all identify with the struggle of recognizing and plucking from our minds the right words to express what we mean to communicate. The task of writing and the persona of the writer relate to the first angle of entrepreneurship. But, it takes more than well-chosen words to produce something that might be bought. It requires editorial skills and representation, the sound judgement of a publisher, the technical skills of a production editor or manager, and marketing and promotion. The table below arranges these roles in relation to the angles we have outlined above and the critical skills required of each.

Each of these angles or roles can be seen as separate parts of an organization or separate parts of more than one organization. They may well be sensibilities required of an individual writer trying to establish themselves, thinking ahead to develop a package more attractive to a desired representative or publisher. But whichever is the case, the entrepreneurship cycle requires an originating/recognizing element, an ability to effectively develop that original idea, a recognition of its value and viability, the technical skills to implement and 'work out' the details, and the capability to launch it.

Moreover, placing the five angles of strategic entrepreneurship into an occupational setting makes it easier to see how the rise of angles leading into a market can also be seen as a replenishing cycle, as in Figure 9.5. A good promoter, producer, publisher, production manager, editor and agent will be able to feed back to the writer (and indeed to each other) how the original 'product' can be regenerated or built upon.

Table 9.1   The angles of entrepreneurship translated into the occupational roles of writing/publishing

Angle of Entrepreneurship	Occupational Roles (Writing/Publishing)	Critical Skills
Recognition	Writer	Creating ideas, boundary-riding, recognizing potential
Development	Editor/Agent	Supporting and exploring the idea
Evaluation	Publisher	Testing the idea, judging potential, directing the idea to market or back to the drawing board
Elaboration	Production editor	Fixing the idea, boundary-setting, matching to distribution channels
Launch	Promoter/Marketer	Delivering the idea, recognizing potential for reinvention

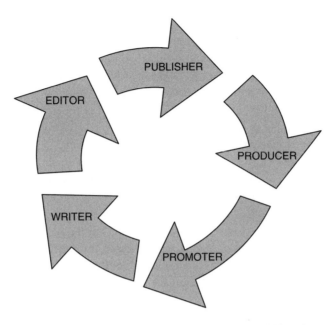

Figure 9.5 A strategic entrepreneurial cycle of writing/publishing roles

From Cycle to Interconnected Star

One of the problems of conceiving of entrepreneurs as in Table 9.1 above as a set of traits or attributes is that one can easily ignore the connections which lie between them. Entrepreneurial individuals or enterprises draw upon multiple capabilities, and it is the ability to switch between them which provides momentum – if we become too locked into one set of characteristics or behaviours, we are unlikely to be able to make the transition between tasks and capabilities. As with the capoeiria dance, a fluidity and flexibility of movement allows the enterprise to generate the necessary momentum.

An individual entrepreneur might well play more than one role – indeed such multitasking is a characteristic of successful entrepreneurs. The most effective publishers, editors, writers, and agents are able to approach an enterprise from more than one angle. In order to move around the cycle, they have to either adapt themselves or forge connections with other mindsets and domains. In the studies of entrepreneurial journeys that are described in the next chapter, some of them will describe this transition between different forms of entrepreneurial behaviour during the course of a career. Just as in Webster's traditional entrepreneurial categories an 'Independent' might eventually become a 'Small business owner', so the editor might become a promoter, or the writer might become his own editor or publisher, and so on. These changes may be planned strategically or they may be forced by external changes imposed upon the business; but for most entrepreneurs or entrepreneurial enterprises, some such transitions will become inevitable.

Analysing the different models or stages of entrepreneurship and the transition points (or angles) between them will help us to understand how enterprises and entrepreneurs evolve. Our cycle diagram enables us to illustrate this more readily than our earlier entrepreneurial rise at the beginning of a product life cycle. By drawing in the lines which connect our five angles together, we can start to see the cycle of entrepreneurship as a dynamic, interconnected network. A given product or idea should both pass around the circle in a linear manner but also be subject to the network of these different forces at each stage. The different players form a collaborative network or entrepreneurial system which turns the raw idea into a finished commodity. In the music industry, for example, collaborative networks between bands, artist management companies, A&R scouts, music publishers, producers and distributors extend between the major record labels and the 'independent' sector and across the industry as a whole to deliver the music to the customer.

Strategic entrepreneurship, as we have defined it, depends upon an ability to connect together different models of entrepreneurship, and to connect these entrepreneurial characteristics and behaviours in turn with strategic processes of innovation, leadership and organization. For the whole system to work effectively, each participant (whether as an individual or a group) must

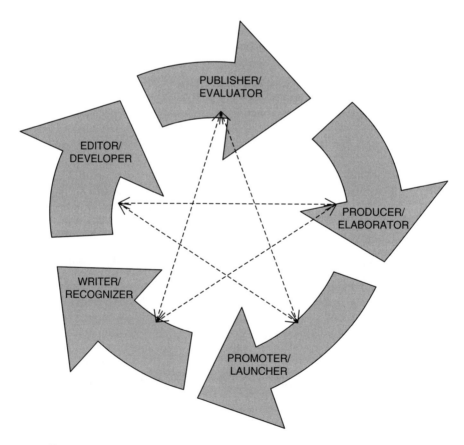

Figure 9.6   Recognizing the interconnection between the roles of strategic entrepreneurship

learn to see the project from different entrepreneurial angles. The transitions and switches in perspective between angles lead to a dynamic process of organizational and personal change. In order to keep the cycle moving, we cannot afford to become locked into one style of thinking or 'character'.

Understanding the other entrepreneurial characters, including our own, is therefore a necessary step to cooperating with them. This leads us to examine the opposing forces which we believe lie at the heart of strategic entrepreneurship: diligence and dilettantism.

The Strategic Entrepreneur as a ¡Diligent Dilettante'

Examining the different angles or roles required to be fulfilled by the strategic entrepreneur and their material differences leads us back to the fundamental dichotomy in this element of creative strategy. Those angles that create the upward momentum depicted in Figure 9.2 (or those elements on the left hand side of the cycle and the star shown in Figures 9.4 and 9.5), require a quite different, indeed opposite, set of characteristics to those angles that bring us downward and into the market (or the elements on the right hand side of the cycle and star).

If we follow the entrepreneurial process sequentially, from recognition to launch, we can see how the process moves between a zone of risk, boundary flitting, experimentation and unfixity, into a zone characterized by experience, focus, application and exploitation (see Figure 9.7, below). The combination of these two sets of attributes is what moves innovation into entrepreneurship, with different roles and capabilities converging to turn the raw idea into a marketable commodity.

We summarize these two 'zones' of characteristics as the *diligent* and the *dilettante*. Diligence refers to the focused, assiduous character of the entrepreneur, driven by a single-minded passion and purpose. Dilettante refers to the impulsive, intuitive and opportunistic aspects of entrepreneurship. Importantly, it is the transition from dilettante to diligent which converts innovative ideas into entrepreneurial applications.

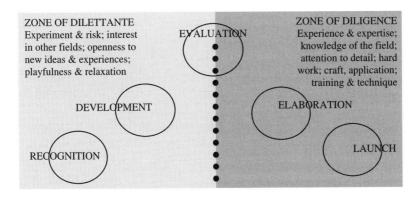

Figure 9.7 The two paradoxical zones of strategic entrepreneurship

It follows that the effective entrepreneur or entrepreneurial enterprise must be at once flighty, amateurish, naïve, flitting from idea to project without fixing for too long and drifting on free of commitment; until, when they happen upon and recognize something of particular interest, they become attentive, assiduous and persevering.

The contrast between breadth of references and depth of attention recalls Edward De Bono's distinction between 'lateral' and 'vertical' thinking, and the contrast between 'divergent' and 'convergent' creative processes described in the opening chapter. Hence, the diligent-dilettante dichotomy is rooted in creativity theory. Arthur Koestler emphasized that creativity requires 'mental cross-fertilisation'. Howard Gruber describes creativity operating across a 'network of enterprises', while Sawyer notes a creative capacity to switch between fields or domains. Through these multiple contacts, creative connections can be made and new ideas emerge. Creative 'field-switching' fits with our description of the 'dilettante' above.

At the same time, creativity theory also emphasizes the importance of domain-specific expertise, a laboriously acquired repertoire of craft, experience and knowledge which allows creative impulses to take root and allows creative people to polish and refine their ideas into a completed form. Contradicting the myth of genius, most entrepreneurs/artists emphasize that ideas are not gifts but the product of assiduous hard work. Edison spoke of the 99% perspiration that he drew upon. Picasso acknowledged the unpredictability of his muse, but also spent long hours in the studio, so that when inspiration comes 'it must find us working'. The dilettante must also be diligent – and creative connections *between* fields must be channelled into expertise and knowledge *within* a designated field.

What this means in practice is that entrepreneurs, like artists, must be both diligent and dilettantes in order to take their work to completion and adapt to different stages in the enterprise. The development of a new idea or project might start from within the field before arcing out into 'mental cross-fertilization', then coming home to roost within a core set of domain-specific skills. They must work within a domain, but also think outside it.

While we can readily see how this paradox works in these examples, even the latest academic theory can struggle with this paradox. A recent paper in the very first issue of the *Strategic Entrepreneurship Journal* does an excellent job of outlining two quite different existing theories of entrepreneurial action: discovery theory and creation theory. Each are logically consistent in their own right, which is perhaps why the authors Alvarez and Barney conclude that future research should carefully examine which context the entrepreneur in focus is operating in. But, we would suggest that, in reality, many entrepreneurs will be operating within elements that are related to both. 'Discovery theory', as it is outlined below in Table 9.2, may relate more to the dilettante or recognition and development phases of entrepreneurship where the idea is being 'found'. 'Creation theory' is more in keeping with the diligence that we have associated with evaluation, elaboration and launch where the entrepreneur or entrepreneurial group is really 'making' the idea. And of course the terminology of 'discovery' and 'creation' connects with our earlier paradox of 'creative discovery' at the heart of innovation.

Table 9.2 Central assumptions of discovery and creation theories of entrepreneurial action (from Alvarez and Barney, 2007)

	Discovery Theory	**Creation Theory**
Nature of Opportunities	Opportunities exist, independent of entrepreneurs. Applies a realist philosophy.	Opportunities do not exist independently of entrepreneurs. Applies an evolutionary realist philosophy.
Nature of Entrepreneurs	Differ in some important ways from non entrepreneurs, ex ante.	May or may not differ from non entrepreneurs, ex ante. Differences may emerge, ex post.
Nature of Decision Making Context	Risky	Uncertain

We would suggest that to divide theories and see them as separate realities in this manner may be to the detriment of our understanding of strategic entrepreneurship. It may offend our academic or scientific sensibilities but, in practice, entrepreneurship rests on a logical contradiction, or paradox.

Whilst entrepreneurs may gravitate towards one end of the diligent/dilettante spectrum as they bring an innovation to market, effective strategic entrepreneurship requires them to switch between these characteristics. Revisiting the entrepreneurial cycle (Figure 9.4), an excess of diligence or dilettantism at any stage in this cycle, or a failure to release from one to the other, can block the evolution of strategic entrepreneurship. For example, momentum is greatly dissipated if a developer/editor becomes too much the dilettante, tinkering and fussing with the book, repeatedly passing the work back up to the writer instead of moving forwards towards evaluation. Instead of forming a unified pattern, the angles flatten out or turn inwards, and the connections between them are broken. In the table below we show how becoming too diligent or too dilettante at each angle of the strategic entrepreneurial cycle can lead to limiting characteristics: turning recognizers into dreamers, developers into tinkerers, and so on. Many of the exercises which claim to 'unblock' creative thinking are designed to switch our brains from one way of thinking to another – from diligent to dilettante or back again, and hence can also be used to help us not get stuck in one zone or another (see the creative thinking games overleaf for some examples).

Recognize/Writer	←	becoming too dilettante	=	Dreamer
Develop/Editor	←	becoming too dilettante	=	Tinkerer
Evaluate/Publisher	←	becoming too dilettante	=	Procrastinator
	→	becoming too diligent	=	Bully
Elaborate/Producer	→	becoming too diligent	=	Obsessive
Launch/Promoter	→	becoming too diligent	=	Pigeonholer

Figure 9.8 Avoiding excesses of dilettantism and diligence

The effective strategic entrepreneur is able to combine dilettante and diligent behaviour and evolve as an individual and as a firm, working across the five angles of entrepreneurship in order to harmonize with the changing needs of the business and the market. At the same time the strategic entrepreneur will be aware of the larger framework of creative strategy, recognizing the

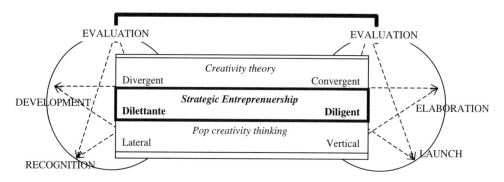

Figure 9.9 The strategic entrepreneurship 'headphones'

importance of *innovation* at the start of the entrepreneurial process and the need to keep the momentum up for those who will provide the *leadership* and *organization* required to sustain the enterprise once the entrepreneurial effort comes to fruition. Momentum comes from a fluid movement through the five angles of entrepreneurship – a commitment and confidence in the initial idea, but directed through a calculated mix of diligent and dilettante attitudes.

Having attempted to capture these difficult to reconcile and conceptualize attitudes graphically using angles, curves and cycles, our last graphic image brings these ideas together in the form of a pair of old walkman headphones. These show the key elements of strategic entrepreneurship, how they relate to both high and low theories of creativity, and how their opposing forces should form something of a balanced 'surround sound' for those who seek to give creative strategy legs.

CREATIVE THINKING GAMES FOR DILIGENT DILETANTTES

Creative thinking exercises are often designed to break up convergent, logical processes by introducing a more spontaneous, divergent alternative – thinking outside the box or 'lateral thinking'. For example, the nine dot problem asks you to join up all of the dots in the diagram below with four straight lines, without removing your pencil from the paper. The solution is at the end of this section. (Hint: the clue here is in the title – 'thinking outside the box'.)

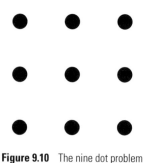

Figure 9.10 The nine dot problem

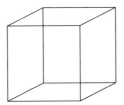

Figure 9.11 Necker's Cube

As we have argued, sometimes it is necessary to reverse this and inject logic and rationality into spontaneous thinking. Accordingly the real purpose of many of these exercises is not to replace one style of thinking with another but to invite us to flip between them – switching the angle of perception. Necker's Cube is a visual exercise which asks you to change the way you see the cube above – is the left hand panel at the front or the back of the cube?

Rather than favouring one style of thinking over another, the purpose of these exercises is to move us out of our comfort zone, allowing us to look at an old problem from a new angle.

Edward De Bono's 'Six Thinking Hats' is one of the best-known methods for animating creative thinking in groups. Six coloured hats correspond to different thinking styles or behaviours as in Table 9.3.

De Bono emphasizes that the purpose of the six thinking hats is not to define behaviour but to change it. By putting on different hats, either individually or as a group, participants can redirect their behaviour, open up new options or pull ideas together. As we have seen, entrepreneurial thinking can become blocked at one phase in the cycle, turning in on itself instead of passing to the next stage in the process. The six thinking hats are a tool for unlocking these negative processes, either by opening out to a more 'dilettante' thinking style or applying a more 'diligent' approach.

The initial phases in the entrepreneurial cycle of recognition and development will tend to draw on new ideas and information (the red, white and green hats) – and will favour a more 'dilettante' approach. The phases of evaluation, development and launch require a more self-conscious, diligent approach – a combination of yellow, black and blue hat thinking. But as Table 9.4 suggests, changing hats throughout the process can change the angle of our thinking, nudging us towards more diligent or dilettante alternatives.

Table 9.3

White hat	Objective	identifying information needs and gaps
Red hat	Intuitive	driven by feeling and emotions
Black hat	Negative	caution, judgement, criticism – why something won't work
Yellow hat	Positive	identifying benefits and value – how something will work
Green hat	Creative	proposing alternatives, provocations, changes
Blue hat	Process	thinking about thinking, not the subject itself

Table 9.4

Become More Dilettante	Angle of Entrepreneurship	Become More Diligent
Red hat	Recognition – creating ideas, boundary-riding, recognizing potential	White hat
Green hat	Development – supporting and exploring the idea	Yellow hat
Blue hat	Evaluation – testing the idea, judging potential, directing the idea to market or back to the drawing board	Black hat
Green hat	Elaboration – fixing the idea, boundary-setting, matching to distribution channels	Yellow hat
Blue hat	Launch – delivering the idea, recognizing potential for reinvention	Yellow hat

The thinking hats are not an attempt to map a linear process – the hats can be taken on or off at any stage in the process, as the situation requires. De Bono has devised a range of exercises and scenarios where exchanging hats can move a creative process forward by giving permission for other types of thinking and unblocking repetitive patterns of behaviour.

Similarly our angles of entrepreneurship are cyclical rather than linear – and the lines which connect the different angles bring together different entrepreneurial behaviours and people in productive combinations. In relation to our 'diligent-dilettante' paradox, the six thinking hats are more useful in combination than in isolation – by pairing up opposing archetypes we can bounce ourselves into a different way of thinking about a problem and bring our idea closer to the market.

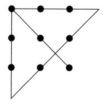

Figure 9.12 Solution to the nine dot problem

CHAPTER 10

Three Angular Journeys of Entrepreneurship

I n the previous chapter we considered how alternating phases of dilettante and diligent behaviours occur in strategic entrepreneurship. Now we consider how these phases, and the ensuing entrepreneurial angles of recognition, development, evaluation, elaboration and launch may be enacted: by presenting three journeys of strategic entrepreneurship. Each comes from what are generally called the creative or cultural industries – from publishing, fashion and video games. While these three journeys are reasonably typical, in our experience, of how strategic entrepreneurship tends to work in almost any industry, their cultural context makes it easy to relate to the type of products they speak of and heightens the drama of strategic entrepreneurship – thus making the journeys memorable.

At one end of the entrepreneurial leap, the cultural industries are characterized by an oversupply of potential products for development and a risky and expensive process of prototype production. The combination of developing, marketing and launching a new video game or a book, for example, requires a major investment in sunk costs, with no guaranteed return. Typically, only around one in ten products pays for itself, and the few successes must bankroll a catalogue of failures. In the era of free online content, that 10% success rate is likely to diminish. In the music industry a 2008 industry survey found that of 13 million tracks available online, 10 million failed to find a single buyer.

At the other end of the entrepreneurial leap to market, once a product has proved itself, the marginal costs of launch and reproduction are becoming increasingly low (especially so in a digital environment), and a successful product can be rolled out through different media, release windows, ancillary merchandising, sequels and spin-off 'franchises'. Here, companies diligently squeeze out every last drop of profit in order to pay for the expensive and risky process of failed experimentation and the search for new talent at the other end of the spectrum.

The most successful cultural enterprises appear to bridge these two alternates in the entrepreneurial cycle. Writing, fashion and gaming provide good examples of this difficult balancing act of diligently getting the most out of the already proven while keeping one's head up enough to recognize the unexpected and unfamiliar, so as to keep the enterprise replenished creatively.

In the following explorations of three distinct entrepreneurial journeys we will consider how the entrepreneurial paradox of the 'diligent dilettante' is manifest And, at the end of each we shall highlight a few essential 'tracks', points that sum up the key things that might be learned from each of their attempts to persevere with the entrepreneurial leap from the recognition of a good innovation to a successful market launch.

About a Writer-Entrepreneur

What makes a successful novelist? According to Nick Hornby, it is not so much the quality of the writer's ideas as the strategic choices the writer applies to those ideas. He routinely comes up with ideas for books, but does not believe he is especially original or prolific in this. Everybody has ideas (especially ideas for novels). Recognizing which of these is worth developing and knowing how long to persevere with them thus become the critical decisions.

Hornby created a new genre of writing for his times. Hornby wrote about something approximating real life, a little bit tragic but quite funny too, for men. Many of his novels, and subsequent film adaptations, *Fever Pitch*, *High Fidelity* and *About a Boy*, are now embedded in popular culture. Hornby's literary innovations emerged symbiotically as he began to sense an unfulfilled market. His first book, the little known collection of critical essays called *Contemporary American Fiction*, provides an insight into where this 'market sense' came from. 'Everything changed for me when I read Anne Tyler, Raymond Carver, Richard Ford, and Lorrie Moore . . . voice, tone, simplicity, humour, soul . . . All of these things seemed to be missing from contemporary English fiction I'd looked at, and I knew then what I wanted to do.'

He explains the gap in more detail in his 'biography' on the Penguin website: 'In the 1980s there was a huge gap between best selling books and literature . . . Jackie Collins stuff on one side, and there was this very difficult dark inaccessible literature on the other . . . there really wasn't anything in between.'

Flitting between a British and an American sensibility enabled Hornby to sharpen his entrepreneurial aim. 'I think there is a general desire to read good books. People read books on the way to work and when they go to bed. We've all had that terrible feeling that you're making no impression on a novel at all and you're 30 pages in and there's 472 pages left and you've been reading it for three weeks already. I think the Americans have always understood that once you have a price on the back of your book there is some kind of contract you are entering into.'

Hornby decided to write a book about his life-story through his relationship with Arsenal football club, developing it by channelling some of his American influences. He intuitively felt that this was a good idea. Working outside the loop of publishers and agents, he was combining several of our entrepreneurial angles himself – writing, developing and self-evaluating.

Indeed, when a senior BBC executive suggested he try writing a different kind of book about football, he ignored the advice. When another friend told him the book would change his life, it simply confirmed his own instincts. As the evaluations of various people were sought he continued to believe in the book against the odds. He knuckled down and ground it out (see the box for a description of Hornby's glamorous creative existence).

After its launch, the book, *Fever Pitch*, did indeed transform Hornby's life, laying the foundations for his own career and even defining a genre of 'Hornby-esque' fiction. Indeed, type Hornby-esque into Google and tens of thousands of hits come back, something that Hornby finds odd given that people seem to be referring to an obsessive relationship with something or a feckless male who's lost a sense of direction and is struggling to achieve emotional maturity, things he hasn't written about for a decade. But, at the same time, today he seems confident enough in his own direction as a writer to shrug off the labels and assumptions which are placed upon him.

Why did Hornby trust his own judgement over others with more experience and knowledge? He finds his own obstinacy rather surprising – at the time he was a first time novelist, and not especially confident or decisive. It is clear too that such a commitment could have become self-destructive if it was misdirected.

NICK HORNBY'S AVERAGE DAY

'I have an office round the corner from my home. I arrive there between 9.30 and 10 a.m., smoke a lot, write in horrible little two-and-three sentence bursts, with five-minute breaks in between. Check for emails during each break, and get irritated if there aren't any. Go home for lunch. If I'm picking up my son I leave at 3.30. If not, I stay till six. It's all pretty grim! And so dull!'

Source: penguin.co.uk

NICK HORNBY'S OTHER AVERAGE DAY

When we spoke to Hornby in 2009, he was promoting his latest novel *Juliet, Naked*, and the film *An Education*. Meanwhile he was also collaborating on a radio sitcom and contributing lyrics to an album, a joint project with the American singer-songwriter Ben Folds. Asked to define an average day, he admitted that he didn't really have one – and that he was unlikely to do much writing until later in the year. Ten years ago such a realization might have prompted anxiety and self-doubt. Perhaps the ability to remain diligent without the reassurance of a daily routine and to focus on multiple tasks and projects simultaneously marks out a maturing of the entrepreneurial character, signalling Hornby's evolving role as a 'diligent dilettante'.

Hornby's decision to write *Fever Pitch* was grounded not in self-confidence or blind faith, but in a measured understanding of the kind of book which would succeed in the market and which he knew he could write. He becomes irritated when artists claim that they do not care about markets – all writers want their books to be read.

On the other hand, his strategic writing decisions are not simply based on market trends either. Sometimes an idea will seem to be 'of the moment' – but he will also sense that it is 'not going anywhere'. He suggests there may be a difference here between novels and screenplays. In film, an idea must be encapsulated in a single phrase – 'giant gorilla invades New York' – which instantly suggests an entire scenario. But for Hornby, while a simple concept may be good, a book idea which appears to predict its own content is not one worth pursuing. And an idea which merely follows an existing market zeitgeist is likely to be drowned out in other voices singing the same tune. Innovation and market should, to some extent at least, emerge in response to each other.

The other element which allows a writer to make good decisions is the availability of alternatives. While Hornby is still primarily a novelist, he juggles a 'network of enterprises' – at the time we spoke to him he was working on a radio series, an animation project, two screenplays and a novel. Like most writers he also spends a lot of time reading. There is an analogy here between the writer and the multi-tasking entrepreneur; Hornby describes his friend and fellow-writer Dave Eggers as 'the most entrepreneurial person I know'. Eggers, best know as author of *A Heart-breaking Work of Staggering Genius* and editor of *McSweeney's*, seems capable of pursuing multiple projects simultaneously, editing, writing, campaigning, producing and publishing other people's projects as well as his own. Like Thomas Edison, having lots on the go increases the set of things that can be drawn upon to create solutions as things unfold.

Such eclecticism facilitates the 'creative connections' noted in earlier parts of this book. It may also provide an underlying source of confidence which frees the decision-making process; if one idea or project is discarded because it is not going to work, there will always be alternatives.

Entrepreneurs, like writers, can become locked into a failed idea or enterprise, becoming inflexible and obsessive. They can also be paralysed by too many possibilities and fail to pursue any one of them with the necessary commitment and confidence. For Hornby, the combination of diligence and dilettantism makes sense not just as a description of some of the paradoxes in the writing process, but also as a kind of cycle or career progression. Recently he took a conscious decision to explore as many different paths as he could, partly through frustration (because he had ideas he was not able to use as books) and partly through wanting to collaborate with other artists. The 'network of enterprises' thus extends into a real network of people and projects which allows him to share some of the responsibilities for originating, selecting and developing ideas. Again there are analogies here between the creative career and the entrepreneurial venture – diversification and renewal eventually require an ability to delegate decision-making and share responsibilities.

For Hornby this new phase of collaborative projects is opening up new possibilities – but he can't entirely escape his diligent past: 'I suppose I think I have earned the right to be a dilettante through my earlier diligence. . .'

ESSENTIAL ENTREPRENEURIAL TRACKS VOL. 1

Trust your intuition: deciding which path to follow has been as much a part of Hornby's creative-entrepreneurial journey as writing. Even if this has meant rejecting other people's advice.

Know your limits (or entrepreneurial range): for Hornby, having a great idea for a book was less important than knowing what kind of book he himself was best able to write.

Dilettantes can be diligent too: working recently with an eclectic range of people and projects has not diluted Hornby's sense of direction and purpose in his own work – quite the reverse.

---

12 000 Miles to Market

Not long ago, an article in *The Economist* magazine profiled what it called 'the unlikely rise of New Zealand's fashion industry'. It explained that when it comes to fashion sense, New Zealand had a reputation – but not in a good way. 'For years Kiwi backpackers recognised each other around the world from their unofficial uniform of black tracksuit-trousers, bush shirts and sneakers.' Their journalists continued on to report visiting diplomats relaying their shock at the New Zealander's standard of dress, accusing their hosts of dressing like soldiers or as if they were going to a funeral. Black (or at least dowdy) appeared to be the national uniform, and not only on the sports field.

But New Zealand is now home to a vibrant and steadily expanding fashion industry, with some fifty established labels, up from just a handful ten years ago, more than half of which sell abroad. The World Trade Organization says clothes exports were worth NZ$315m ($216m) in the year to June 2007, up from NZ$194m a decade earlier. Labels such as Karen Walker, Kate Sylvester, World and Trelise Cooper are becoming increasingly well known in Australia, Hong Kong, Japan, the USA and even as far a field as Britain some 12 000 miles from New Zealand.

Why might people be interested in fashion from the edge of the earth, as far away from the traditional fashion centres as one could possibly get? And why have the entrepreneurs behind these labels been successful? Charles Haddrell of New Zealand Trade and Enterprise says New Zealand benefits from an unusual combination of Pacific and urban cultures, an emphasis on natural fibres that appeal to environmentally conscious buyers, and a fresh and quirky approach.

Trelise Cooper is one of New Zealand's most successful fashion designers. Her clothes are sold extensively in the UK, Paris, Rome, Singapore, Australasia, and the United States where she sells more than all other New Zealand designer labels combined. In 2002, Cooper was awarded a Trade New Zealand Export award. At the end of 2009, at the height of a recession, Cooper is pleased to report that her order books, against all expectations, are between 10 and 20% up on the previous year.

Picking up on Haddrell's themes, Cooper told *The Economist* that because New Zealanders are geographically remote and have little exposure to mass labels, like Gucci and the Gap, its designers ignore the rules. 'This produces a different, quite edgy style', she says.

When we spoke to her she expanded on this idea. 'New Zealand is so small that it doesn't have big department stores. And it's so remote that until recently most of the big high-end fashion labels didn't have a presence here. So, designers grew up with very different influences, and a need to satisfy a range of people to survive.'

This leads to a second characteristic of New Zealand fashion entrepreneurs: point of view. Cooper relates a story of seeing a fantastic collection in Paris by a designer she greatly admires. 'There was such a strong singular point of view; everything was a subtle variation on a single theme.' This designer responded that what she liked about Cooper's collections was that there were a number of different perspectives at play. It may be that the strength of the New Zealand fashion point of view, if there is such a thing, embraces multiple perspectives more than is often the case elsewhere.

Trelise Cooper is known for her richly detailed, textured and colourful designer pieces which characterize her exclusive *Trelise Cooper* label. Her diffusion label *Cooper by Trelise* also reflects a distinctive feminine look but with a more casual orientation. Cooper's most recent label diversification *Trelise Cooper Kids* shows a similar design quality and philosophy for the children's-wear market. An associated concept store seeks to create a new direction in retailing by providing a 'fantasy world' for the 2 to 8 year old market. Her designs often make historical references and are refined to express a quirky directional quality and an emotive, positive experience for the customer has always been a core part of Cooper's design philosophy.

The third aspect that makes fashion from the edge popular now, Cooper believes, is that consumers, particularly at the high-end, are also becoming more daring and creative. 'People like the idea that they might buy a dress in a store in Hong Kong by a designer from another end of the world that nobody else they know is aware of. This is exciting for them.'

Like Nick Hornby in our previous case, Cooper can relate to the notion of the creative entrepreneur as a diligent dilettante.

'When people look at me, they tend to see and focus on the frizzy hair, the frivolous side, the flippant "ditzy" me, but there's the other side: the side that has to be focussed, determined, persistent.'

'There's a whole business and a lot of people now who rely upon me being able to "get myself together". To get, in other words, the two sides of strategic entrepreneurship working together to ensure that something that is going to sell gets off the ground and makes it to market.'

'I never had a problem with the [more overtly] "creative" side', says Cooper. 'I still tend to be late for things, always squeezing out the last few minutes of creative time, playing around with ideas, you have to do this, but only five minutes late, never an hour ... Over time I've learnt a lot about how to get it together.'

The first and most important thing, Cooper explains, is 'visioning', having a strong point of view and being able to communicate this. This provides an important starting point for the entrepreneurial journey which helps guide decisions about which ideas to develop beyond the 'drawing board'.

A strong vision or point of view makes it easier to make 'gut' decisions. And the gut is generally the best guide for selecting which of the ideas that are sketched by Trelise and her team will be taken to prototype. 'It's a collective gut now', she explains. 'We look at things as a team, but it's still about gut feel.'

'Those items that turn out to be "winners", that sell really deep, are always those everybody on the team is excited about. They want to see what it's going to look like made up. They think they want to own one.' Like Hornby in the previous case, Cooper wants the entrepreneurial journey to take her somewhere – and the winning ideas are the ones which don't signal their final destination in advance, but leave Cooper and her team curious as to how their journey will 'turn out'.

The Trelise Cooper brand relies upon finding 'deep niches' in the market, items that are distinctive, uniquely in tune with the Cooper point of view, but which people in different markets can easily relate to, without hesitation. Hence, Cooper explains that evaluating which items to develop beyond the prototype stage is not about asking if there 'is anything wrong with it.' But rather thinking 'Is everything right with it?'

This doesn't mean that there will not be further elaboration at this stage. 'It's only when we start to look at the prototype on the fit model that we can really begin to see how a prototype works;

then it becomes very physical. We rip and tear and modify and re-stitch. Then we photograph the changes and communicate with our people in Hong Kong and India. With language and distance barriers it's much better to communicate physically and visually so that we all get to the same point of view.'

This elaboration is important for another reason too. It is only now that Trelise and her team can really experience how the garment feels when it is put on. This is crucially important. Cooper believes that if a woman decides to give up her time and step into a changing cubicle (a very vulnerable space) with a Trelise Cooper item it must feel great, whether that customer decides to buy that item or not. A bad changing room experience can be devastating for a good brand.

Cooper finds the launch of any new collection 'nail-biting', but reckons that if an entrepreneur doesn't find a launch nail-biting then they should be worried. Without that sense of urgency and anticipation it may be that the boat isn't being pushed out far enough, or that there isn't enough of the entrepreneur being put on the line.

For her the key dimension that enables a successful launch is her relationship with retailers, and for one week every year she tries to bring representatives from all her main retail partners together in Sydney. Here many conversations take place, ongoing relationships are reinvigorated, and new ones established. This is crucial because without retail support it's very hard to get the Trelise Cooper point of view across to the customer consistently.

She must get a lot of feedback and suggestions for next season's ranges in this setting, we suggest. Does she take it?

She explores this question for some time. Then she focusses: 'Feedback, yes. Suggestions, no. It's a conversation, but ultimately they have to realise that taking on board lots of different suggestions would dilute the Trelise Cooper point of view.'

ESSENTIAL ENTREPRENEURIAL TRACKS VOL. 2

Strong point of view: a consistent point of view allows Cooper to draw upon an eclectic range of influences and 'suggestions', and to communicate with her customers through language and distance barriers.

Devil in the detail: how a project 'turns out' through the process of 'elaborating' the original idea is often more important than the prototype. Hence Cooper's question: 'Is everything right with it?'

Empathy with the customer: understanding how customers will use the product at the point of consumption feeds back into the process of elaboration and launch.

Deciphering Codemasters

The games industry is still relatively young, but is already beginning to challenge the film industry in terms of revenues. As gaming has matured, the stakes have become higher. With each new console raising the bar in terms of graphics, technology and gameplay, there is a corresponding increase in the time and budget needed to create a new game. Today's best-selling games have budgets similar to Hollywood movies, and typically demand a two to three year development cycle. The industry comes close to John Howkins' definition of the creative economy as 'creativity plus electronics', demanding a mix of imaginative vision and technical skill. A new release game will command a premium price and enjoys a relatively long product life cycle. Consequently reviews are more influential than in the music and film industries, and there is a direct correlation between sales and online ratings by players.

Codemasters is a games developer and publisher based in a converted farm near Leamington Spa in Warwickshire. The business was set up in 1986 by two brothers, Richard and David Darling, both games enthusiasts, who began to write games while they were still at school. Seeing the potential of the business, their father Jim supported them and the business expanded from the boys' bedroom to take over the family farm. When we visited in 2008, one of the development studios was a converted cow shed, while some of the management team are based in the old farmhouse. Today the company has offices in Birmingham, Guildford and Kuala Lumpur and employs over 800 people worldwide.

Codemasters develops four or five new games every year, as well as publishing up to ten 'external' products. The company is perhaps best known for its racing simulations (TOCA Racer, DiRT, Colin McRae Rally, F1) but also specializes in battlefield games (Operation Flashpoint – Dragon Rising) and sports simulations (Ashes Cricket 2009). In 2009 Codemasters won a BAFTA award for its GRID racing game. The most successful franchises are handled by a brand manager who aims to balance innovation with continuity. Straightforward sequels are considered to be less attractive to consumers than they are to retailers – consumers expect games to evolve within a framework of rules and expectations, but also to offer a unique experience.

Codemasters is unusual in maintaining its own 'engine', the software architecture around which each game is built. This architecture provides a technological resource which can be drawn upon to develop specific capabilities in gameplay, interactivity and artificial intelligence. These technical possibilities are in turn combined with the work of art directors, programmers and sound designers to deliver the look and feel of the game to the user.

The different parts of the business appear to run to different rhythms, yet they must also mesh together, like a set of cogs turning at different speeds. A game's designer is responsible for connecting the wheels together as well as acting as the game's 'vision keeper' and ensuring that it is driven by the player's gaming experience rather than by technical and aesthetic possibilities. There are echoes here of Cooper's emphasis on 'visioning' and establishing a 'strong point of view' from the outset. Former programmer and art director Clive Lindop is one of Codemasters' designers. As the game develops it passes through different zones of experiment and application to a finished product. Lindop's job is to guide it through different departments and capabilities, ensuring it remains true to its own internal logic and to the requirements and expectations of the player.

Many of Codemasters' most successful games simulate real environments, from battle scenarios to racing simulations. Players have come to expect a high level of realistic detail in the look and feel of the game. Typically it will take 300 man hours to create the environment for a game – leaving aside the weapons, cars or figures which populate it. For example, in the background for a racing game, the trees around the track each contain around 5000 leaves and as the cars drive past, the swishing movement of the trees helps create a feeling of speed and motion. The artists and programmers we met were dedicated to the craft of their work, with a strong intrinsic task motivation. Their line managers, responsible for production schedules and budgets, would occasionally have to rein them in and force a compromise, but for the most part this obsessive dedication was nurtured. On the one hand, game development follows a strict schedule of targets and deadlines; on the other, the detailed work takes place in a timeless zone where unconstrained perfectionism is actively encouraged.

Whereas the technical and art departments are characterized by painstaking diligence bordering on the obsessive, Lindop is more of a dilettante. But he is also, like Cooper, responsible for 'getting it together'. As lead designer, he has to decide whether technical and artistic details are necessary to the player, or can be discarded as 'fluff' – desirable, but not essential if the budgets and schedules are tight. Moving between departments and perspectives, he must 'listen to other ideas and bind them together'. A programmer working on a game's artificial intelligence might not be able to deliver a particular interaction, but might suggest an alternative – 'here's a cooler way of doing it, here's a more efficient way of doing it'. Equally he might find himself mediating between the programmer and the art director – a novel solution from one department allowing a short cut in the other. In these situations, the designer's lack of specialist knowledge can be an advantage. For example, Lindop was able to give feedback on some of Codemasters' racing titles precisely because he could not drive himself (something he shares with many of the game's users). A lack of immersion in the technical detail of the game allows the designer to see the game from the player's point of view. Lindop acknowledges 'the need to know what you don't know' in order to avoid 'taking the technology down a dead end'.

In these negotiations the expectations and needs of the player are Lindop's trump card. The game must create a world within which the player can understand and negotiate their own experiences – consistency with the internal 'rule set' is more important than realism. In a battlefield game, the process of loading a mortar is not realistic – the ammunition would in reality be too heavy for an individual soldier to handle – but it is necessary to the player's expectations of how the game works.

The strategic entrepreneurship of a games designer like Lindop rests on his ability to negotiate between multiple constraints and sources of ideas and to move between the internal divisions and hierarchies of the organization. The designer is the dilettante who flits between technical specialisms. In a business where much of the work is locked into its own rituals of craft and technique, Lindop's job is 'to know everything that's going on'. At the same time he must work within a 'boundary box' defined by technological and artistic limitations – and these boundaries are perpetually shifting, the only constants being time and budgets.

Strategic entrepreneurship is driven by a combination of attributes and attitudes across the spectrum from diligence to dilettantism. Occasionally these converge in one individual but more often they must be connected and orchestrated by 'intrapreneurs' who mine the organization's internal resources and configure and direct its talents. Strategic entrepreneurship consists in connecting up competences internally and aligning these externally to the changing demands of markets and customers. Codemasters is successful because it allows its 'diligents' and 'dilettantes' to cohabit the same space and helps them to adapt to each other. Design and technical teams work side by side in a converted cow shed. According to the company's CEO, Rod Couzens, the long-term goal is to build a 'campus' where there can be cross-fertilization of ideas and talents between the best programmers and artists recruited from around the world – 'you need a big playing field'. Since our visit, the recent changes to the company's premises are turning this vision into a reality.

The creative industries are characterized by highly specialized, individualized work. 'Dilettantes' like Lindop play a crucial role in knitting these diligent strands of expertise and craftsmanship into coherent products. As we will see in the next chapter, the role played by Lindop can also be seen as 'leading from the middle' – toggling between different leadership positions to manage the technical experts and line managers around him, as well 'managing up' to the senior management.

Videogames, especially the first person shooters and racing games favoured by Codemasters, spend much of their development process in a diligent zone of technical expertise, painstaking attention to detail and laborious craftsmanship. Yet the game begins as a blueprint drawn up by a designer. This is not just a concept, it is closer to a screenplay, with the mechanical and aesthetic elements clearly mapped out – Lindop may not know how to deliver all of this, but he knows what he wants. He admits the need to be 'relatively egotistical' in order to oversee the game's progress – as a dilettante he must also be diligent, and manage the diligence of others. In the end he is the one who must weave all of the technical and aesthetic specialisms into a marketable product.

ESSENTIAL ENTREPRENEURIAL TRACKS VOL. 3

Champion the customer: Lindop's role in the development process is to see the game from the player's point of view. Ideas are evaluated not against internal criteria or logic, but against player expectations: will it be fun to play?

Don't over-elaborate: One of Lindop's key roles is to discard 'fluff' and prevent the core experience of the game being diluted by an excess of detail. Elaboration can be taken too far.

Get different disciplines/departments together: As a 'diligent-dilettante' Lindop has to provide a focal point between different disciplines and departments. As a self-professed non-expert, he knows a little about a lot of the process rather than a lot about a little. This allows him to empathize and adjudicate between different points of view.

The development process passes through different phases where rigorous attention to detail alternates with imaginative vision. In the end the key to Lindop's role is empathy – an ability to understand and interpret the ideas and demands of diverse colleagues, but also an identification with the mind of the player, who will want a game that is not just technically realistic but delivers an immersive, satisfying experience. Game players have their own mix of logical and illogical expectations, from a demand for painstaking realism to complete suspension of disbelief. The diligent dilettante's job is to reproduce this mix in the game itself.

All three of our entrepreneurial journeys clearly connect innovation with markets, like the 19th century promoters who would 'get up' an entertainment for a public. The value of an idea, at the point of recognition and development, is evaluated with half an eye on the later stages of elaboration and launch, which will determine how that idea will 'turn out' and how it will be used by readers, wearers or players.

Our entrepreneurial journeys also chart an upward and outward trajectory for the individual and the enterprise. Hornby and Cooper, whilst continuing to make their own creative decisions, have used collaboration as a way of expanding their range. Most of Hornby's current projects (the screenplay, the radio sitcom, the album) are collaborations. Meanwhile Cooper has diversified her individual 'point of view' into separate labels or brands, and works with her 'collective gut'. Lindop's colleagues have seen Codemasters expand in the year since we first met them, taking on new staff and a new building and increasing their output, while Lindop himself has recently taken on a new role as lead designer with the German games company Crytek.

The trajectory of the entrepreneurial leap, which these journeys illustrate, connects with the next two dimensions of creative strategy: leadership and organization. In the transition from individual projects and one-off enterprises towards more complex networks and developing careers, leadership provides a direction to the enterprise and organization provides a sustaining context for renewed cycles of innovation and entrepreneurship. Strategic entrepreneurship provides the energy and momentum to connect the other dimensions of creative strategy, and the three journeys described in this chapter have provided an interesting 'mix-tape' of insights to take with us as we move forward.

STRATEGIC ENTREPRENEURSHIP 'MIX-TAPE'.

SIDE 1 (DILIGENT SIDE)	SIDE 2 (DILETTANTE SIDE)
Have a strong point of view	Trust your intuition
Know your limits (or entrepreneurial range)	Get different disciplines/departments together
The devil is in the detail	Champion/empathize with the customer (medley)
Don't over-elaborate	Dilettantes can be diligent too

THE ROYAL SHAKESPEARE COMPANY
ACT II: THE ENTREPRENEURIAL ACT

Previously, in Act 1, we considered how innovative processes combine discovery with creation in order to develop new ideas in rehearsal. Revisiting the RSC rehearsal room, it is time now to consider the 'entrepreneurial' motives and characteristics which drive this innovation process.

Creative thinking combines divergent processes of idea generation with convergent processes of application and verification. This creative interplay between imaginative play and technical skill is driven by entrepreneurial attitudes, from dilettante playfulness to diligent, obsessive attention to detail. The strategic entrepreneur has a special ability to combine or switch between these attitudes.

In his New York speech describing his approach to 'ensemble' theatre, Boyd emphasized the technical discipline of acting. Actors are trained in verse, voice and text through their time with the company. Boyd reintroduced a movement department to the company and the musical director was part of the rehearsals we observed. For Boyd's history plays there was a further technical challenge in the trapeze-like use of ropes in the battle scenes, which placed additional physical demands on the actors.

At the same time Boyd also emphasizes risk-taking and playfulness. He sees himself and the actors 'walking a tightrope between reckless irresponsibility and playing it safe'. Risk is essential to innovation and demands trust between actors, director and audience. Without taking entrepreneurial risks and taking innovations to market, Boyd suggests that theatre will 'retreat into well-trodden failure'. The ensemble principles listed in our prologue section make frequent reference to risk, experiment and failure.

Rehearsals move from an expansive exploration of possibilities, gradually focussing on the details of the scenario as the opening night approaches. Several members of the *Richard III* ensemble noted this 'gear change', with an escalating speed and intensity in the later stages of rehearsal. The transition from an upward curve of recognition and development in the early rehearsals towards a downward curve of elaboration and launch maps the entrepreneurship cycle outlined earlier in this chapter. These two trajectories draw upon the imaginative and technical aspects of acting referred to above. For the actors there is a gradual shift in emphasis from *what* a scene is about in the early, exploratory rehearsals towards a technical emphasis on *how* that scene is communicated to an audience.

However, this transition from dilettante risk to diligent certainty is far from straightforward. First of all the actors themselves are continually dipping in and out of these two modes in rehearsal. As outlined in Act 1, the Innovative Act, the rehearsal process requires an ability to step in and out of the present tense and point of view of the character. Secondly, each technical 'working out' of an idea triggers a fresh round of exploration, recognition and development. For the actors, a confidence in the technical details of the scene paradoxically allows a greater imaginative freedom in interpretation.

An example of this occurred midway through the rehearsals for *Richard III*. For a scene in the court, the director and his assistant set out some chairs in the rehearsal area – this was the first time chairs had been used on the set. The chairs were arranged down either side of the room, adding a new formality to the staging. The actors had to be more calculated in their decision-making – when and where to stand, when to move up or downstage, whether to stand or sit in response to another actor, and so on. Through this concentration on the technical aspects of the performance, the actors were able to explore and improvise the complex shifts in status and allegiance between Richard and the other members of the court. By literally 'fixing' one aspect of the staging, the director was able to free the actors to recognize and develop a new set of interpretations.

Throughout the rehearsal process the director orchestrates these shifts between diligent attention to detail and experimental risk-taking. Sometimes the actors are encouraged to take risks and flick between multiple options; at other times they must work through the technical details of a defined scenario. So whilst we did observe the promised 'gear change' over the six weeks of rehearsal, the experimental, risk-taking approach of the early rehearsals never entirely disappeared. As the rehearsals progress, the space and time for decision-making shrinks, focussing the actors on the technical details of performance rather than expansive exploration of meaning. Yet these two modes of rehearsal feed off each other, so there is always some scope for renegotiation and reinvention.

For the actors avoiding closure and embracing risk translates as a reluctance to fix every aspect of the performance in advance. One member of the *Richard III* ensemble, Richard Cordery, has written of the Elizabethan actors' practice of taking (or learning) only their own 'sides' – their own lines – and argues this approach allowed them to be 'much more in the moment'. Thus unprepared, the actor must respond in character to what is happening around him on the stage in real time, unaffected by a pre-emptive knowledge of what other characters are thinking or what might happen later in the scene. Cordery claims that this allows the actor to discover less obvious meanings in the lines which he or she might otherwise overlook. The paradox here is a deliberately planned state of unpreparedness or 'diligent dilettantism'.

Comparing the RSC rehearsal process to the entrepreneurial cycle, the key moment of evaluation is continually deferred. Evaluation is the high point in the entrepreneur's leap, when he/she decides whether to land the jump, readjust or start again. In rehearsal, the actors and director prolong or defer this point of decision for as long as possible. By resisting the temptation to 'nail down' every aspect of the performance, the actors and director give themselves more time and space to recognize and develop ideas. So Boyd would repeatedly invite the actors to 'try it and see' and referred to run-throughs of scenes as 'drafts', to be repeatedly picked open and rewritten.

In terms of our entrepreneurial cycle then, the actors attempt to inhabit all five phases – recognition, development, evaluation, elaboration, launch – simultaneously. As with the entrepreneurial journeys in the preceding chapter, these different ways of thinking about ideas and projects feed off each other and provide energy and dynamism. The danger, of course, is that the circular, iterative process of rehearsal becomes an end in itself. Instead of an upward spiral, with successive 'drafts' building upon each other, the cycle becomes endless and repetitive.

Converting this entrepreneurial energy and momentum into a clear direction is the task of leadership. From a strategic perspective, the actor's ability to switch focus, from close-up to long shot, will connect with the leader's ability to move from 'interacting' to 'envisioning' in the next chapter. In rehearsal and in performance, the actors must pursue parallel processes. They have to remain imaginatively and emotionally 'in the moment' while at the same time remaining intellectually aware and technically in control. They become 'diligent dilettantes'. Their special gift may be the ability to control their level of immersion in a situation. The Elizabethan actor was able to focus on the immediate reality by excluding knowledge of context, cause and effect. The RSC actors we observed could achieve this intensity, but could also see the bigger picture of the performance. This connection between different angles and attitudes of entrepreneurship, and between innovation, entrepreneurship and leadership, may be the defining feature of what we have called 'strategic' entrepreneurship.

'SPARK-NOTES'

- Like entrepreneurs in business, RSC actors in rehearsal combine a *'diligent'* attention to detail with a *'dilettante'* approach to experiment and risk in order to animate and drive the innovation process.
- There is a move from a *'zone of experiment'* towards a *'zone of experience'* as the actors start to focus on the technical details of the performance. However, the technical and imaginative aspects of acting feed off each other – and the possibility for experiment and reinvention should never entirely disappear, as this would breed complacency.
- Actors must be both technically aware and 'in the moment' – actors and director use various techniques to achieve a state of *'planned unpreparedness'*.
- Actors and director tend to delay evaluating or 'fixing' a scene to allow more scope for further exploration. And fixing on details should not be seen as an endpoint, it can be a *springboard for further reinvention*.
- The RSC rehearsals fit our definitions of **strategic entrepreneurship**:
  - the actors are 'diligent dilettantes', combining attention to detail with playfulness in order to **drive** the innovation process.
  - the rehearsal process follows an arc or **entrepreneurial cycle** from *recognition* and *development* of ideas in the early rehearsals, through *evaluation* towards *elaboration* in later rehearsals and eventual *launch* into performance.
  - these five angles of entrepreneurship are mutually supporting, forming a network or cycle rather than a linear process.
  - entrepreneurial attitudes form part of the bigger picture of creative strategy – **entrepreneurial** behaviour in rehearsal provides momentum for **innovation**, and relies in turn on **leadership** to provide direction.

STRATEGIC LEADERSHIP: ENVISIONING AND INTERACTING

CHAPTER 11

Leading from the Middle

You say that you have no keenness of wit. Be it so; but there are many other things of which you cannot say that nature has not endowed you. Show those qualities then which are perfectly in your power: sincerity, gravity, patience, contentment with your lot, frankness, dislike of superfluity, freedom from pettiness. Do you not see how many [leadership] qualities you are immediately able to exhibit, as to which you have no excuse of natural incapacity and unfitness?

Marcus Aurelius, *Meditations*

At the time of the Beijing Olympics in 2008, one of the best selling books in China was Marcus Aurelius' *Meditations*. This seems unlikely, but if you read what may be one the earliest complete treatises on the nature of leadership you can see how Aurelius' writings, ascetic, rational, almost Confucian in tone, might appeal to both East and West. But while *Meditations* is currently well known in China, it is now largely overlooked in the English speaking world. This is a great shame, given that it contains a passage that we believe best sums up the qualities required for leading the development of a creative enterprise: in two centring ways.

Firstly, while innovation gives a creative strategy a heart and entrepreneurial drive gives it legs, it takes a quite different set of abilities to establish and lead an enterprise beyond the beachhead established through a successful launch. In the next and final part of the book we will explore how moving on from the entrepreneurial launch to consolidate, sustain and move on to other beachheads requires a fertile organizational environment for the creators and dilettantes, the discoverers and the diligents, to continue to flourish and recreate. But holding this chaotically diverse and often necessarily egotistical band together requires a quiet, strong and relatively ego-free, *centre*. The strategic leadership that coordinates and inspires innovation, entrepreneurship and organization, comes from 'the middle', providing a solid centre for the diverse band that inspires creativity to hitch on to. If strategic entrepreneurship is about providing force or impetus to the innovation that lies at the heart of the creative enterprise, strategic leadership is about providing a gravitational hub to ensure that things don't spin out in conflicting orbits.

Secondly, the strategic leadership of a creative enterprise requires someone, or a group, that is *centred*.

A question often asked is 'are leaders born or made?' Aurelius provides us with what we think is the best answer with regard to forming the lynchpin between innovation, entrepreneurship and organization: they are none of these.

Often people will claim that they are not leaders. They were not born with, or they failed to acquire, the attributes we routinely associate with our leaders: charisma, searing intellect, a strong jaw. However, this misses Aurelius's important point. We may lack an innate 'keenness of wit', for example. But the qualities Aurelius describes – sincerity, gravity, patience, contentment with your lot, frankness, dislike of superfluity, freedom from pettiness – are not God-given traits; nor are they skills which can be acquired from training, consultants or business schools. These qualities are more like habits than traits or skills. They come slowly, and they come with experience and use. Aurelius would probably class them as 'virtues'; we must continue to restrain our baser instincts to enact them. They come to us as we become more 'centred'. Leaders are not born. Nor are they made. Leaders mature.

Hence, it is not so much, as is commonly purported now, that everybody is a leader. Or, alternatively, that nobody can lead apart from a sainted few. Aurelius indicates that everybody has the *potential* to mature into a leader. The qualities he describes are possible for any human; the challenge is to enact them consistently to the point where they become habitual and we become centred in this way.

In *Leading Quietly* Joseph Badaracco paints a picture of how this type of leader may appear: 'They're often not at the top of organizations. They often don't have the spotlight or publicity on them. They think of themselves modestly; they often don't think of themselves as leaders. But they are acting *quietly*, effectively, with political astuteness, to basically make things better, sometimes much better than they would be otherwise.' It is a picture, like that painted by Marcus Aurelius, that requires us to think differently about what it means to be a leader of creative strategy.

Creative strategy requires leadership that quietly joins the diverse elements and energies that contribute to innovation, entrepreneurship and organization. Creative strategy needs leadership not from the top, but from the middle. In the remainder of this chapter we explore some recent arguments and ideas that are all pointing us towards the importance of 'leading from the middle'. We will relate these arguments to the paradoxical combination of 'envisioning' and 'interacting' which we identify with strategic leadership. And we provide a framework that will enable you to conceptualize how leading from the middle can connect with these different approaches to leadership. In the following chapter we shall explore some practical examples of leaders who lead from the middle and switch between different leadership styles or 'keys'. Whereas in previous parts of the book we have used examples from music, science, fashion, writing and the performing arts, here we draw on analogies and stories from the world of sports, where 'leading from the middle' may be more easily recognized than in business.

All Roads Lead to the Middle

In a 2007 article in *Scientific American Mind* called 'The New Psychology of Leadership', Stephen Riechler and his co-authors outlined the case for leading not from the top or the front, but leading instead from the middle. In a world where leadership is about working to enable and shape what people want to do, rather than telling them or showing them what to do, leaders rely upon constituent support and cooperation. Leadership can thus no longer be a 'top-down' process, relying on the leader's intelligence, charisma or other extraordinary traits to captivate and dominate the minds of followers. Rather, to gain the credibility necessary to attract followers, leaders must position themselves among the group not above it. It follows then that the best leaders are those who best personify the shared values of a group rather than being in some way superior or extraordinary.

This new concept of leadership was backed up by a growing number of research studies showing that most people would prefer a leader who is considerate and dedicated over one who is highly intelligent, and that they value the sort of mature leadership qualities that Marcus Aurelius alluded to, like being down-to-earth, trustworthy or dependable.

---

1. A new psychology of leadership suggests that effective leaders must understand the values and opinions of their followers – rather than assuming absolute authority – to enable a productive dialogue with team members about what the group stands for and thus how it should act.

2. According to this new approach, no fixed set of personality traits can assure good leadership because the most desirable traits depend on the nature of the group being led.

3. Leaders who adopt this strategy must try not only to fit in with their group but also to shape the group's identity in a way that makes their own agenda and policies appear to be an expression of that identity.

From *The New Psychology of Leadership* by Stephen Reicher, Alexander Haslam and Michael Platow, *Scientific American Mind*, August/September 2007.

The box above contains more details about the research behind the article, but it is also clear that this notion of leading from the middle, rather than just from the top, is part of a groundswell of changes in business thinking about leadership. In the following pages, we highlight some of these trends. From different starting points, each of these eight 'routes' has taken us further towards our understanding of 'leadership from the middle'. They are:

- recognizing the rise of the 'knowledge age';
- working with the 'wisdom of crowds';
- rediscovering the importance of the 'gut instinct' and intuition;
- appreciating 'tipping points' rather than charging into the fray;
- knowing the power of networks and relationships;
- moving from IQ to many Qs;
- adopting 'post-heroic' leadership styles; and
- remembering how strategy can develop from the middle.

Route 1: The Rise of the 'Knowledge Age'

In 1990 Arie De Geus declared that we live in a new 'knowledge society' in a book called *The Living Company*. He describes this historical development as follows:

I. Economic theory suggests that there are three sources of wealth: land and natural resources, capital, and labour. Until the late Middle Ages, the critical factor was *land*. Those who possessed and controlled land controlled the accumulation of wealth.

II. But as nation-states formed and became concerned with expansion, the *capital* to finance expansionary endeavours became more valuable. During the 'Age of Capitalism' that ensued, the modern company developed. Capital was made available for the wealth-creating processes of the venturer and tradesperson and old craft guilds broke apart. There evolved competing companies and enterprises and a market which gave the speculative owners of capital great control over human resources. Capital now held greater utility than land or labour.

III. The past fifty years, however, have seen a shift from one dominated by capital to one based on labour, and in particular the *knowledge* possessed by labour. Changes in the banking system since 1945, globalization and technological advances have made capital easier to access, move around, share and invest. At the same time restrictions on land and natural resource-use mean that possession of land has become less of a driver. Increasing cross-border competition and the subsequent complexity of work have fed the need for inventiveness or creativity, leading people rather than land or capital to become the dominant economic resource for companies. Those people who had knowledge and knew how to apply it (and the firms which recruited them) would henceforth be the wealthiest. This shift has become visible in the rise, since the 1950s, of material asset-poor but knowledge-rich companies such as international auditing firms, management consultancies, advertising and media businesses, and IT providers.

The effects of globalization, 'footloose' labour and the growth in information technology mean that organizational knowledge is now not only the most valuable commodity, it is also more mobile than ever. David Ogilvy famously remarked that the assets of his advertising agency went up and down in the lifts. More recently an advertising executive described his business to us as engaging in a 'war for talent', with each agency competing to recruit the brightest people before their rivals, then leasing them out to clients. And this war for talent presents some unique challenges for strategic leadership.

With an increase in the value and power of the 'knowledge worker' leaders have had to become less 'command and control' oriented and more facilitators, enablers, mentors and coaches. Successful firms are 'middle-men' or brokers between the owners of capital and the owners of knowledge. Indeed, a recent study of the academic business literature confirms a massive spike in interest in 'knowledge' in the 1990s and early 2000s and predicts that strategic leadership will need to become more dexterous and 'political' to be effective in an environment where knowledge is king. This applies especially to the creative industries, where people are valuable but volatile assets and keeping 'the talent' happy has long been a key task for leaders. But as we enter De Geus's 'knowledge society', knowledge, and in particular knowing how to retain and use knowledgeable people, will become everybody's business.

Route 2: Working with the 'Wisdom of Crowds'

In 2004 *New Yorker* columnist James Surowiecki began his book *The Wisdom of Crowds* (with the cumbersome but descriptive sub-title: 'Why the Many are Smarter than the Few and How Collective Wisdom Shapes Business, Economies, Societies, and Nations') with a one hundred year old story of a sprightly 85 year old scientist and a fat ox. British scientist Francis Galton's studies of human behaviour, and his fascination with the new science of eugenics, had left him with little faith in the intelligence of the 'average' person. As he walked around a country fair near his home in Plymouth he observed a weight-judging competition where around 800 bystanders wrote what they guessed as the weight of an ox on display on a ticket. Some were expert breeders, but most were interested laypeople. This struck Galton as an interesting set of data, and once the contest was complete he asked the organizers if he could have the tickets. He carried out a number of statistical experiments and found, to his surprise, that the mean of all 800 estimates was extremely accurate. The mean was 1197 pounds. The actual weight: 1198 pounds. The scientist conceded that 'The result seems more creditable to the trustworthiness of a democratic judgement than might have been expected.'

Surowiecki connected this story to a range of subsequent anecdotes and more recent experiments and research that explained how collective wisdom is generally better than individual guess-work.

More recently some have questioned Suroweicki's faith in crowds, citing failing financial markets as examples of crowd-think gone awry. But this is to miss Surowiecki's emphasis on the pluralism and diversity of crowds, and Galton's stress on 'democratic' judgement. Crowds are wise only if they are diverse and paying attention (we might say curious, as we did at the end of Part I). The problem with financial markets in the global financial crisis was that too many people weren't paying proper attention, and there was not a critical mass of divergent dissenters among those who were.

Since *The Wisdom of Crowds* was published, further studies have pointed to the power of plurality in helping guide decision making. Indeed, one study published in 2008 in *Psychological Science* showed that the average of two guesses made by the same person at different times are also significantly better than one.

What does this tell us about leadership today? First, notwithstanding the need for leaders to make judgement calls at particular points (see the comments of Jeffrey Immelt on the 3rd and 7th routes below), it leads us to a view that gung-ho leadership from the top or front may not be such a good thing. Inclusive consulting across a range of people is useful. And, it is good to pause before making those judgement calls.

Route 3: Rediscovering the Importance of the 'Gut Instinct' and Intuition

A third route brings leadership to the middle in a physiological sense. This is the rediscovery of the positive influence of the 'gut' or instinct and intuition in management. The primary popularizer of this view is another *New Yorker* columnist: Malcolm Gladwell. Gladwell's book *Blink: The Power of Thinking Without Thinking* instantly gained a huge readership, partly because of the fervour that his previous work, *The Tipping Point*, generated (see the 4th route, below).

Gladwell organized a fantastic array of examples to demonstrate that decisions seemingly made in an instant can be as good, if not better, than those made more consciously or deliberately because of a phenomenon that Gladwell terms 'thin-slicing'. This is where our 'gut instinct' very quickly senses a pattern that enables us to sift out irrelevant information, develop a 'hunch', and then act on this very quickly. Because our unconscious mind, or gut, is so good at this it often delivers a better response than more protracted forms of rational analysis.

It is important to point out, however, that some have been misled by *Blink* and the simplistic interpretations it has spawned. The title, and subsequent associations with making 'snap judge-ments', not looking before leaping, and acting impulsively, can lead people to forget that intuition is not just based on impulse. Quite the opposite. In actual fact, relying more on our gut instinct is about accessing *deeper* feelings and memories and getting beyond experiences that may be at the top of our conscious minds and wider into a series of other physiological senses tuned by millennia of evolutionary instincts. Those works and scientists that Gladwell drew upon, such as *Gut Feelings: The Intelligence of the Unconscious* by Gerd Gigerenzer and *The Second Brain: The Scientific Basis of Gut Instinct* by Michael Gershon, go into greater detail about the mechanics of how the hundreds of millions of nerve cells in and around our guts can act independently from and in association with our brains as we make decisions. There is now a wide range of evidence suggesting that the stomach (particularly in combination with a mind that knows how to use it) can be a source of very good judgement. It is not so much that less thinking is better but that thinking should incorporate and value a diversity of senses.

Gershon in particular is credited with rediscovering the existence of the gut as a 'second brain' in the 1960s (it was widely discussed decades before this but the subsequent knowledge that was developed was side-lined, eclipsed and forgotten by medicine). Now he is at the forefront of the field exploring this phenomenon: neurogastroenterology.

Intuition is also being rediscovered in leadership studies too. Noel Tichy and Warren Bennis's recently published book *How Winning Leaders Make Great Calls* looks extensively at the importance of good judgement with regard to decision making and the role that intuition plays in this. Good leaders in this respect, they argue, need to gain experience and gather 'domain knowledge', but self-knowledge and self-confidence must be a corollary. As the new CEO of General Electric, Jeffrey Immelt, tells them: 'I make every decision, but get lots of advice. . . It's 'What do you think?' What do you think? What do you think? Then boom. I decide.'

There is a parallel between the heroic leader at 'the top' and the 'genius' artist. Robert Weisberg has noted that when artists appear to be making impulsive creative decisions, they are very often drawing upon domain-specific expertise, accumulated wisdom and memory – but they don't always acknowledge these less glamorous precedents. The other authors cited here remind us that individual, intuitive 'judgement calls' very often draw upon exposure to a wider range of collective experiences and perspectives than the conscious mind might allow or admit. Leading from the middle will help us to access some of these resources.

Route 4: Tipping Rather than Charging

Gladwell's previous book had an even more pervasive effect on modern culture than *Blink*. *The Tipping Point*'s big idea is that big ideas aren't really that different from other ideas: it's just that they reach a tipping point, a critical mass or threshold at which their momentum becomes unstoppable, like a virus that becomes an epidemic. Gladwell describes the 'three rules of epidemics', or the three agents of change that lead to the tipping points of epidemics, as 'the law of the few', 'the stickiness factor' and 'the power of context'.

Understanding these rules, claims Gladwell, can help people manage toward desired tipping points. Hence, it pays to know that, as with systems thinking's '80/20' principle (where it is generally 20% of the system's components that account for 80% of its value) or marketing's focus on 'early adopters' (who will influence others to follow them into using a new product or service), it is much more effective to target those people who have the power to influence others than rely on a formal hierarchy, random selection or treating all things equally. Secondly, it pays to know that no idea will spread unless it is communicated in a way that resonates and 'sticks' with people, particularly with that key 20% (more on this in the next chapter). Finally, it pays to know that no idea will spread quickly unless it fits with and can latch onto the environment or context in which it is seeking to embed itself.

It is easy to see how the tipping point logic would contribute to a 'new psychology' of leading from the middle. Instead of issuing blanket proclamations from on high, leaders should position themselves near the centre of an organization, understand that organization's key players, identity and context, and then seek to attract the influencers and connectors (see the next route) toward a vision in order to virally spread messages that tip the organization toward the desired direction.

Route 5: The Power of Networks and Relationships

One of Gladwell's most memorable examples in *The Tipping Point* compares the two men who rode out simultaneously on the night of 18 April 1775 to raise the alarm that America's Revolutionary War had begun. William Dawes rode South. Paul Revere rode North. But despite both men coming from similar backgrounds and the towns they rode through being demographically alike, only one man raised an army. Gladwell, like many others before him, asked what might account for the difference.

The answer, according to Gladwell, and to the authors of a *Harvard Business Review Paper* entitled 'How to Build Your Network', was that Revere was at once a gatherer of information and a connector of people and a great salesman or communicator. He knew what to say, how best to say it, and the best people to say it to. Whereas Dawes spread the word in a linear fashion with an additive effect, Revere created an exponential multiplier that had the effect of a virus. Revere was like a super conductor: a connector who connected to other connectors. Like that famous shampoo commercial from the 1970s: '*She told 2 friends, who told 2 friends, who told 2 friends...*', networks of connectors allow information and influence to multiply geometrically ($4 \times 4 \times 4 = 64$) rather than progress arithmetically ($4 + 4 + 4 = 12$).

A 2009 paper applies this network thinking to recessionary times ('Start Networking Right Away – Even if you Hate it' by William Byham) and recommends that prospective leaders should engage in 'courageous networking'. To gain information, Byham recommends you get to know those people who know things that can help you to connect and grow your network. Those people may not be 'bosses'. As Byham explains, it's better to think about who are the critical people in a supply chain or an information system. Knowing somebody in the legal department may open up a network of contacts able to provide insights into major problems an organization is facing. Knowing the person who implements office moves can help you to connect with people who are being promoted within the organization. Knowing someone who knows how to 'read' social networking sites may help you to gather multiple insights into what is about to be hot and what is about to be not.

There is now much evidence, both high and low brow, about the value of networking for a leader. From the world of neural science we now understand that adults can reason, recall and combine ideas more effectively than children, despite having brains that are more 'set in their ways' and which are the same physical size (the human brain stops getting larger at six years), because they have grown more than one neural network, and these networks can operate both independently and collaboratively. In the world of pop management, guru-extraordinaire Tom Peters has updated

Bill Clinton's famous slogan 'It's the economy, stupid' into a mantra for what should matter to the strategic leader: 'It's relationships, stupid'. The value of networks in the creative industries is often described in terms of a shift from 'know-how' to 'know-who'.

Leading from the middle means being able, through one's abilities *and* through one's networks, to move quickly from the top to the bottom of an organization, or from the organization to the wider environment to capture the mood and spread the word.

Route 6: From IQ to Many Qs

In simpler times there was one widely recognized quotient of how effective or bright a person might be: IQ. Reflective of the changes outlined above, there are now many 'Q's' to compete with cerebral intelligence. Most of these can be related to what were once seen as more humble or 'lower order' faculties.

Intelligence Quotient (IQ): A measure of *intellectual* proficiency.

Technical Quotient (TQ): A measure of *technical* proficiency in achieving certain tasks.

Experience Quotient (XQ): A measure of types of *experience* related to the task or role.

Motivational Quotient (MQ): A measure of one's *motivation* to achieve and to grow.

People Quotient (PQ or EQ): A measure of *emotional* awareness and, subsequently, of a person's ability to work cooperatively with others.

Learning Quotient (LQ): A measure of one's ability to *learn* and adapt to new skills, behaviours and beliefs.

Cultural Quotient (CQ): A measure of a person's ability to understand and operate across different *cultures* and situations.

Social Quotient (SQ): A measure of one's ability to *socialize*, mix and get on with others.

The list will no doubt continue to grow. Indeed, we could develop a case for an additional PolQ (political quotient), IntQ (intuition quotient), TipQ (tipping quotient) and NQ (networking quotient) based on the preceding paragraphs.

While it may be helpful for a strategic leader to have all of these characteristics, the latest research seems to suggest that for future leaders a relatively low score in the first three categories (intelligence, technical proficiency and relevant experience) will be less important than any deficiencies in the last five Qs (motivation, emotional intelligence, learning ability, cultural awareness, social skills).

The major management consultancies have changed their recruitment profiles and advertising accordingly. When it comes to leadership, recruiters are less interested in measuring extraordinary abilities and achievements, and more interested in the leader's ability to facilitate the achievements of others, like a good sherpa or caddy.

Route 7: 'Post-Heroic' Leadership

At the beginning of the last century, Max Weber conceptualized three types of leaders: traditional leaders, those who gained their authority from their traditional associations with power (monarchs, Popes and so on); rational-legal leaders, those who ruled by secular decrees and appeals to rational frameworks (prime ministers, scientists, etc.); and those whose charisma furnished them with followers, for better or for worse (Jesus, Nelson Mandela, Bono, Hitler, etc.). Weber believed that only charismatic leaders might deliver us from the rather gloomy and cold bureaucratic world that his social history foretold.

In the chaos that surrounded World War I and beyond, the notion of charismatic leaders as saviours gained further support. The dictatorships which led the world into a second war did undermine enthusiasm for the charismatic hero leader. But work that emerged in the 1970s and beyond (particularly that of James McGregor Burns on transformational leaders and their special attributes) reignited the Western world's belief in great leaders, standing on a podium or leading from the front, promising salvation.

The first decade of the 21st century has seen another shift, however. There is now a solid body of work shaping a fourth archetype: the less-elevated, 'anti-heroic' or 'post-heroic', leader.

Jim Collins, author of *Built to Last* and *From Good to Great*, was recently asked for some leadership tips based on his research for these books. Collins suggests that two of the best things that good new leaders do is to create a 'not-to-do list' and increase their 'questions-to-statements ratio'. Old-style, charismatic hero-leaders tended to take on huge workloads and proclaim their own decisions and points of view. In today's complex business environments the post-heroic leader can no longer monopolize all the key decisions – other lower-level managers want to be heard and are looking to create or make their own marks. So for every new ongoing task put on their 'to-do list' Collins argues that one must be put, like an accounting balance, on the 'not-to-do-list' and delegated. In a similar vein, the good leaders in Collins' studies were Socratic – they lead by asking questions and debating the answers.

In theatre rehearsals too, we observe the great directors asking lots of questions. This model of leadership is concerned primarily with the way that problems are framed rather than attempting to solve them. The distinction between 'problem-solving' and 'problem-engagement' is echoed in creativity theory; a genuinely creative approach to a problem does not merely provide an answer, it fundamentally changes the way we think.

The arrival of the post-heroic era can be seen in the most observed CEO transition over the past twenty years. When Jeffrey Immelt replaced Jack Welch at GE that contrast could not have seemed starker. The jumper-wearing Immelt appears altogether softer, more empathetic, calm, humble, unflappable than the hard-nosed, 'heroic' Welch. Immelt was recently named by the *International Herald Tribune* as the 'prototype CEO' for a world in which people follow 'not because they have to, but because they want to': a good listener, consensus builder and ambassador.

Indeed, what is remarkable about GE, and one of the main reasons it has continued to prosper (relatively speaking) while the conglomerate has been pronounced an archaic organizational form, may be that it has a great talent for bringing forth the right leader for the context of the times. In its 130 years it has only had nine chief executives and only one might be considered less than successful. He was the star of the second part of this book: innovator Thomas Edison. Post-heroic times call for post-heroic leaders.

This is not to say that post-heroic leaders don't have to make tough calls, rather that they know when to and when not to. As Immelt told the *Herald Tribune*, 'When you run General Electric, there are seven to twelve times a year when you have to say, "You're doing it my way". If you do it eighteen times, the good people will leave. If you do it three times, the company falls apart.' The secret of post-heroic leadership may be knowing where this middle ground is.

Route 8: Strategy from the Middle

In addition to these seven arguments for leading from the middle, we might reflect back on earlier parts of this book to note an eighth. In Part I we described the view that strategy should not be seen as the capstone at the top of an organization but the keystone in the middle, that which connects and turns the whole organization. If strategy is seen to be moving from the top of organizations to the centre, then leadership should be moving that way too.

Figure 11.1 offers a summary of the theoretical routes leading to our view of the growing importance of leading from the middle.

This is well and good, in theory; but what about strategic leadership in practice? The next chapter develops a framework, based on the theoretical perspectives described above, which can be applied to the practical tasks of leadership.

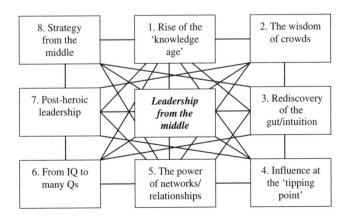

Figure 11.1 Eight routes to leading creative strategy from the middle

CHAPTER 12

The Strategic Leadership Keypad

I n the last chapter we examined a shift in theoretical perceptions of leadership from 'leading from the top' towards 'leading from the middle'. But how does this relate to strategic leadership in practice?

Throughout this book we have argued that each of the dimensions of creative strategy requires the embrace of dichotomous elements. Here we will argue that strategic leadership means switching between two paradoxical processes. Strategic leadership, whether by an individual leader or a leadership team, depends upon *interacting* with people and ideas inside and outside the organization, and at the same time *envisioning* a clear way forward by abstracting away from these detailed interactions and seeing the bigger picture. To understand how this strategic leadership dichotomy plays out, we have developed a framework that identifies four practical dimensions or keys to strategic leadership, linked by a central 'shift key', which allows leaders to move back and forth between them.

Switching Positions: Introducing the Strategic Leadership Keypad

We can better grasp this idea of strategic leadership as a combination of envisioning and interacting through a sporting analogy. In sport, it is standard practice for the playing captain to be positioned in the midfield in football or as quarterback in American football, or down the spine of a team (hooker, number 8, halfback, centre) in rugby. By leading from the middle they can see the game develop and are better positioned to interact with team-mates.

But there are many other leadership positions in a professional sports organization, from the managers and CEOs to the coaches, stars and scouts. Typically the coaches and managers will take a broader, more conceptual perspective, *envisioning* strategies and future targets, whilst those closer to the action will take a more specialized and detailed view, *interacting* with others and with the immediate tasks of running the team. For the team to perform, all these positions must function in harmony.

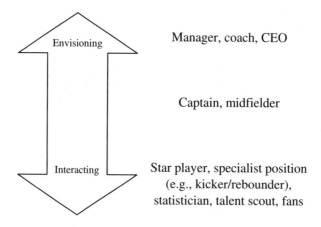

While the diagram above explains the spread from envisioning to interacting, the positions outlined on the right also point to a second dichotomy, between an *internal* and an *external* orientation to the organization or team. At the envisioning level, a coach should be focussed on the internal world of the team; but the CEO or management team must be mindful of the wider commercial and competitive environment. At the level of interaction, particular players will be immersed in particular games, whereas the scout and the statistician must be looking outside and ahead.

We think the leadership of business organizations is analogous. Leaders here must also shift from an internal orientation focussing on what is happening inside the organization to an external orientation connecting to the wider world, to customers (who like fans can be inspiring or distracting), financial stakeholders and 'the wisdom of crowds'. And as a successful sports team will require more than one leader if it is to create effective results, so a successful business will need to tap more than one leadership 'key' to keep a creative strategy on track.

Layering this internal/external dialectic across our envisioning/interacting dichotomy creates a picture of four keys that can, and should, be accessed by effective strategic leadership. Leading from the middle thus occupies a position midway along either axis, the best place from which to switch in an agile fashion between internal and external perspectives, and between envisioning and interactive 'leading by doing'. The different leadership keys are illustrated in the figure below,

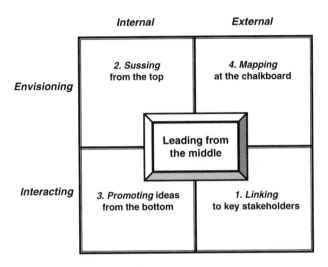

Figure 12.1   The strategic leadership keypad

with 'leading from the middle' depicted as a shift key (we could have termed it a 'joy-stick'), allowing us to toggle up and down and across the other leadership approaches.

We now consider each of these leadership keys in more detail, before examining how strategic leaders can switch between them.

Key 1. Linking with the Outside

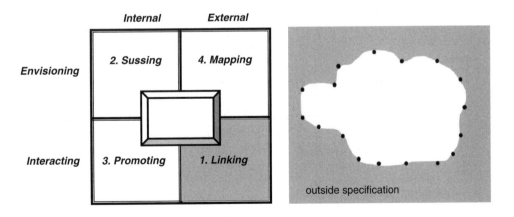

In an interesting example of *boundary* and *market* innovation (see Chapter 7), Procter & Gamble CEO A. G. Lafely recently set a goal of having 50% of its innovations being sourced from outside of the company. The decision fits with Lafely's view of the leadership priorities of the CEO.

In an article called 'What Only the CEO Can Do' published in the *Harvard Business Review* in 2009, Lafely pays tribute to his leadership mentor, the great Peter Drucker. In 2004 Drucker outlined that 'The CEO is the link between the Inside that is 'the organization', and the Outside of society, economy, technology, and customers.'

Building on this perspective, Lafely summarizes his view of the CEOs primary function as follows:

- Conventional wisdom suggests that the CEO is primarily a coach and a utility infielder, dropping in to solve problems where they crop up.
- In fact, however, the CEO has a very specific job that only he or she can do: link the external world with the internal organization.
- It's a job that *only* the CEO can do because everybody else in the organization focusses much more narrowly and almost always internally.
- It's a job that the CEO *must* do because without the outside there is no inside.

Hence, the primary task of the CEO is to 'define the meaningful outside' for their organization, determining who the external stakeholders are, prioritizing the ones that matter the most, and consequently determining how those key interactions might be evaluated. We define this leadership approach as *linking*.

Indeed, research carried out in the late 1990s emphasizes the importance of this prioritization. It found that firms who used stakeholder analysis indiscriminately generally performed worse than those who ignored their stakeholders. The implication is that attempting to satisfy too many and too varied a group of stakeholder demands instead of prioritizing between them can paralyse an organization.

In order to assess which stakeholders should be prioritised, it is useful first to map them. One way of doing this is to use a power/interest grid which identifies the level of power a stakeholder has to influence the firm and the level of interest they have in supporting or opposing a particular strategy. Those with high interest in influencing and high power to influence are key and they should be given top priority with regard to relationship building and lobbying efforts.

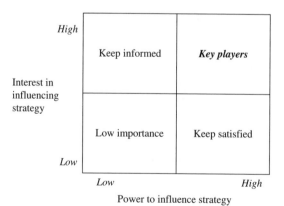

Figure 12.2 Stakeholder power/interest matrix

In the Trelise Cooper story in Part II, we could see how her 'key players' were her own point of view and the 'collective we' of her design team that enacts and develops that view. As she moved from an entrepreneurial to a leadership perspective, this was where the most meaningful strategic interactions would occur. Retailers, while very important and potentially enabling or disruptive to a launch strategy, were less interested in influencing strategy provided Cooper could keep them *satisfied* by delivering a good product. On the other hand, her manufacturing partners in India and Hong Kong were more involved but less powerful, and here Cooper needed to keep them *informed* about her strategic decisions, with good communication being essential.

Similarly, when Steve Jobs says: 'We do no market research. We just want to make great products'; it is an indication that Apple's key stakeholders are the design team and its links with the wider world of design and design influences, rather than customers or competitors in the technology market.

For Proctor & Gamble, focussing on defining the meaningful outside helped Lafely to understand that the key external interaction was with customers. 'Without consumers, there is no P&G', he explained. 'Therefore, our [most] meaningful results come from two critical moments of truth: first, when a consumer chooses to buy a P&G product over all others in the store, and second, when she or a family member uses the product at home. Although other external stakeholders have important demands, when there's a conflict, we resolve it in favour of the one who matters most: the consumer.' This perspective is similar to that of Clive Lindop at Codemasters in one of our other entrepreneurial journeys in Part II, with Clive seeing himself as 'championing the player' against other stakeholders in the development of a game.

Subsequently, this is why and how Lafely came to see the importance of half of P&G's innovations coming from outside the organization: they should be driven by consumers, or, more accurately, from the interaction between P&G employees and consumers. Hence, almost every P&G office and innovation centre now has consumers working inside with employees.

Having identified the primary task of the CEO as defining the meaningful outside, Lafely then outlines the other imperatives for the CEO:

- Deciding what business you are in. 'Where should you play to win? Where should you not play at all?' This resonates with the view that strategy is as much about knowing what the organization doesn't do as it is about what the organization does;
- Balancing present and future – being satisfied with short-term goals which are 'good enough' and prioritising long-term aims, so that you are not tempted to sacrifice your future at the altar of the quick win; and
- Shaping values and standards.

The last of these priorities leads us on to the second key on our strategic leadership pad: sussing.

Key 2. Sussing the Overarching Vision

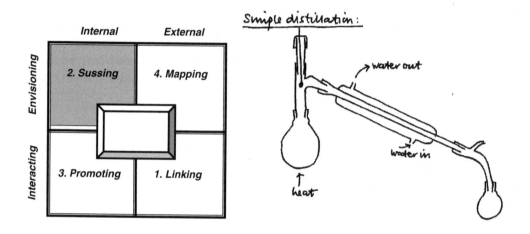

to suss 1. (New Zealand, British, Australian) To discover, infer or figure out something (often used with 'out'.) 2. (New Zealand, British) To study or size up something.

Work done on the external/interactive key of *linking* (identifying and prioritising stakeholders) will help when the leadership toggles up and across to the internal/envisioning key: a perspective that we term 'sussing'. This word may be less familiar to American readers (we provide a British dictionary definition above for this reason). We have chosen to use 'sussing' rather than 'distilling' or 'abstracting' because the word suss is also an acronym for a desired outcome of this key: *Simple Unifying Strategic Statements*. Such a statement can function like a good vision – see the box below for a good vision's characteristics (most company visions fail to meet this definition). However, the 'SUSS' is generally more colloquial and shorter than a vision statement: it 'sizes up' a strategy and distils its essence into an internal rallying call that is memorable and unifying.

A Peter Drucker inspired view of the five principles of a good vision:

1. **brief** (not a long-winded hero sandwiches of good intentions);
2. **true** to the particular company's focus and character;
3. **understandable** to all employees;
4. **inspirational**; and
5. **verifiable**, so that progress and ultimately success can be determined.

The first characteristic of sussing is simplicity, boiling down complex ideas into a distilled essence. When Mark Wood became CEO of The Prudential in the UK a few years ago, he inherited an organization with a formal statement of purpose much like any large financial services company: *Prudential plc provides retail financial products and services and fund management to many millions of customers worldwide. . . .* And on it went for another 150 words. But it was also a company that seemed to lack a clear view of how it was different and what it, in particular, was trying to achieve.

While Wood recognized the necessity of the professional looking statement of purpose quoted above, he also appreciated the need to distil something that could focus the minds of people internally on what the company actually stood for which could enable clear decision making. In a speech to employees not long after he became CEO he began to grasp the nettle:

> . . . Above all else we have worked, first and foremost, to ensure that our customers, in their old age, can afford to eat, to heat their homes, to take the style of holiday they are used to, replace worn out clothes, and continue to tend the garden they love and live in the home in which they are comfortable.

This was what made the Pru different. It wasn't playing the quick high-risk, high-return game that most of its competitors were. It should be focussed on the solid, good-growth, for the long-term, nest-egg investments. Wood went on to distil the following SUSS-line for the Pru: Helping Old People Eat. It doesn't sound much like a corporate vision statement and it was never promoted externally as such, but Helping Old People Eat (and the ensuing acronym HOPE) struck a chord with an ever-increasing number within the company and went on to tip the Pru toward a much clearer strategic vision, even beyond Wood's tenure as leader.

The New Zealand police had a great SUSS-line for nearly 100 years: *'To work with the community to maintain the peace.'* Then in the 1990s consultants were brought in to replace this motto with a more professional sounding mission statement. They came up with this:

> *To contribute to the provision of a safe and secure environment where people may go about their lawful business unhindered and which is conducive to the enhancement of the quality of life and economic performance.*

After ten years of bemusement and disquiet it was a senior sergeant who advocated moving back to the future by reverting to a simple statement 'Safer communities together'.

Senior management within the force had the vision to promote this idea (see Key 3 below). Not only does it connect the organization to a proud tradition, offer a clear view of who the key stakeholders are for the future (community groups), and clearly distil a strategy into three words, it's a lot easier to paint on the side of a police car!

Four words for HOPE, three words for SCT. . . Can it be done in less than three words? J.P. Dru's book *Disruption* advocates leaders reducing strategies to single words. Whereas we suggested that one route to value innovation might be to think of the adjective that you might add to a conventional product or service, Dru challenges us to think of the verb that best captures the organization's desired distinctiveness. Dru says that the best brands are easy to associate with singular verbs: Apple opposes, IBM solves, Virgin enlightens, Sony dreams.

The simplicity of SUSS-lines gives them clarity and purpose. SUSS-lines must strike right to the point, delivering a message which is memorable and easily understood. And rather than being overly intellectual, they should inspire action. As the Roman politician Cato reminds us: 'When Cicero spoke, people marvelled. When Caesar spoke, people marched.' But also, and importantly, because simple statements tend to be brief and evocative rather than prescriptive, they leave space for people to work within them and grow into them, interpreting them differently for new times, new situations and different personalities. The 'unifying' element of sussing means articulating a vision which works across different scenarios and perspectives.

Theatre provides some good examples of this inclusive, unifying vision. Successful theatre directors are often described as 'visionary' – their productions provide a new way of seeing a text or performance, reframing ideas, characters and story. Yet our conversations with directors and observations of directors in rehearsal suggest that they do not, indeed could not, set out with a 'vision statement'. Their first aim is to provide a simple frame within which the visions, ideas and decisions of others (the actors, but also the designer, musical director, lighting designer) can converge. In the end, the actors are the ones implementing the performance – and they will be more convincing if they are presenting ideas which they have co-created organically during rehearsals, rather than parroting somebody else's vision. The director's role in rehearsals is to cajole and coach the actors towards their own shared understanding of the play rather than impose his own preconceived vision.

And yet the director is more than a receptacle for everybody else's views. As with the mapping of stakeholders in the previous leadership key, 'sussing' requires us to prioritise selectively. In theatre rehearsals we observe directors either holding a distorting mirror up to the actors – appearing to endorse their suggestions whilst turning them into something else – or bouncing the suggestion back to them. The reflection is a critical one, questioning the bases and assumptions through which decisions are made. This reflects a key function of leadership – sussing out the values and capabilities of other people's values and capabilities in order to better articulate them. Neither Mark Wood nor the police sergeant invented their SUSS-lines: all the elements were there already, they simply articulated them. Like a good surfer they picked out a naturally occurring wave and rode it.

Articulating a unifying vision for the New Zealand police force involved distilling not only the present priorities but also drawing on the past. Hewlett-Packard's SUSS-line works in a similar way. Recognizing that they couldn't win an all-out price war, Hewlett-Packard saw the need to distil what set them apart. The phrase they came up with, 'the rules of the garage', drew together the individualistic pioneering spirit of the company's founders, Bill Hewlett and Dave Packard, toiling away in their little inventor's shed in Palo Alto, and the company's subsequent history of significant innovation. Like Apple, IBM, Virgin and Sony, they managed to boil this all down to one underlying verb: 'Invention' and have subsequently ensured that wherever one sees the HP symbol it stands upon the word 'Invent'.

While it may not be possible to suss your organization's strategy into a word, brevity is certainly the aim. A simple word or phrase is usually more inclusive, adapatable and unifying than a lengthy mission statement. It also forces you to be strategic by focussing on what's important. Seth Godin outlines the challenge thus: 'If you can't explain your strategic position in eight words or less, then you don't have one'. But Samuel Goldwyn probably said it better a long time ago: *If you can't write down your movie idea on the back of a business card then you ain't got a movie.*

Key 3. Promoting from Below

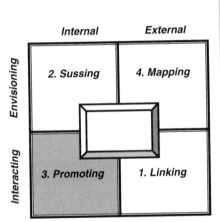

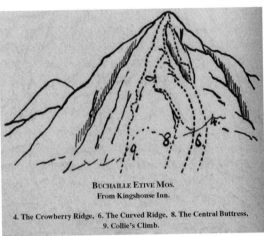

BUCHAILLE ETIVE MOS.
From Kingshouse Inn.

4. The Crowberry Ridge, 6. The Curved Ridge, 8. The Central Buttress, 9. Collie's Climb.

We have already provided a number of examples in the book that relate to promoting the ideas of people at 'lower levels': the idea of strategy as emergent, the tales of how Post-It Notes came into existence and how Honda established itself in the USA; the story of the email from the CEO to all staff saying 'any ideas?' and the notion of identifying and sponsoring promising practices as a more enlivening approach than telling people to copy so-called 'best practice'. We do not need, therefore, to go over that ground again. Here we propose a framework to describe the conditions which support the promotion of good ideas across all areas of a business.

First, promoting from below depends on the other keys we have discussed already. Linking with external stakeholders and 'sussing' the internal vision provide a context for promoting ideas from within. Many ideas may appear promising but it is hard to define which of these are best suited to a particular organization unless these other two keys are also being played. Conversely both sussing and linking are both supported by interacting with people and promoting ideas.

But beyond this, there are three conditions, or 3 Ts, that are crucial to enable good 'leadership by promotion':

- **Trust** – people must believe that their thinking will be treated with respect and that due credit will be given as their ideas come to fruition.

- **Teamwork** – trust leads to teamwork in that a good idea freely given up by an individual (or individuals) can then be knocked around and developed by others, this also entails that all parties have an ability to switch between leading and supporting or promoting, as the situation demands.
- **The 'traverse'** – trust and teamwork will be enhanced if people can see some pathways to the top and recognize some ideas which have filtered up to the highest levels. They are less likely to put effort into developing and sharing new ideas if they can't see how good ideas can climb within the company.

One of the biggest obstacles to these conditions in large companies is that those in formal leadership positions are hardly seen. The age of e-mail gives senior managers an illusion of connection, without other people in their organization actually feeling their presence. In Jack Welch's words: to inspire trust and 'rally the team, you need to see, hear and feel the team, and they need a regular dose of the real you'. Without connection then, it is difficult for ideas to traverse the organization, because there is no trust or team to nurture them.

But these three conditions are common in team sports and in the arts. In arts organizations, for example, leadership functions typically traverse the company, rather than being invested in single individuals. The individualistic culture and project-based nature of creative enterprise means that fixed roles and functions are shared, exchanged or combined – in theatre there are directors who act, actors and designers who direct, writers who do both. This overlap and exchange between roles reflects the boundary innovations described in Chapter 7. It also allows different types of leaders at different levels of the organization to delegate to each other's strengths. From the outside it is sometimes difficult to tell who is leading and who is following. Without a fixed hierarchy and without identifiable leaders taking control, leadership comes from unexpected places – a deputy director or head of department might be driving key decisions as much as the nominal leader.

Sadly, in our experience, this 3T environment with its absence of visible hierarchies or strong charismatic leaders, has prompted suggestions that arts organizations are suffering from a leadership 'crisis'. External bodies have subsequently sought to professionalize the arts by bringing in management consultants and executives from other industries to create more business-like structures. Unfortunately though, parachuting in 'business' trouble-shooters in this way has generally done more harm than good. In the UK arts sector, changes in leadership driven by external stakeholders (the board of the Royal Opera House, the BBC governors) have led to appointed leaders having to battle internal suspicions (and dwindling trust and teamwork) before they can even begin to address the external challenges. In a situation where conventional businesses might have learned from a leadership model in the arts which effectively promotes ideas from within, the imposition of a model in the other direction has only exacerbated the mutually destructive animosity between 'creatives' and 'suits' (the two dead men on the first page of this book). A 'crisis in arts leadership' can become a self-fulfilling prophecy.

A major difference, however, between most arts or sporting organizations and many conventional businesses is size. It's a lot easier for trust, team, and traversing to flow in a smaller arts

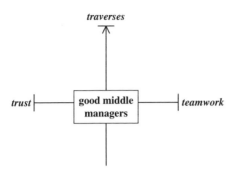

Figure 12.3   The three T's of leading by promoting

organization, where people know each other and have a singular set of values. This is why we would add one final crucial part to successful leading by promotion: good middle managers. We described the role of middle managers in 'sponsoring' innovation in Chapter 8. They fulfil a similarly important function in a leadership context. Much maligned in the past two decades, a really good middle manager plays an essential role in communicating broader visions and political realities downwards and helping to develop and promote good ideas from below. There may be nobody as strategic in creative strategy as a good middle-manager.

Key 4. Mapping: at the chalkboard

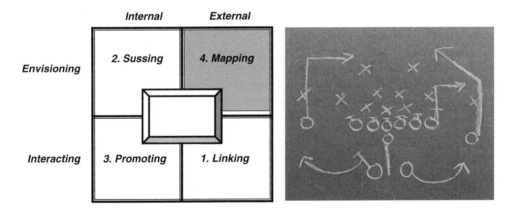

Whereas 'sussing' distils the internal values and aims of the organization to a single line, our other envisioning key maps a more complex external reality. 'Mapping' is comparable to the chalkboard used by coaches to translate a simple objective into a detailed game-plan. Coaches, managers and players stand outside the action, using graphical tools to communicate how they see the play unfolding and to demonstrate which moves may be the most effective. TV sports commentators often draw on interactive screens to demonstrate this 'eye of God' perspective. White boards, flip charts, freeze frames from TV footage, play books, game cards are all useful vehicles for conveying positions and dynamics in a contested space over time.

A recent survey asked executives which areas of strategy required greater emphasis. The most common response, according to 79% of respondents, was the need to 'more effectively communicate their strategy internally'. As we have already noted, one of the biggest problems in this regard is that leaders generally capture and communicate strategy in a strategic planning document packed with text and numbers. Graphics tend to be used to communicate technical data, not ideas. A vision is hardly ever communicated through effective pictures or graphics in business.

Consequently, many strategies fail to create effectively not because they are poorly planned or implemented without enthusiasm, but because they are poorly expressed. Those in the organization are not sure what the leaders envision, or how to put that vision into practice. All too often they carry their own mental picture of the strategy which may not tally with that of other people in the organization.

Visual communication can work at a more intuitive, direct level:

- Tennis coach Bob Brett, who has trained champions such as Boris Becker and Goran Ivanisevic, tells us of how he often finds it better to coach without talking. He starts by hitting in a way that mimics what he sees as the player's 'problem', and asks them to copy his stroke. He then gradually seeks to evolve to a better swing, taking his charge with him on a physical journey from flawed to good. Talking or writing this down can often be far less productive, he explains.
- Ben Rich of Lockheed's legendary Skunk Works could never get the Pentagon generals whom he relied upon for sponsorship to grasp the completely revolutionary nature of the Stealth aircraft until he took a ball bearing (with the same radar profile as the Stealth) to a meeting, rolled it across the table to them and said 'Here's your airplane!' Rich knew he 'had them' when a general caught the ball, held it in his hand and looked up at him.
- HP is able to use the tiny SUSS-line 'invent' because it is connected to a visual image of 'the garage' in employees' minds, which is then connected to HP's 'laws of the garage'.

Research in education confirms that people have better recall of pictures and that printed words receive less 'processing attention'. We know that young children learn maths concepts better if they use hand gestures as well as words to convey ideas. In Chapter 3 of this book we referred to the research by Piaget and Bruner which demonstrates that learning is best achieved through combining three elements. One element is the *concrete* or 'hands-on' doing of tasks. Another is associating these things with abstract representative *symbols*: language and numbers. But in between these two elements is an important link: *pictorial or graphical* aids to help conceptualize. These insights are familiar to most primary school teachers. Without pictorial and concrete learning, learning through language and numbers alone is not particularly effective.

'Mapping' (map-making and map-reading) thus forms a crucial link in the communication of strategy, connecting up the language and numbers of strategic vision to the concrete actions which must be performed towards it. Below we offer some examples of how mapping allows a company to envision and communicate a strategy.

Our first two examples show how mapping can elaborate outwards from a simple 'SUSS-line' and make that message more memorable and engaging. When Rob Fyfe became CEO of Air New Zealand he wanted a wider range of employees and other stakeholders to feel connected to the company's emerging strategy. He and his strategy team distilled the strategy into a few lines, and then used doodles and drawings to sketch out the details. The inclusion of common office objects and stains made it less daunting and more intimate than a normal strategic planning document: as if you were sitting at a desk or coffee table with Fyfe as he is taking you through it.

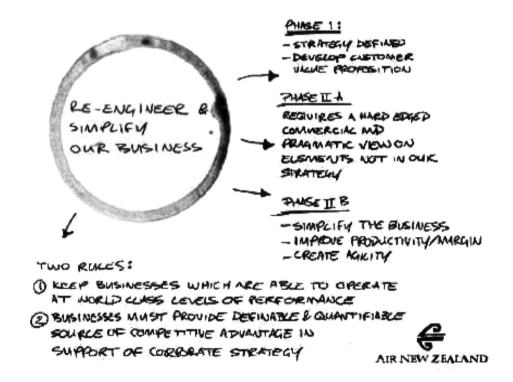

The next picture shows multi-national supermarket giant Tesco's strategy steering wheel. Again a simple message is extended outwards and made more immediate using colour and layout. The strong red segment (top left) draws the eye to the top left with the primary focus on the customer. The eye is then steered around and across the circle by the band of text around the outside, to relate all of the other segments back to the customer perspective. The eye is also drawn to the cool blue in the centre showing how each element connects to Tesco's/SUSS-line:

'Every little helps'. The shape, colours and simplicity (six basic zones) emphasize the connections between the different parts of the business, Tesco's core strategy and its customers' perspective.

The next example, a map of Australian company Alinta's growth strategy, again depicts expansion in different directions out from its core capabilities, but this time organized into three time horizons, indicating priorities, sequencing and where resources will need to be allocated and when. This is a more complex map than the previous two, using colours and shapes to arrest and lead the eye, allowing us to see the big and smaller pictures and the connections between them. It is hard to imagine words and numbers capturing this complex strategy in such a simple and memorable way. The minimal detail and open spaces add a further dimension, inviting the viewer to customize or add to the picture.

Komatsu is a construction and mining equipment company. Many years ago a Komatsu executive explained his company's vision of the future by whiteboarding the matrix below. He began by outlining a typical strategy framework contrasting market share against quality, and drew a big circle to show how Komatsu's main rival, Caterpillar, dominated the industry with the biggest market

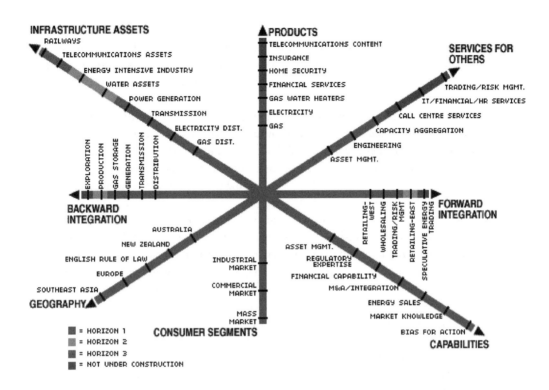

share and highest perceived quality. This was acting as a barrier against Eastern competitors like Komatsu. However, Komatsu's strategy, which had focussed on low cost segments (which he drew as a circle to the left of the Caterpillar circle), was to break this perception. Komatsu would seek to invest heavily in R&D to target particular high-quality niches as a way to showcase their technological prowess (he drew smaller circles with Ks in them underneath the Caterpillar circle to show this). They would then seek to deploy different product ranges to *encircle* and nibble away at Caterpillar's business on *two* fronts: cost, translated into lower prices, but also quality (he depicted this with arrows directed toward 'nibble marks' on the Caterpillar circle from Komatsu's circles below and left).

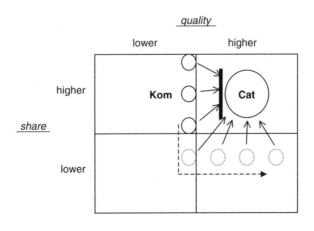

What is it that these effective envisioning maps share? They are simple. They are engaging. They could be manipulated and changed to grow with newly promoted ideas. And, they appear unique and particular to the leadership teams that have developed them. Unlike a lot of vision statements or strategic plans, they are personal.

But also they enable envisioning the relationship between the micro and the macro, the big picture and the detail. They connect an internal core strategy or SUSS-line with a wider set of perspectives and stakeholders, mapping out the behaviours which will translate that idea into action. This is a particularly important aspect of strategic mapping. As Edward Tufte explains, people respond to this macro/micro effect: 'We love to [be able to] see the big picture *and* personalize the data.' Any device that enables this is thus extremely engaging (Google Maps, for example).

Because incorporating too much detail can turn people off or paralyse them, strategic mapping should focus on just the few dimensions necessary to aid decision making in a particular arena. Certainly, while three dimensions may enable us to better represent reality, we find it much better to work with a two-dimensional map or graphic. And, within two dimensions, a useful general rule is to aim for no more than seven colours, no more than seven directions or seven value categories and not to introduce too many different shapes. By simplifying complexity in this way, we contribute to the ability to see both the micro and macro, to see a particular detail that may relate specifically to a particular part of the system while seeing the system as a whole. We can move in and out of focus, on a vertical plane – like a zoom lens.

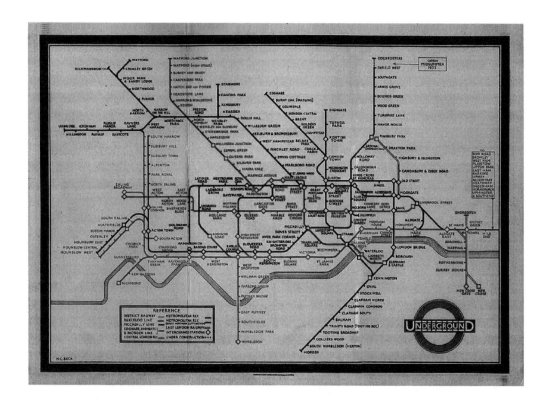

An exemplar of this characteristic is Harry Beck's London Underground map, first published in 1933. Beck's quirky diagram was far less representatively accurate than the map it replaced – the actual location of objects has been manipulated to aid visibility, so whilst Morden and Wimbledon appear close together on the map you would not want to walk between them in practice – but it was a more effective tool for providing confidence that one was 'on the right track', as a good envisioning map should be.

The simplifications incorporated into Beck's diagram enabled travellers to quickly place themselves within it, plan, discuss and take action, picking out particular lines while easily seeing key relationships between lines and the Underground as a whole. Thanks to the white space within the map, many people have been able develop it for different purposes (as Beck explained, the map should be 'a living and changing thing, with schematic "manipulation" and spare part osteopathy going on all the time') – like the spaces on the Alinta strategy map, or Komatsu's customization of a standard strategy template, the tube map invites us to step inside it.

A good creative strategy map invites such interactions. Beck's tube map invites you to trace your route with your finger, to share your perspective on it with your travelling companions, to annotate it with additions, reminders and doodles particular to individual aims and goals. And as with any map, once you have added to it physically you (and your co-customizers) have a greater mental connection with it.

Our previous leadership key, 'sussing', showed how strategic leaders distil an organization's internal values and aims into a clear vision. 'Mapping' takes this vision a stage further, connecting it to a complex and changing reality, radiating outwards into actual scenarios and situations. If 'sussing' presents a vision of the organization to the world, 'mapping' presents a vision of the world to the organization. That vision has to engage its users. As with Karl Weick's description of narrative sense-making, the 'mapping' leader not only makes sense of the wider world, she/he invites us to envision our own place within it.

Unfortunately, just as most 'visions' fail to meet the criteria of a 'good vision' or a 'simple unifying strategic statement', so too in our experience, most strategic plans fail to 'map' a strategy in this way. They are either so generalised as to have little real meaning or resonance to employees on the ground, or they are so detailed that people can't readily zoom in to see how it relates to them and zoom out to where they are in relation to the big picture. Mapping is not part of an MBA student or manager's formal education. But it could have been . . . as the box below shows.

THE LEE KEY

The first business school established in a university was very nearly launched at Washington College (now Washington and Lee University) by College President Robert E. Lee. The former general had a particular interest in what he termed 'practical education'. On 8 January 1869,

(Continued)

(*Continued*)

he presented a report to Washington College's Board of Trustees outlining a plan for a 'Business School'. His proposed curriculum included some subjects which might be less familiar in today's business school, especially the last one:

> Mathematics, book-keeping and penmanship, correspondence and the correct use of the English language, geography, technology, law, economy, history and biography, modern languages, geometry and drawing. Ten subject areas, to be studied as equal parts.

In 1869 the *New York Herald* predicted that Lee's initiatives were 'likely to make as great an impression upon our old fogy schools and colleges as [General Lee] did in military tactics upon our old fogy commanders in the palmy days of the rebellion'. From our point of view, Lee's English language, geometry and drawing would have formed a basis for future generations' sussing and mapping skills.

Alas, Lee became seriously ill just a few weeks after presenting his proposal. The College foundered without Lee as its figurehead, and the business school did not come to pass. Modern business schools have been built upon the 'scientific' foundations established near the turn of the 20th century, where the experts involved were less interested in Lee's practical and broad-based approach to business education.

As a salute to General Lee, we might name the 'mapping' key on the strategic leadership key pad for him: the Lee key.

CHAPTER 13

Shifting Keys: Leadership as Envisioning and Interacting

The key distinctive role of leadership at the outset is that leaders take the initiative. They address their creative insights to potential followers, seize their attention, spark further interaction. The first act is decisive because it breaks up a static situation and establishes a relationship. It is, in every sense, a creative act.

James McGregor Burns

B urns' definition above is a classic, and well worth referring back to. Strategic leaders do provide a creative spark and they build relationships. But a critical difference between the context within which Burns wrote and now is that today's leaders must do more than address their creative insights *at* followers, they need to be able to follow and weave the creative sparks of others. They must act in the middle, as a conduit for sparks, as well as a maker of them.

Leading from the middle is our fifth leadership key – we use it to describe the shift between the different leadership styles we have described in the previous chapter. Specifically, the 'shift key' of leading from the middle allows the leader to toggle between 'envisioning' (mapping and sussing a vision) and 'interacting' (linking and promoting with ideas and perspectives inside and outside the organization). This connection between envisioning and interacting is articulated by two other modern leaders. Terry Leahy, CEO of supermarket giant Tesco, claims that leadership to him 'means enabling people to achieve more than they could on their own. In a practical sense, this means having vision, leading by example, motivating and inspiring.' Michael Stedman, CEO of Natural History New Zealand, one of the world's largest makers of documentary programming, puts it this way: 'The way I like to think of my job [as a leader] is that it's like being a squash ball. I'm doing my job when I'm bouncing around the different parts of this company, connecting ideas and sparking things off.'

The 'shift key' of leading from the middle unlocks the other four keys that it sits between, connecting Stedman's interactive style with Leahy's vision. This ability to shift between perspectives fits with our definitions of creativity in the first part of this book. And as with the other dimensions of creative strategy in this book, it is the ability to combine different elements within leadership as well as with other dimensions (innovation, entrepreneurship, organization) which makes leadership 'strategic'.

The tales we tell here to illustrate leading from the middle follow a sporting and trans-Atlantic arc. The first examines a baseball GM who has turned what leadership means in that field on its head. The second reflects on the two most successful British football managers in recent years. The third is about an American football player and coach who has become one of the most influential (but unknown) leaders in Silicon Valley. And the final tale brings us back to creativity in a traditional business setting: the London office of advertising agency Saatchi & Saatchi. Examining this diverse group of leaders can offer some practical perspectives on leading from the middle without prescribing a single 'best practice' model – we hope they can spark strategic leadership in organizations that you are familiar with.

1. Leading Ugly: Billy Beane

In baseball, as in most modern sports, money talks. The teams with the most cash sign the most expensive players and win the trophies, building the brand and becoming even richer as a result. Yet over the past decade the Oakland Athletics regularly outperformed the bigger, richer teams in the professional leagues. They did this with a team of misfits and mis-shapes, passed over by the scouts from the other clubs. How did they do this? The answer may be a rather unconventional leader: Billy Beane. The story of Beane's unique perspective on the game was told by Michael Lewis in his book *Moneyball: the Art of Winning an Unfair Game*.

As a promising young player, Beane was a 'five tool' guy. He ran fast, threw strong, fielded skilfully, hit well and he could hit with power. In the mind of the scouts who selected players for the major league clubs, he was the full package. The icing on the cake was that he looked great: tall, lean, square-jawed. The scouts had a term for this: Billy Beane had 'the good face'. He joined the New York Mets straight from high school. The Mets considered him a better prospect than Daryl Strawberry, whom they signed in the same draft.

And then Beane's playing career slowly fell apart. After toiling away between various major league club rosters and their feeder teams for nearly ten years, he ended up with the A's.

He then walked a path seldom trod, from the field to the front office. And there Beane found the Oakland A's GM, Sandy Alderson. He asked Alderson an unheard of question: could he hand in his glove and become an advance scout, going out on the road ahead of the team to watch and report back on future opponents. Alderson liked Beane. Beane treated him with a respect that baseball people often didn't afford somebody who hadn't played pro ball. Plus, Alderson admitted, 'I didn't think there was much risk in [it] because I didn't think an advance scout did anything.' By 1998 Beane was in Alderson's job.

Asked his advice to anybody seeking to make it as a leader, Beane's answer points to one of the keys to his own success: his humility and lack of ego: 'I think too many people put a timetable on themselves. They are more in a hurry to get to the next job, and sometimes they aren't concentrating on [learning from] the current job they have... when people look beyond a job they currently have, it's probably a mistake... If you are good at what you're doing and you show a lot of passion, ultimately, you will rise, probably quicker than you think.'

Beane drew lessons from his own travails and his unique collection of perspectives. He was the first major league GM to have been a future all-star, a failed player, an advance scout and intensely curious about things outside of baseball. This enabled him to suss that certain types of players and skills were overvalued in baseball. Others, however, were not valued highly enough.

Beane failed as a player because he didn't have it in the head. He was so good as a young man that he'd never really failed at anything. Subsequently, he crumbled under the pressure of the big leagues. He seemed unable to make minor adjustments that might have helped him, and became, in turn, paralysed by over-analysis and engaged in making wholesale changes that confused himself and his coaches until his self-confidence was sapped.

Such an embedded deficit was not apparent to a scout watching a high school star. As a player, 'I was sort of misjudged', Beane would later explain. '[T]hey were measuring the wrong things, like running speed and strength, and they were undervaluing guys who actually did things (such as get on base and score runs) that contributed to winning games...There were a lot of guys who maybe weren't the natural athlete I was, but they were much better [pro] baseball players.'

A case in point was his former Mets roommate Lenny Dykstra, a player as physically unimpressive as Beane was grand. But Dykstra, Beane reflects, didn't think about failure, he had no doubt that despite only being a thirteenth round draft pick he would be a great player. Apart from thinking that, Lenny didn't seem to think much at all. He would come back to their room late at night and admonish his roommate for reading books, claiming it would ruin his eyes. Dykstra went on to write a book about his brilliant career. As Michael Lewis puts it in *Moneyball*, 'Lenny didn't read books; he wrote them.'

Beane claimed that by rooming with Dykstra, 'I started to get a sense of what a [good] baseball player was. I could see it wasn't me. It was Lenny.'

Beane's emerging views about what was over- and undervalued in baseball and his elevation within the A's front office emerged at a fortunate time. Former A's team owner Walter A. Haas Jr.

was prepared to sink his own fortune into keeping up with the big clubs' spending. New owners Stephen Schott and Ken Hofmann weren't. As a business proposition, pumping millions into a team that relatively few people supported (the population of Oakland is just over 400,000) made no sense to them. Scott and Hofmann made innovation a matter of urgency. Beane was the right leader in the right place at the right time to revolutionize the A's strategy, and, subsequently, the way professional baseball teams are led.

Together, the new owners and Beane worked out a new approach, and what seemed a source of perennial shame became a rallying call for the underdogs: 'We can't do the same things the Yankees do', Beane said. 'Given the economics, we'll lose.' Unable to *join* them, or follow what was best practice for the big clubs, Beane set about seeing if they could *beat* them at a different game: trading.

He would assemble a team that would sign the players nobody else wanted – 'fat guys who don't make outs'. After buying low, Beane would look to sell high as his players became established and successful, by which time he would have another 'ugly' and cheap cohort rising through the ranks.

This was the strategy, but achieving it would require promoting a number of things that baseball insiders currently didn't value, and, subsequently, demoting a number of others that had long gone unquestioned.

Beane's former boss Alderson had never played pro ball, but he was a smart executive who could see the big picture. Alderson mentored Beane and turned him on to Bill James, a little-known amateur publisher of pamphlets of baseball statistics that most baseball insiders considered unimportant. Beane saw in these numbers an ability to map something that he had been gradually sussing for some time. James provided proof that what matters most in terms of winning baseball matches were the ugly things: primarily scrambling to first base by whatever means, particularly through walks. Consequently, the stats that most people in baseball did focus on, like batting average (which does not include walks), were the wrong ones.

Alderson could see this and the consequent arbitrage possibilities it might afford, but found it hard to push the envelope without a baseball pedigree and under Haas' free-spending ownership. The stars aligned far more favourably for Beane to build upon his mentor's insight and put James' numbers into practice.

But there was still a battle to be fought against the old baseball thinking. Whereas the kingpin at a baseball club was generally the first team manager or coach, the A's new owners supported Beane's installation of a different kind of man in this role. Coach Art Howe was put in place to follow Beane's strategy. This team would be led from the front office, not from the dugout.

Beane then set about dismantling the monopoly that the scouting team had on recruitment. The secret weapon in Beane's armoury was Paul Podesta, a Harvard graduate with a laptop. Beane subtly promoted Podesta, a statistician with no track record in the game, into the mix when prospective new players were being evaluated and when the front office was deciding who to buy ahead of the draft.

Perhaps the most evocative passage of Lewis's *Moneyball* book is a fly on the wall description of how Beane would steer these sessions.

The discussions had as their focal point a big whiteboard with the names of players to be ranked in order of desirability. Beane would begin by listening to the scouts outline their top picks. Then he would use Paul's stats to critique their ideas.

Podesta and the influence of Bill James led Beane to begin by promoting a particular kind of prospect: college players. Scouts tended to be enamoured with high-school stars and measured themselves on picking those high school prospects who had then gone on to achieve a potential that only the wizened scout could have foreseen – no matter how long the odds of this were. As Beane would say, 'We [used to] take fifty guys and celebrate if two of them made it. In what other business is two for fifty a success?' Because college players played in leagues with a large number of games played to a good standard, they had meaningful stats. Podesta used these stats to assess the investment risk.

So, down came most of the high school players from the white board. Unlike other clubs, the A's no longer saw those potential stakeholders as key. Then, Beane would set about critiquing what was left and introducing his own players.

In 2002, Jeremy Brown provided a case in point. Brown was an 'ugly' catcher from Alabama who just made the last page of the lists of hundreds of possible players compiled by the scouts. Where the scouts saw only 'a bad body catcher', Paul's laptop enabled him to counter that 'He's the only player in the history of the SEC with three hundred hits and two hundred walks.' Beane moved Brown's name from obscurity to the top of the list. And a new map began to take shape.

By the end of the discussion, Beane had a list of eight players on the white board very different from the list of names the scouts had started with, but gradually some of the scouts started to appreciate Beane's vision and buy in. 'We've got three guys at the top of the board that no one has ever heard of', said one, with a trace of pride. 'There isn't a board in the game that looks like this one', said another.

All the scouts and players and coaches, from the top team to the dozens of semi-pro feeder teams that contributed to the A's franchise, were now expected to understand the significance of the diagrams and the numbers churned out by Podesta's laptop – even if it looked ugly, getting a free walk to first base was as valuable as a spectacular hit. Players were taught to play to a new creative strategy, a new percentages game, not just to swing and hope to be a hero.

Beane's revolution from the middle redefined success and talent in baseball. When it came to plays and players, what looked good on the field did not win games. He sussed out that while appearances could be deceiving, certain statistics gathered over a long enough period of time,

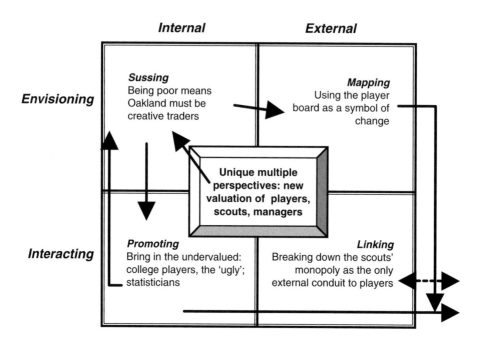

Internal   **External**

Envisioning

Sussing
Being poor means
Oakland must be
creative traders

Mapping
Using the player
board as a symbol of
change

**Unique multiple
perspectives: new
valuation of players,
scouts, managers**

Interacting

Promoting
Bring in the undervalued:
college players, the 'ugly';
statisticians

Linking
Breaking down the scouts'
monopoly as the only
external conduit to players

Figure 13.1   Billy Beane's strategic leadership keypad

generally weren't. Indeed, one of Beane's quirks is that he won't watch live games, because he doesn't want particular events and emotions in the heat of the moment unduly influencing his reading of the game. Current A's owner Lewis Wolff sees Beane's ability to suss and chart the 'objective variables more than most people in baseball do' as his key strength as a leader.

But relating the tale of Billy Beane to our leadership keypad shows that Beane was able to play to a number of different strengths, or leadership keys – envisioning by sussing and mapping but also interacting by promoting and linking. His use of the white board and aggregated statistics, his promotion of Bill James, business school grads, college players and 'bad bodies'; his breaking down of the monopoly that scouts had as the link between the club and future players – it was the combination of all these things that made Beane successful. And, moreover, because Beane's experience and open-mindedness enabled him to see how domains that others kept separate, baseball-bleeding dirt kickers and business school graduates, jocks and nerds, could be creatively combined, he was well placed to move between and link the four keys.

Beane's leadership from the middle took the A's from also-rans to perennial contenders. They won ninety-one games in 2000, 102 in 2001 and 103 in 2002, more games than any other club in baseball (except the big-spending Atlanta Braves), and they made it to the play-offs three years straight. While the Beane revolution has now spread and other teams have caught up by learning the A's lessons, for a period of four or five years, Beane's strategic leadership put his team well ahead on baseball measures, and on some seemingly obvious but seldom applied 'business measures' too, like dollars spent on players per win. At the top of this scale the Texas Rangers were paying nearly $3 million per win. The A's were paying $500,000, or six times less.

Beane was offered $12.5 million to take his approach to the Boston Red Sox, a big and storied club, but one whose stories were mostly about failure. They hadn't won a World Series for eighty-five years. But Beane stayed put. Oakland allowed him to be himself and Beane acknowledges that the level of open-mindedness and acceptance in the Bay Area, which encourages innovative leadership in sports and business, makes him feel very much at home. Having failed to appoint Beane, Boston hired Theo Epstein, a twenty-eight year old Yale graduate and baseball outsider in the Paul Podesta mould. They also hired Bill James, the formerly unheralded statistical guru promoted by Beane. In 2004 the Red Sox won the World Series. In 2007 they won it again. Billy Beane's unconventional leadership may have changed the way baseball is played for ever.

2. Leading Without 'Leadership': Arsène Wenger

I don't believe too much in leadership. I believe more in good passing than a guy who jumps around with the hands in the air and plays the leader.

Arsène Wenger, Arsenal manager, November 2008

Arsène Wenger, manager of Arsenal Football Club, is widely acknowledged to be one of the most effective football club managers in the world, and one of the two most effective English club managers of the past decade. He was one of the first 'continental' managers to come into the English premier league in the 1990s, bringing a new emphasis to the technical aspects of the game both on the pitch (where passing and keeping the ball became more important than effort and energy) and off it (importing nutritionists and psychologists and sophisticated tactics).

Wenger's remarks on leadership in 2008 were partly a response to criticisms of the club's captain at the time, William Gallas, and a perception that his team, suffering a run of poor games, lacked inner strength and character. He was implicitly distancing himself from an English tradition, embodied in the heroic captain who gets 'stuck in' and leads by example, throwing himself around the pitch and yelling at his team-mates. Most of the British-born managers (ex-players themselves) and the British sports media preferred this 'passionate' approach. Leadership in English football, especially in the England national team, has followed the role-model of Shakespeare's Henry V, a warrior-prince who interacts with his troops and leads from the front.

However, Wenger's captain, William Gallas, had responded to a crucial late penalty against his team towards the end of the previous season by retreating in tears to the other end of the pitch and collapsing onto the ground. More recently he had launched a scathing attack on his team-mates, an indiscretion for which Wenger suspended him from the captaincy and (temporarily) from the team. According to the English media, the unpredictable Frenchman was a cowardly Dauphin, sulking on the field of Agincourt when he should have been rallying the troops, failing to fulfil his responsibilities as club captain and team leader.

But it is not that Wenger doesn't believe in leadership, rather he just comes from a different tradition. This European tradition promotes a more calculated, deliberate approach to leadership based on tactical awareness rather than fist-pumping English enthusiasm. Consequently, Wenger believed that 'leadership' was too important to be entrusted to one individual, nor should the concept be confined to leadership on the pitch.

On the pitch, Wenger argued that teams need 'five or six' leaders, allowing different players to take the initiative from different positions at different times as the situation requires. What he wanted from his team was a combination of leaders capable of 'sussing' the big picture and interacting with each other, in order to adapt to rapid changes in the balance of the game and the team. This had been the hallmark of previous successful Wenger teams – an intelligence and fluency which allowed them to switch rapidly from defence to attack and to promote and support each other's visions and initiatives.

What probably helped move Wenger towards this view of leadership may be that unlike most English coaches, he had not enjoyed a successful playing career. Like Billy Beane, Wenger could hold an outsider's perspective on the game. From this vantage point, strategic leaders seem to recognize that the team depends on a combination of 'envisioners' and 'interacters' on the pitch as well as off it. Wenger did not want his captain to be the hero. He wanted every member of his team to contribute to leadership.

By contrast, the English national team, even under foreign management, has tended to trust in a single leader to command the troops on the pitch. The captain inspires through his passion, commitment and energy – and the team prizes energy and effort over coordination and cohesion. England's teams have been flawed by an excess of 'mucking in' over seeing the big picture, full of sound and fury, but all too often failing to cohere as a unit and failing to win important games in international tournaments. Of course the England team manager is not able to manage in the all-seeing sense enjoyed by Wenger – the England manager selects the players (provided the English clubs will release them), organizes a few training sessions and presides over the press conferences. Consequently, even those England teams who have now been coached by a Swede or an Italian still bend back to a style of heroic, 'ball and all', leadership demanded by most English media and fans. Not surprisingly, Wenger has rejected any 'opportunity' to manage the English national team. Wenger could only consider leading the English team if its sponsors and supporters were to embrace Wenger's approach to leadership, rather than see it as just a bit soft, a bit 'continental'.

But wait. Gruff old Scotsman Alex Ferguson (the other best football manager in Britain) could not be described as soft. Nor continental. However, a recent article in the *Irish Times* outlined what

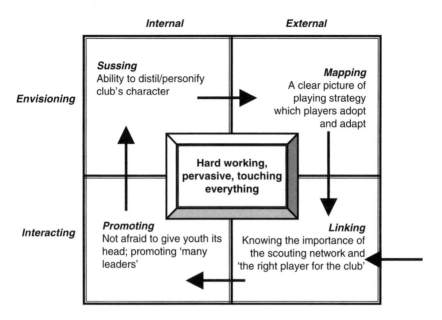

Figure 13.2   The Wenger/Ferguson strategic leadership keypad

may be easier to see from across the Irish Sea – Ferguson and Wenger are cut from the same cloth when it comes to leadership. Both exhibit:

- A realization of the importance of scouting to keep new blood flowing through their clubs and oversee scouting networks unrivalled in scope and in depth.
- The ability to build, understand and subsequently trust a scouting network gives them the confidence to promote youth when others might stick with the tried and true.
- '20th century characters' with long memories and a gravitas that enables them to understand, distil, communicate, even personify, the essence of their clubs and what makes them distinctive.
- They communicate a clear picture of team strategy, chalkboards characterized by variations on a consistent theme developed over time, rather than fad and fancy, thereby making it easier for players to know what is expected of them and to create within clearly understood parameters. This makes it easier for the scouting network to find what the club wants/ needs.
- Hard work and perseverance. They get involved in their own styles. A very visible track-suited presence at training (one barking and pointing, the other watching and thinking), they also pervade all aspects of their clubs (from the board of directors to the building of a new stadium, from the training ground to the club's medical facilities and the reserve and youth teams) while letting others get on with what they do. Nobody doubts that Ferguson and Wenger are in this for the long haul.

The keypad above enables us to connect up these Wenger/Ferguson characteristics into a matrix of strategic leadership. What the keypad matrix doesn't capture, and neither does the *Irish Times* article, is a sixth similarity between Ferguson and Wenger that is worth reflecting on. Ferguson too has said he will never manage England.

3. Leading by Whispering: Bill Campbell

Bill (Coach) Campbell is shaping the future of Silicon Valley, and, subsequently, much of how the world relates to technology. He doesn't have a high profile. He prefers his mentoring work to go uncredited in official documents and regularly shuns media attention, deferring and deflecting glory on to those that he coaches. And he is no computer whiz – he has never written a line of code. Campbell is not a nerd. He is the nerd-whisperer.

But the former player and coach of Columbia University's football team has high profile supporters. Eric Schmidt claims Campbell's contribution to Google 'is literally not possible to overstate'. In an industry that people see as deeply technological, Steve Jobs describes Campbell as 'deeply human' and regularly talks with him about 'the things that have got me concerned and things I haven't yet figured out'.

'He loves people, and he loves growing people', says Jobs.

How did Campbell come to be so heavily relied upon by companies such as Google, Apple, YouTube, Intuit, Netscape and Opsware? Campbell helps them to 'lead from the middle', playing across the four leadership keys of linking sussing, promoting and mapping. 'We work as a tag team', explains Schmidt. 'He's [certainly] not trying to overwhelm the management.' Rather, Campbell just helps to get things linked up right.

It is an approach that works especially well for those companies that are seeking to make the transition from the initial innovation and entrepreneurial drive of a start-up to an organization that can sustain itself and grow as a smooth, well-run operation.

While Campbell himself is largely unknown, his playbook for enabling leaders to enable their organizations is gradually becoming apparent.

First, Campbell never allows his leaders to forget that engineering must always be the heart of a successful technology organization. Engineering is 'where the crazy guys have stature', Campbell told *The McKinsey Quarterly* in 2007. 'There's not a product idea that I'll ever have that's going to amount to anything', he told *Fortune* the following year. 'But what I'll [help] do is make sure that the right people are in the room and that [necessary] lunatic fringe has an opportunity to contribute.' Promoting engineers so that they have the freedom to create, free of marketing dictates, is particularly critical in this respect.

After coaching football, Campbell got his first corporate job at the ad agency J. Walter Thompson through a friend. He showed enough flair for sales and marketing on the Kodak account for Kodak to hire him. Next, John Sculley persuaded him to take a job at Apple in 1983, after giving his new recruit a look at a top-secret new product called the Macintosh.

'It would be pretty unusual today to hire a football coach to be your VP of sales', says Sculley. 'But what I was looking for was someone who could help develop Apple into an organization. We had a dealer network in those days, and he gained trust both inside the company and in the dealer channel. He was just a natural.' He also played a key role in getting the Mac's famous '1984' campaign to air.

It is said that Jobs primarily rates Campbell for his marketing intuition and savvy. This allows Campbell to access a second key to leadership – linking. As well as promoting engineers, by encouraging them to create, Campbell understands the importance of linking to the outside world through marketing.

Thirdly, Campbell helps CEOs not to get lost in the detail or stuck with their heads in the clouds too far away from the action, by linking them only to their most important stakeholders. In this regard, Campbell has served as the secret glue helping bind Schmidt to Google's founders, Larry Page and Sergey Brin, enabling them to make decisions together despite their different perspectives. Chris Sacca, Google's former head of special initiatives says that it was as if 'they had just been taught this amazing art of decision-making where you express your dissent, lobby each other, hear everyone out, and then get to a decision. There's no doubt that it was all Coach.' Campbell helped mould a process where the three work out issues privately, then come together as a united front behind the best choice.

Beyond working with these key stakeholders, Campbell also encouraged Schmidt to always keep sussing the company's vision by asking what Google's most interesting problems are. When Schmidt asked, for example, what should we focus about at a board meeting? Campbell replied: setting the overall tone and the three most interesting things facing the company.

Fourth, Campbell advocates removing the layers that prevent most CEOs from linking, bringing them closer to people and ideas in the organization. Most companies Campbell coaches tend to drop their chief operating officers. Campbell thinks that the COO often takes over management details that the CEO should be deeply involved in. However, COOs can themselves end up being bypassed, with star managers insisting on reporting to the CEO. Either way, the COO tends to break the links in an organization rather than building them, adding to uncertainty. Campbell encourages his CEOs to lead from the middle rather than downwards through a hierarchy.

Fifth, if a CEO is to lead from the middle they have to be open. Remember some of those things that Marcus Aurelius wrote of: sincerity, gravity, frankness, dislike of superfluity, freedom from pettiness? Campbell inspires here by leading through acting out these virtues. 'I remember him describing me as a human missile', says Danny Shader, CEO of Jasper Wireless and victim of what some light-heartedly refer to as an example of Campbell's technique of 'management by

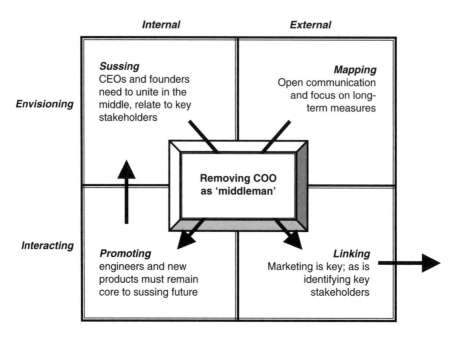

Figure 13.3   The Coach's strategic leadership keypad

insult'. Campbell sat Shader down, saying, 'Here are a bunch of things you need to do to improve yourself, and things that I need to do.' By encouraging frankness with employees – and committing to helping them succeed and being there when they fail – Campbell helps leaders create a team dynamic, and to map the strengths and weaknesses in the organization.

Sixth, like A.G. Lafely, Campbell argues that leaders must measure not against short-term financial goals, but against what is important to the organization's long-term future. Campbell encourages leaders to focus on a healthy balance in the organization, based on four measures:

- On-the-job performance (which includes the typical quantitative goals);
- Peer group relationships (Campbell's influence on hiring at Google has helped make being intelligent not the only criterion for getting a job there; you also have to have those other Q's described in Chapter 11);
- Management and leadership (defined as how well you develop – or act as a conduit for – the people around you); and
- Innovating or encouraging innovation

Randy Komisar, a partner at Kleiner Perkins who has worked with Campbell at several companies, sums up Silicon Valley's view of Campbell: 'Bill's impact in the end will be very hard to measure, but it is really important. It won't be in the legacy of a GE; it won't be in the more classic sense of putting points on the board. It will be in seeing the people he's touched go off to do great things.' It is a nice summary of what leading from the middle is about.

4. Reconnecting Leadership: Saatchi & Saatchi

In 2008 Saatchi & Saatchi's website announced 'Thirty-eight years of history. Ten months into its reinvention.' We see five people, the new senior management team, with the slogan 'This time it's personal. . .'

Richard Huntington is Director of Strategy at Saatchi & Saatchi's London office, appointed in December 2007 to join a young management team charged with reinventing the company. His, and their, strategic leadership story is one of reinvention, rediscovery, reconnection and reinvigoration.

At its zenith in the 1980s, Saatchi was the biggest and best known agency in the world, employing 1000 people in its London headquarters under the charismatic leadership of the brothers Saatchi. Today the company is owned by Publicis, its headquarters are in New York and the brothers left the company in 1995. With only 230 employees, the London office earns part of its income from renting out unused space in its still impressive building. When Huntington and his colleagues arrived, the company was still part of a powerful network and heir to a formidable reputation. But, despite sporadic successes and repeated reincarnations, Huntington concedes that the company had been 'off its game' since the late 1990s.

Saatchi's success in the 1980s was based on its commitment to creative excellence as well as pure self-confident chutzpah. But over the last twenty years, that confidence had dissipated as new players and new priorities shook up the industry's priorities. Media planning agencies had become increasingly important, and a well-chosen media strategy could trump creative excellence. The kind of grandiose 30-second television mini-movie format on which Saatchi had staked much of its reputation was being challenged by other formats. Shrinking budgets and a more cautious clientele meant that clients were more demanding and sceptical. And a new generation of smaller creative shops (Fallon, HHCL, Weiden) had challenged Saatchi's creative pre-eminence.

At the same time, creativity had taken on a different meaning in the advertising industry. The centre of gravity had shifted from the creative teams to the planners and media departments – and creativity in advertising had become as much about consumer insight and clever ways of engaging with customers as about great content. As a former planner, Huntington could recognize these changes, especially the importance of giving creative teams a clear brief, not just expecting them to blow the client away with their creative ideas.

If the style of advertising had changed, so had the style of leadership. Huntington recalls Maurice Saatchi's refusal to shake hands with staff. He would shake hands with the clients; the staff were instructed to stand when Saatchi entered, in order to be politely ignored. Everything in the creative agency – the architecture, the clothes, the décor, the CEO's handshake – was calculated to reinforce the agency's mystique and to subtly intimidate the client. Whilst this aura of self-confidence impressed clients, it also reinforced tacit internal hierarchies and kept staff in their place.

The challenge for the new management team was to reinvent Saatchi's confident culture and instil a belief among staff and among clients that this was a genuinely exciting place to work, where people could produce great creative advertising. The company's motto, 'Nothing is Impossible', is carved into the steps of the London office. But the boast no longer seemed to ring true when we first met Huntington in 2008 – the agency, according to Huntington, seemed to have lost its spiritual core and its self belief. Huntington spoke to us of rediscovering 'the unreasonable power of creativity' inscribed in that message, encouraging staff to release talents they didn't know they had, inspired by a feeling of 'joy, energy and danger'. The mantra of creative ambition remained the same, but it was made more inclusive and vivid by mapping that message outwards, into the company's culture and relationships.

One of the first symbolic changes Huntington made was to remove the clocks from the reception area which were used to show the times in Saatchi's corporate offices around the world – a classic symbol of global corporate power. Huntington wanted to break down the symbolic distance between managers and staff. He spent his first weeks 'walking the agency', bouncing around the building, fuelled by countless espressos, talking to people, inspiring and enthusing them. He admits that this display of Tigger-like energy took its toll and he eventually had to slow down. But those first weeks set a pattern of expectations and relationships which formed the baseline for subsequent communication, allowing him to comment on results rather than performance. By commenting honestly on a piece of work, by saying that a presentation was merely acceptable, Huntington encourages his staff to take responsibility – they want to impress him. 'Selective disappointment' and 'the withdrawal of love' are here more effective, more intrinsic motivators than a public dressing-down.

Huntington's approach to leadership is perhaps the reverse of Saatchi's charismatic style. He is deliberately upbeat and approachable with his staff. The effect is calculated to inspire confidence in those around him by being constantly interested in their work, 'bigging up' people when they do well. He has tried the same approach with clients – Huntington even claims that he has been able to win accounts by seeming to be more enthusiastic about their business than the clients themselves. He deliberately spends 'wasted' time 'hanging out' with his staff in a bid not only to be more approachable but also to allow his enthusiasm to rub off on people. 'If somebody says "how are you?" and I say "f***ing brilliant" then it makes them think there's a reason to feel optimistic about the business. There's a direct correlation between my mood and the attitude of the people working for me.'

Huntington explains that his approach to people-management is partly a reflection of the industry he works with. Everybody from senior management downwards, craves praise. There is another rationale for his approach: 'creativity isn't something you can order up like a ham sandwich'. It is extremely difficult to legislate for quality, because controlling the process does not guarantee successful results. For example, some agencies have attempted to introduce standardized mechanisms for briefing the creative team – but whilst such systems might eliminate basic errors, they still cannot provide an inspiring brief. This is important because if a brief is designed correctly it saves the agency money – get the brief right and you provide the best possible beginning for the creative work. Get it wrong and you condemn your creative teams to several weeks of painful and time-consuming reworking. In the end the people working in the agency have to be motivated by their own sense of the quality of the work. Huntington comments on the need to develop a 'muscle memory' (a popular term in sports) – meaning that people come to understand what producing outstanding creative work feels like by doing it so often it becomes a habit; thereby 'getting to know what good looks and feels like'.

Huntington believes that his role as a leader is to inspire those around him to produce their best work, and that to achieve this, direct interaction is worth any number of directives and briefings. The day after we meet him, he is due to talk to his planners about how to produce a creative brief – to crystallize their ideas on a single piece of paper in order to inspire the creative team. It's probably the hardest, and most important, task in advertising. He admits that he does not know whether this will work – but if even a handful of them develop some understanding of that process, he will have achieved something any amount of policy documents and strategy blueprints could not. He suggests that this may represent a distinction between leadership and management – leaders inspire by focussing on the often intangible outcome (quality), managers are responsible for process and delivery (quantitative targets). In his own role he has delegated some of the managerial responsibilities to a newly appointed head of planning, freeing him up to focus on the 'intellectual output' of the agency, meaning both 'the beginnings we give our creatives' and 'shaping the future of the agency'. Of course, leaders still need managers and vice versa. But leaders have to prioritize – they have to inspire, to set the agenda, to provide momentum and energy. Echoing Lafely's advice to the CEO, Huntington argues that leaders should concentrate on doing what only leaders can do.

Like many in advertising, Huntington leads by example. He continues to work on two major accounts as a planner and believes that 'the ability to do' is a necessary underpinning of his ability to lead; restaurants and chefs listen to Gordon Ramsay's advice 'because they know that he can cook'. This emphasis on senior managers retaining their credibility as practitioners is not uncommon in the creative industries. It makes perfect sense in relation to Huntington's own style of interactive leadership. There is of course the dilemma that many leader-practitioners secretly want to do the work themselves – everybody in advertising wants to take credit for the good ideas. One of the problems here is that leaders seldom receive credit or praise for 'getting other people to be brilliant'. Huntington himself makes a point of 'praising upwards', crediting the company's CEO when occasion allows 'because nobody else has the right to praise him, so he doesn't get any credit'.

Huntington also runs a popular blog on advertising, and cites a mantra popular among bloggers: 'sacrifice control in order to gain influence'. This is a maxim which many organizations fail to understand at the corporate level, since it means handing over control of their brands to consumers in the hope of winning their loyalty and trust. On his own blog, Huntington recognizes the need to give away his ideas in the hope of getting something back. The maxim provides a reasonably accurate summary of his approach to leadership. Rather than seeking to lead from the top by setting a target, he attempts to lead from the middle by inspiring and promoting other people's creativity, encouraging his staff to see the leadership as 'resources not bosses' and to surprise themselves by their own abilities.

In 2009, nine months after our first interview, the agency's reinvention seems to be working. An enthusiastic piece in the industry paper *Campaign* has suggested that Saatchi 'is back'. The

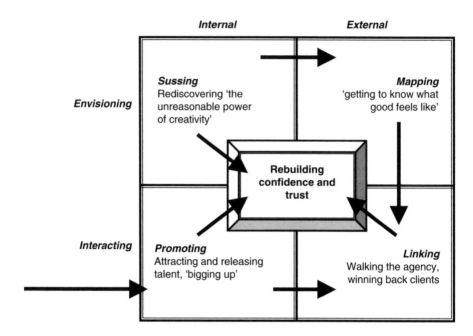

Figure 13.4   The Saatchi strategic leadership keypad

judgement is based not only on successful campaigns like the T-Mobile campaign (filming thousands of people singing along to 'Hey Jude' in Trafalgar Square), but also a feeling that the agency is once again a fun place to work.

Reputation in advertising is volatile. One year previously, Huntington and his colleagues took a risk in joining an agency whose reputation was at the bottom of the market; today that reputation is riding high. New recruits are attracted to an agency which seems to have reinvented itself and promises to be a place where others can do the same. Clients too have a new confidence in the agency's creative output. As Huntington notes, this changes the negotiating position – once clients know that they can't get this type of campaign anywhere else, 'you decommodify the offer'. Instead of arguing over costs and control, or playing one agency off against another, the client trusts in the agency to deliver. It also means that Saatchi attracts clients who share Saatchi's creative ambitions and can prioritise its efforts accordingly. Confidence begets more confidence, inside and outside the agency. The reinvention of Saatchi is succeeding not through a top down vision, but through a gradual rebuilding of trust and self-belief, starting with the staff in the building, then radiating outwards to draw in clients, new recruits and others in the industry. Nothing is impossible.

From Strategic Leadership to Strategic Organization. . .

Leading from the middle requires adopting a clear perspective or position at the centre of the organization, and working outwards to access the other leadership keys. In particular, interaction with other ideas and perspectives inside and outside the organization unlocks a vision of the future and allows that vision to be communicated outwards. The arrows in the leadership keypads for each case indicate that this cycle can flow in more than one direction, but the central idea of 'leading from the middle' remains the critical junction, allowing leaders to toggle up and down and across the other leadership perspectives.

Leading from the middle also connects to innovation and entrepreneurship. Sussing and mapping for our leaders have often started with the discovery or creation of a new perspective on the organization or the recasting of an old one. Interaction triggers the entrepreneurial energies and networks inside the organization; mapping and sussing the vision combines 'zooming in' and 'zooming out' in the same way as entrepreneurs alternate between diligent and dilettante perspectives. The external side of the leadership keypad (linking and mapping) builds upon the entrepreneur's 'network of enterprises' and the innovator's boundary and market innovations, and characteristics of diversity and curiosity. The 'internal' keys (sussing and promoting) draw upon the internal processes of discovery and the diligent entrepreneurial character which first brings ideas to the boil then distils them down into a marketable commodity. These connections are further elaborated in the creative strategy helix at the start of this book. However, a final connections remains to complete the picture. It is worth stressing that without this final piece in the puzzle, many creative strategies are not sustainable or renewable.

For example, we might conclude Part III by looking at the leadership qualities of Thomas Alva Edison. Not only was Edison a great innovator and entrepreneur, he was often described in terms that would make him appear to be a great leader too. When President Coolidge awarded him the Congressional Medal of Honor he said of the recipient: 'Few men have possessed to such a striking degree the blending of the imagination of the dreamer with the practical driving force of the doer.'

One of Edison's assistants at Menlo Park, Francis Upton, went into greater detail about Edison's leadership from the middle, glowing about Edison's ability to 'delegate and inspire simultaneously, his discipline of mind, and facility to save energy when one goal is reached, even cutting the thought, abandoning one line of enterprise temporarily, parenthetically delving into another area. . . and then picking up at the same point later on; marshalling crudities, raw ideas, and refining them through his power to draw analogies; and by his healthy balancing act, to be sanguine and confident, and yet doubting at the same time, taking nothing for granted.'

And yet, Edison is regarded by many as the least effective GM in General Electric's history. It may be that what Edison lost a grip on in his later years was the fourth part of creative strategy: strategic organization.

THE ROYAL SHAKESPEARE COMPANY
ACT III: THE LEADERSHIP ACT

Good theatre directors develop a vision of the play through the interactions of rehearsal. In order to allow the innovative ideas and entrepreneurial behaviours to take flight, directors must hold back any pre-emptive vision of their own. The director Sam Mendes has commented on the need 'to go into it with as little as possible' and 'to make as few decisions as possible when you begin the rehearsal process'. Another director and RSC associate, Tim Supple, describes his attempts to 'dilute' the decision-making process in rehearsals, encouraging the actors to accept 'a situation where the attitude of not knowing is embraced'. In our terms, the director must lead from the middle.

There are exceptions to this of course, from Alfred Hitchcock's famous claim that 'actors are like cattle' to Mendes' acknowledgement that working in musical theatre on Broadway or the West End, 'you have to basically make the work in your head before you start rehearsal', an approach to rehearsal he describes as 'my least favoured way of working'. But generally, working in a collaborative medium, theatre directors cannot afford to be dictators.

Leadership in rehearsal begins through a process of promoting ideas upwards and linking to other people, ideas and realities outside the rehearsal room. A vision of the play emerges through these interactions, and only then does the director move on to 'sussing' or distilling that vision and mapping out its implications.

Like the football teams described earlier in this chapter, theatre uses a plurality of leaders. The actors are encouraged to develop and act upon their own vision. For an ensemble like the RSC, this process of collective discovery and creation, as has already been noted, is especially important. The RSC actors are comfortable with textual analysis, and many of them have experience of directing and devising theatre themselves. As a leader, the director Michael Boyd is a coach or editor of other leaders, encouraging and promoting their ideas selectively.

Boyd's position at the centre of a semi-circle in the early text-based rehearsals, or sitting at a table in the centre of the room when the actors are running through a scene, underpinned his position as a focal point for other people's ideas. Throughout the rehearsals, Boyd gave the impression of following rather than leading the process, picking up on other people's comments and suggestions and using these to initiate another 'draft' of a scene.

Of course, there is a selection and filtering process at work. Having given permission for actors to learn by interacting ('try it and see'), the director's vision prioritizes one action over another, or redirects the actor's suggestion ('what would make that absolutely perfect would be...'). Because of the trust between Boyd and his team, such interventions were often very subtle. It was sometimes unclear whether Boyd was accepting an idea or charming the actor into doing something entirely different. This phase of the rehearsal fits Amabile's description of organizational creativity as agreement on strategic goals but 'autonomy around process'. Again the director's 'vision' would generally follow rather than precede the action, with the director withholding comment until after a scene or sequence had run its course.

Without imposing a singular vision on the play, the director is able shape the emerging consensus, using the story of the play to define what Supple calls 'a culture of seeing'. Here the director's *linking* supports the selection process. Whereas the actors tended to speak of their character in the first person ('what am I doing in this scene?'), Boyd would link the individual character to the broader historical and political meaning of the play ('what is Shakespeare telling us here?'). And as the vision of the play emerges, Boyd was able to 'map' the relationship between individual and collective stories, relating individual scenarios and interactions to the big picture.

Linking also extended outside the rehearsal room. On the second day of rehearsal the director of Liberty (the National Council for Civil Liberties) was invited to address the entire company on the subject of tyranny. Over two hours she embedded the play's themes in a discussion of contemporary human rights. Phrases like 'on the sofa' (describing a complicity between democratic and non-democratic leaders in government) or 'frog in the water' (describing the delayed reaction to tyranny – a frog in a pan of water will not react to a gradual change in temperature, allowing itself to be slowly boiled alive) would recur in the rehearsals, forming a kind of shorthand for talking about the play's themes.

Linking to other characters, other plays in the cycle and to historical and contemporary events, provides a framework for making sense of and filtering the ideas generated in rehearsal. Linking outwards allows the leader to *promote* ideas inwards and upwards.

Boyd's linking also took place in a broader context, firstly with other members of the production team; the associate director, Richard Twyman, and the musical director, James Jones, were actively involved throughout rehearsals, the set design was on display and wardrobe sketches were pinned up on the wall. Secondly, as Artistic Director of the company as well as director of this production, Boyd's links extended outwards to audiences, press interviews, the management team and the relationship between the theatre and the town of Stratford. Prioritizing which of these connections to bring back into the rehearsal room and which to exclude was a crucial task.

The leader's *promoting* role likewise extends beyond the rehearsal room. The trust and teamwork ethos of the ensemble encouraged the RSC actors to feel part of a bigger project, from the acting company to the education department, to the redesign of the building. Apart from the exchange of ideas, there was also a reshuffling of the acting company, with actors taking their turn to be cast in the more prominent roles. Boyd has made a particular point of promoting understudies at the RSC, staging full performances by the understudy company in front of an audience, presenting them as an ensemble in their own right rather than a collection of substitutes. Again there are echoes here of sport, as when the younger players in a football squad take centre stage during a cup game.

These interactions, inside and outside the rehearsal room, lay the foundations for *sussing* and mapping the vision of the play. Here the director's role shifts to distilling and articulating a vision of the play – in the rehearsal room this would often be achieved by constructing a shared vocabulary or shorthand communication. Actors and director continued to add to a repertoire of phrases to encapsulate iconic metaphors, ideas, emotions or scenarios. The shared stock of ideas and phrases provided an implicit logical framework within which ideas could be rapidly communicated and evaluated.

Having established a 'core understanding' of the play, much of the rehearsal is concerned with *mapping* that vision and making sense of it for both actors and audiences. A single concept in *Richard III*, like 'tyranny' or 'power', had to be elaborated through more detailed explorations of particular scenes. The director was continually 'zooming in' and 'zooming out', relating the micro to the macro and vice versa. During the later rehearsals, Boyd would sometimes be moving around the room, interacting with the actors and giving detailed notes on a particular move or line, whilst at others he would talk more generally about the meaning of a scene or the play as a whole. What was striking here was Boyd's ability to see different sections of the rehearsal 'map' simultaneously and to tailor his remarks accordingly. This in turn encouraged the actors to switch focus between specific actions and the bigger picture. Mapping thus connects collective vision to specific points of view and concrete actions.

Because *Richard III* was part of a longer cycle of plays ('The Histories'), some of the smaller roles had been combined into a single composite character whilst some of the major roles recurred across four plays. Mapping and making sense of these individual journeys and the overall sweep of the Histories tetralogy required reference to lines and actions from previous rehearsals and performances, as well as to family trees and prophecies. Mapping thus takes us back to the earlier leadership task of 'linking' different characters and ideas, moving beyond individual perspectives to a joined-up interpretation of the play as a whole.

The promoting, linking, sussing and mapping functions of leadership thus form a cycle through the rehearsal process. Rather than setting a vision of the play at the start of the rehearsal, the director deliberately withholds any pre-emptive decision. Interactions inside the rehearsal room and with the world outside it allow a collective vision to emerge. Promoting these ideas upwards allows the director to distil an essential message about a scene or about the play as a whole, then to map these out in more detailed instructions to the actors. This returns to the problem of linking the different viewpoints and stories of the play to each other and eventually to an interpretation the audience will engage with. The director leads from the middle, switching between responding to specific interactions and articulating a framework within which these interactions can be evaluated, filtered and channelled.

This sharing of leadership between actors and director reflects the RSC's ensemble principles. Leadership in the rehearsal room consists in setting the boundaries around a collective process, linking, promoting and mapping individual decisions, and 'sussing' the collective vision of the play which emerges from these interactions. Leading from the middle in this way depends upon organization – as we will see in the next section, leadership in rehearsal ultimately depends upon constructing a culture or value system within which leadership at all levels can occur.

'SPARK-NOTES'

- The 'director's vision' does not come from the leader but from the group. The director 'leads from the middle' to connect together the interactive process of rehearsal with an emergent vision of the play.
- Leadership in theatre tends to be **collective** rather than individual. Most artistic enterprises, like sports teams, tend to distribute leadership responsibilities through the organization rather than investing it in one person. Business organizations could learn from this.
- **Envisioning** is dependent on **interacting**. The vision of the play emerges from a 'try it and see' approach, and is tested and made vivid through action.
- Strategic leadership in rehearsals follows a pattern of **linking, promoting, sussing** and **mapping** (connecting ideas inside the rehearsal room and linking to perspectives outside it).
  - **Linking:** the director connects the actors' ideas to each other and to broader perspectives of the play as well as to other contexts like human rights
  - **Promoting:** this linking framework allows the director to selectively promote interpretations which the actors 'try out' in rehearsal
  - **Sussing:** the director articulates the interactions and experiments as a coherent vision of the meaning of the play
  - **Mapping:** the director elaborates this core understanding into a series of instructions which the actors can understand and a series of actions which the audience can engage with, by 'zooming in' and 'zooming out' of the action

PART IV

STRATEGIC ORGANIZATION: FOCUSSING AND LOOSENING

CHAPTER 14

From Principles of Excellent Organizations to Organizational 'Virtues'

The test of a first-rate intelligence is the ability to hold two opposed ideas in mind at the same time and still retain the ability to function.

F. Scott Fitzgerald, *The Crack-up*

Simultaneous loose-tight properties, the last of our eight basics of excellent management practice... is about organizations being on the one hand rigidly controlled, yet at the same time allowing (indeed insisting on) autonomy, entrepreneurship, and innovation from the rank and file.

Tom Peters and Robert Waterman, *In Search of Excellence*

*I*n Search of Excellence, by Tom Peters and Robert Waterman, was the first management 'blockbuster'. Over 5 million copies were sold in the four years after its publication in 1982. Despite this, most of the eight themes of excellent organizations that it promoted have not stood the test of time. By 1990 two-thirds of the forty-three companies identified by Peters and Waterman were no longer 'excellent'. Many were no longer solvent. The book has subsequently been criticized for lacking a rigorous methodology and in certain instances not even being 'based on fact'.

IN SEARCH OF EXCELLENCE'S EIGHT PRINCIPLES OF EXCELLENT ORGANIZATIONS

1. **A bias for action**, active decision making – 'getting on with it'.
2. **Close to the customer** – learning from the people served by the business.
3. **Autonomy and entrepreneurship** – fostering innovation and nurturing 'champions'.
4. **Productivity through people** – treating rank and file employees as a source of quality.
5. **Hands-on, value-driven** – management philosophy that guides everyday practice – management showing its commitment.
6. **Stick to the knitting** – stay with the business that you know.
7. **Simple form, lean staff** – some of the best companies have minimal HQ staff.
8. **Simultaneous loose-tight properties** – autonomy in shop-floor activities plus centralized values.

Indeed, Tom Peters confessed to *Fast Company* magazine in 2007 that when the McKinsey project on organizational traits had been passed on to him and Waterman, they had no idea what they were doing. The project was considered small beer compared to a much larger comparative project on business strategy (at McKinsey, according to Peters, *organization* was always the 'weak-sister' of *strategy*). He also admitted that he arrived at the eight principles (shown above) by closing his eyes and thinking about how to reduce a 700-slide presentation for a short meeting with a CEO of Pepsi, whom he thought would only give him a few minutes of his time. The eight 'principles' were those that surfaced in his mind from the masses of data they had compiled. And, he also agreed that they had 'faked' the way the data was collated.

Nevertheless, *In Search of Excellence* was built on a huge database of McKinsey studies and experiences from around the world, and some good gut instinct. And, it is widely regarded as having changed the way people thought and wrote about business. Moreover, while many of the eight organizational excellence principles have not held up over the past quarter of a century, one of them certainly has. As has the espoused guiding philosophy outlined at the beginning of *In Search. . . .*

That philosophy highlights the importance of managing ambiguity and paradox in management, something that readers will be well aware by now is the keystone of this book. Unfortunately, the first seven organizational principles of excellent companies do not seem to fit with this fundamental philosophy. Instead of recognizing ambiguity, they promote one best way. And many of those companies that have subsequently 'fallen' from excellence have done so by following one or more of those first seven principles too single-mindedly. Focussing too much on 'getting on with it', for example, will lead to rushed and ill-informed decision making.

The exception is Peters and Waterman's last 'excellence principle'. The principle of being simultaneously loose and tight avoids oversimplification, and dovetails with that espoused guiding philosophy, because it is itself a paradox, an example of the sort of intelligence that the quotation from F. Scott Fitzgerald promotes at the head of this chapter. Organizations with simultaneous loose-tight (or SLT) properties promote both autonomy *and* centralized control. The SLT paradox works against creeping or lurching towards one extreme or the other.

Peters and Waterman's eighth principle of SLT properties, adheres to the original and insightful philosophy of managing ambiguity. Because of this, we believe, it has stood the test of time. It is also a revolutionary insight that directly challenges a tendency in organization theory before and since to promote the 'one best way'.

In Search's SLT principle is still prescient today, and it also has a long history predating Peters and Waterman's articulation of it.

SLT

Much has been made of Google's unique, revolutionary and autonomous organizational structure. Many hold it up as a beacon that should be leading other organizations away from the traditional, harder aspects of organization. In a recent exchange, Andy Grove of Intel described Google's structure as appearing to be like Brownian motion; as though ideas were constantly being bumped around and taken to new levels by Google staffers colliding with them and one another like dodgems or bumper cars.

Brownian motion
noun

Random motion of particles suspended in a fluid, arising from those particles being struck by individual molecules of the fluid. Etymology: *Named after botanist Robert Brown (1773-1858) who investigated the movement of pollen suspended in water.*

The reality is more complex. Google CEO Eric Schmidt agreed with Grove, but only in part. There is indeed a small part of Google that does work like this: the parts where new ideas and innovations are developed. But most of the organization, Schmidt explained almost apologetically, is very 'tight' and very conventional. The company could not function otherwise. The revolutionary organizational structure developing Google's creative strategies turns out to be not that revolutionary after all. It is simply an evolution of what *In Search* outlined twenty-five years ago. It is SLT.

But Google is just the latest incarnation of an SLT approach to organization as a means of fostering creativity. Long before current SLT stars like Google, Genentech and Honda, 3M encouraged staff to use 15% of their time on their own free thinking projects (the most famous idea to emerge, eventually, from this structure was the Post-It Notes described earlier). Before that, Lockheed had developed its Skunkworks, a much faster, looser and unbound organization within its more normal and tightly structured organization. The World Wide Web, integrated circuits and bubble gum were all invented during loose or 'slack time' at the CERN Institute, Texas Instruments and Philadelphia's Fleer Chewing Gum Company respectively.

The SLT line goes all the way back to Edison, who had the knack of pairing his own manic, unstructured style with byzantine controllers like Charles Batchelor (although Edison did seem

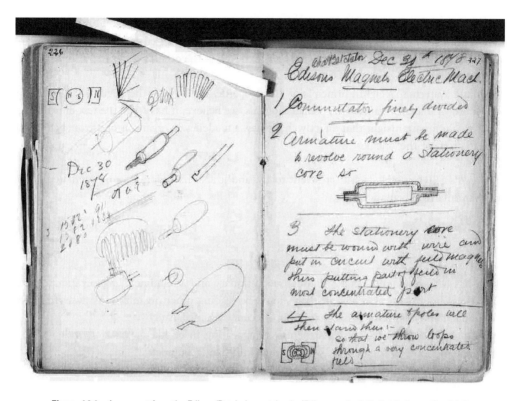

Figure 14.1   An excerpt from the Edison/Batchelor notebooks (Edison on the left, Batchelor on the right)

to lose this knack somewhat in his later years). We can observe their combined personalities in their co-created notebooks, an example of which is provided above. Batchelor's precise decipher-ing (on the right) of Edison's scrawled drawings (on the left) provides focus and order alongside Edison's free thinking. This combination of order and chaos characterized the research facility established by Edison at Menlo Park in 1876, which might be considered the world's first research and development lab.

Trailing behind these practical developments is a developing body of theory that attempts to conceptualize the loose-tight paradox. This body includes: theories of ambidextrous organization, where both bureaucratic and free-flowing elements co-exist; semistructures and underspecified structures, where both mechanistic and organic orientations are promoted; and a new emphasis on simple organizational rules, where reduced structure sets enable and encourage individuals and teams to act with certainty on baseline principles and adapt to particular circumstances as they see fit (much like the leadership SUSS statements we discussed in Part III).

This new appreciation of the SLT principle coincides with a revaluation of the worth of bureau-cracy after a period where it became the norm to dismiss it with contempt. Esteemed Stanford business professor Harold Leavitt, who died in 2007 at 85 years of age (and so had a far greater perspective on organizational developments over the past century than most), wrote his last book,

Top Down, as something of an ode to bureaucracies. Leavitt argued that modern organizations had not necessarily become 'flatter', as many pundits claimed and as many gurus opined, but rather were just new types of hierarchies. In an article in the *Harvard Business Review* prior to the book being released (called 'Why Hierarchies Thrive'), he argued that:

> the intensity with which we struggle against hierarchies only serves to highlight their durability . . . The organization of the knowledge economy – whether loosely coupled, networked, or federalized – seem to be no more than modifications of the same basic design. The new flatter, faster organizations certainly reflect some important changes in the way business is done, but the basic blueprint is unchanged.

Leavitt passed away before the financial crisis that began in 2008, but what we may add to the list of bureaucracy's virtues as the coals of that recession are raked over is that a good bureaucracy incorporates the sort of checks and balances that can prevent the escalation of laxness, or looseness to levels where this virtue becomes a vice.

Icarus, Aristotle and the Virtue of Virtues

The SLT principle supports, and is supported by, our ideas about creativity and strategy developed to this point. Creative strategy, we have argued, requires innovation, entrepreneurship and leadership. Strategic innovation is spurred by actively going out and seeking to discover the new, *and* letting it emerge from the elements that may coalesce on one's doorstep. Strategic entrepreneurship entails a grinding, attentive diligence, *and* the promiscuous enthusiasms of the dilettante. Strategic leadership is about an ability to understand, simplify and loosely outline the big picture, *and* connect this to the minutiae at every level. To enable these elements and, importantly, to enable them to evolve and recur, requires an organization that is in some ways loosely structured *and* in others tightly bounded.

The processes and characteristics we have described in the first three parts of this book require a certain fluidity to allow individuals and individual elements to switch roles and explore oppositions and paradoxes. Organization frames and guides these processes. If we accept the paradoxical nature of creative thinking and creative strategy, the organization around them must be flexible enough to allow individuals to switch roles and relationships, but focussed enough to provide boundaries and constraints around them. If the organization is too tightly structured, these roles and relationships harden into habits and stereotypes, with no space for experiment or interaction. If the organization is too loose, individuals become self-absorbed and isolated, never quite meshing together into a coherent purpose. 'Looseness' is needed to allow ideas to take shape and evolve at their own pace from discovery through dilettantism to envisioning. Focus or 'tightness' forces these ideas together into new patterns through the processes and characteristics of creation, diligence and interaction. In this final part of *Creative Strategy*, we consider how an organization can be designed to facilitate and encourage creative strategy by allowing individual and collective looseness and focus to adjust to each other, avoiding the extremes of chaotic individualism and collective over-organization.

The content of strategic organization is clear enough: SLT properties, or what we call a dichotomous emphasis on focussing *and* loosening. As we have noted above, there has been a convergence of opinion on the strategic importance of SLT principles (or variants on them) for organizations. What's missing is any clear expression of *how* to develop a well-designed SLT organization. Unfortunately, *In Search of Excellence's* chapter on SLT is the slimmest in the book. It appears almost as an afterthought, or, rather, a loose collection of afterthoughts, lacking focus. And the other works that we have referred to in this chapter provide little in the way of practical guidance here either.

We seek now to fill this gap. Having drawn upon Peters and Waterman's reasonably old (by management's standards) framework, we now combine some slightly newer thinking (from Danny Miller's *Icarus Paradox*) with a truly ancient framework (from Aristotle). Adding these insights to our own recent observations drawn from a wide range of organizations, in the next chapter we will present seven organizational virtues that can help to promote innovation, entrepreneurship, and leadership – or creative strategy.

At the beginning of the 1990s, ten years after *In Search of Excellence,* Danny Miller developed a profound but simple philosophy cautioning against the sort of claims being made by Peters and Waterman. Miller's book, *The Icarus Paradox*, related the Icarus fable from Greek mythology to the relationship between strategic success and failure.

Icarus was a young man who achieved astounding feats with his wax wings. Emboldened by success, his pride became vanity and he failed to heed the warning signs as he flew higher and higher. Eventually he flew so close to the sun that his wings melted and he crashed to his death. The Icarus paradox, Miller argued, can apply to outstanding companies: their achievements seduce them into the excesses that cause their downfall. In other words, Miller discovered that success, or the pursuit of 'excellence', imperils an organization through the momentum and blind confidence that it engenders. Successful organizations specialise and simplify their operations around what they consider to be their strategic innovations. This strips out their complexity and their ability to reinvent themselves or reinnovate, locking them into stereotypical and destructive versions of themselves. What was once a strength becomes a limitation, and by pursuing excellence the organization sinks into excess.

In 1991, Miller was able to point to four types of companies which followed this trajectory from 'excellence' to excess. Craft-based organizations with excellent engineering or technological capabilities, such as Ford and Texas Instruments, turn into 'tinkerers', focussing inwards on products and technology. Entrepreneurial 'builders' become seduced by the growth of their companies and become greedy 'imperialists', acquiring businesses they do not understand – much like some of our financial institutions in recent times. Pioneering companies with superb R&D get carried away by their inventiveness and turn into 'escapists', pursuing improbable ideas which have no market value. Companies driven by excellent sales and marketing start to neglect the product, becoming 'drifters' who focus on the package instead of the content. Each of these trajectories has also led the companies towards an excessively 'loose' or 'tight' organization; and it was precisely their pursuit of 'excellence' which led them in this direction. Echoing *In Search*'s legacy, Miller's companies have failed to manage paradox and ambiguity, by focussing on simplicity and 'one best way'.

Miller argued that any principle of organization, excessively pursued, warps into vices. The challenge is to find a happy medium between pursuing one's strengths and being prepared to rethink them. Not surprisingly, his use of the Icarus fable resonates with the ethics and philosophy of the ancient culture from which it derives. The notion of ethics as being associated with the pursuit of a 'golden mean', constituted by virtues that avoid excess, is often attributed to Aristotle and, in particular, his *Nichomachean Ethics* written in the 4th century BC. But the notion of the 'Right Mean' had been investigated by Plato and it is likely that both philosophers drew on the Pythagorean analogy between the sound mind, the healthy body and the tuned string, which inspired most of the Greek Moralists.

In Plato's *Philebus*, we are told that all good things in life belong to the class of the mixed and that in the application of intelligence to any kind of activity, the supreme wisdom is to know just where to stop. The Aristotelian development of the 'right mean' as the basis for a good or ethical life considers how virtues can be reached by training ourselves over time to behave in balance between the pairs of vices that constitute virtue in a particular domain. Here virtuous actions require reasonable moderation where both excess and defect are avoided. Take the domain of 'fear', for example. Here acting with courage (the virtue that one hopes to achieve when experiencing fear) requires avoiding a lack of fear which would result in foolhardiness, and avoiding being overtaken by too much fear, which would result in cowardice. The table below shows a fuller list of Aristotle's virtues, the domains they relate to, and their relationships to the vices that would result from either a deficit or an excess of the virtue in question.

Many today would not have drawn things in quite the same way as Aristotle (righteous indignation, for example, does not sound like a virtue to us); and, others still would not consider this ancient Greek approach to ethics to be particularly ethical (in modern times we tend to associate

Table 14.1   The Aristotelian virtues

Domain	Deficit	Virtue	Excess
Fear	Foolhardiness	*Courage*	Cowardice
Desire for Pleasure	Insensibility	*Temperance*	Self-Indulgence
Giving Money Away	Stinginess	*Generosity*	Extravagance
Desire for Honours	Humility	*Pride*	Vanity
Proneness to Anger	Apathy	*Good Temper*	Irascibility
Self-Presentation	Self-Deprecation	*Truthfulness*	Boastfulness
Desire to Amuse Others	Boorishness	*Wittiness*	Buffoonery
Desire to Please Others	Unpleasantness	*Friendliness*	Obsequiousness
Susceptibility to Shame	Shamelessness	*Modesty*	Bashfulness
Reaction to Other's Fortunes	Spite	*Righteous Indignation*	Envy

ethics with general codes rather than particular individual practices). But despite such differences of sensibility we believe that the framework for thinking provided by the Aristotelian approach is extremely useful in working out how an organization might develop the kind of 'loosening and focussing' structure and environment necessary for promoting and replenishing creative strategies.

Two aspects of Aristotle's ethics are particularly worth remembering. The first is that Aristotelian virtues are context specific. Aristotle outlined how acting virtuously only made sense within a particular community, hence an understanding of this particular community and how one fits within it is crucial, and different individuals (or organizations) will need to do different things to be virtuous. 'Excellence' is not something we can prescribe, and trying to follow a set of abstract principles or 'best practice' will more likely lead us into vices.

The second consideration is that virtues are related to the history of the individual or organization concerned. Here Aristotle explained how we need to understand in which direction of vice our particular predispositions might steer us, so as to be mindful of countering these potential excesses. We shall return to how the pursuit of the virtues should be tailored to particular organizations in Chapter 16, following the description of seven organizational virtues for creative strategy in the next chapter. At this point it is enough to note that you should read them not as a linear prescription for all organizations, but as a framework for thinking about organizing for creative strategy.

CHAPTER 15

Seven Virtues of Strategic Organization

If there is some end of the things we do... clearly this must be 'the good'. Will not knowledge of it, then, have a great influence on life? Shall we not, like archers who have a mark to aim at, be more likely to hit upon what we should?

Aristotle, *Nichomachean Ethics*

M indful of the fate of *In Search of Excellence*'s first seven principles, the fate of Icarus, and following Aristotle's approach to mapping virtue, we outline seven virtues of strategic organization. These are what we, in our experience across a wide range of creative and commercial enterprises, believe to be important organizational characteristics for fostering creative strategy. They should not be the last word, and there will be many exceptions to these seven virtues. But, as Aristotle suggests, it is useful to give the content of good organizing (loosening and focussing) an aim.

As the summary table below shows, each requires finding a balance between two extremes rather than pursuing excellence, and that balance will be relative to the organization and its context. Our virtues of strategic organization relate to seven domains: culture, politics, learning, idea generation, job orientation, organizational architecture and orientation to change.

- The first organizational virtue is a strong culture that holds things together and provides focus but which is also adaptive to environmental changes and new ideas.

Table 15.1 The seven virtues of strategic organization

Domain	Too Loose	Virtue	Too Tight
1. Culture	Disintegrating	*Adaptive*	Homogenizing
2. Politics	Democracy	*Meritocratic*	Dictatorship
3. Learning	Naive	*Deutero-learning*	Expert (or bounded) rationality
4. Idea generation	Disembodied	*From everywhere*	Subjective
5. Job orientation	Distracted	*Multi-tasked*	Blinkered
6. Architecture	Open ended	*Ambidextrous*	Closed minded
7. Change	Static	*Poise*	Flux

- The second virtue is a political environment that recognizes good ideas from anybody, can evaluate these ideas on their merits, and promote them accordingly.
- The third virtue is a learning environment that balances the value of expert knowledge with naïve and curious 'blue-sky' thinking.
- The fourth virtue is an approach to idea generation that can draw on people external to the organization and retain an active body of engaged internal people.
- The fifth virtue is multi-tasking to mitigate against blinkered or 'silo' thinking, without people becoming too distracted or scattered.
- The sixth virtue is an ambidextrous architecture or work environment that allows both closed and open spaces for engagement, to avoid closed door environments while working against completely unbounded working relationships.
- The seventh virtue is to be always poised for change, should change be needed, to avoid the traps of constant change for change's sake and becoming complacent and static.

The paragraphs that follow explain each of the virtues in more detail.

The 1st Virtue: Integrating and Fragmenting: Adaptive Culture

Just a year before *In Search of Excellence* hit the shelves, another book by two McKinsey staffers was making waves. In *The Art of Japanese Management* Richard Pascale and Anthony Athos argued that American business was being overtaken by Japanese business and this was down to one major factor: culture. Japanese corporate culture provided strong 'glue', a devotion to the company, a collective purpose, a drive for continual improvement and a coherence that gave them a huge advantage over Western organizations.

Throughout the 1980s, *The Art of Japanese Management* and related works spurred a wave of Western companies seeking to mimic their Japanese counterparts with respect to culture, and from this time the notion of a 'strong' or positive culture came to be associated with a culture that was unified, homogenized and integrated. However, as we might expect having reflected on creative processes in earlier parts of this book, a major negative with this kind of 'strong culture' is that its homogeneity generally works against innovation and change. Over time, as with Icarus, this kind of 'strength' actually becomes a weakness.

The 'discovery' of the 'New World' provides a good example here. In the 15th century China may have been the most powerful empire in the world. It certainly had what might appear to have been a unified culture. When their all-powerful emperor ordered that its ocean-going ships be destroyed there was no significant opposition. China subsequently lost its connection to the changing world around it, lost the possibility of being challenged, and gradually lost its techno-logical lead. Meanwhile, in Europe, Columbus (like many other adventurers or entrepreneurs) could challenge a variety of heads to sponsor his fantastic voyage. After four unsuccessful pitches, his fifth audience agreed to set him on his way. The competing cultures which made his voyage possible were further enriched and diversified by what Columbus found there.

The first virtue of strategic organization relates to the domain of culture. It suggests that an organization's culture should integrate enough to provide a clear sense of identity, but should at the same time be loose enough to enable diversity, challenge and adaptation to a world that will be changing around it. We take the term 'adaptive' from a recently published paper in the *Academy of Management Review* entitled 'Organizational Identity, Image, and Adaptive Instability'. Here, Dennis Gioia and his co-authors argue that while those who focus on organi-zational identity tend to highlight what is core, distinctive and enduring about an organization, another important school of thought focusses on organizational image (marketing, stakeholder management, etc.) and encourages a 'presentation of self' that moves with the times. In recog-nizing the interplay between these two forces, one for consistency and the other for change, Gioia et al. suggest that we must take a more paradoxical view of cultural identity: to pre-serve a culture we must change it. To be true to our pasts and move with the times we must aim, in their words, for dynamic consistency or adaptive instability. Hence, when it comes to corporate culture there should be, in the words of Max McKeown: 'just enough disunity for progress'.

One of the earliest and still one of the best challenges to the dominance of the hegemonic or 'strongly homogenized' view of culture is Peter Frost's book *Reframing Organizational Culture*. Here Frost and his co-authors outline three different perspectives of culture, each with their particular strengths and weaknesses. They are summarized in the table below.

The first, the integrative perspective, maps on the view of 'strong' culture we have already outlined here. The second perspective, differentiation, suggests that a corporate culture is more likely to be made up of different subcultures. Each subculture may display the characteristics ascribed to integrative cultures, but they will diverge, compete and struggle with one another within the organization. The third view questions the notion of any sort of cultural or even subcultural unity. The fragmentation perspective suggests that integrating cultures are constructs that we assume

Table 15.2   Defining characteristics of three perspectives on organizational culture

Features	Integration	Differentiation	Fragmentation
Orientation to consensus	Organization-wide consensus	Subcultural consensus	Lack of consensus
Relation among manifestations	Consistency	Inconsistency	Not clearly consistent or inconsistent
Orientation to ambiguity	Exclude it	Channel it outside or to subcultures	Acknowledge it

exist, or would like to believe in, but, in reality, things are much more ambiguous and contested and driven by fragmented individual interests.

As Frost et al. argued, we suggest that it is useful for the strategic organization to look at culture in each of these ways. It is useful to try to develop an understanding of the cultural glue that binds the organization's corporate identity and seek to protect and enhance this. But this glue should not set and it is also useful to encourage subcultures and individuals to challenge cultural norms as things evolve. If we were to depict this in a diagram it might look like Figure 15.1 below. The culture of a strategic organization should have a significant core, but this should be both strong and malleable: open to challenge and change from subcultural and maverick individual forces. It might be useful to use this diagram as a template and draw in the integrating, differentiating

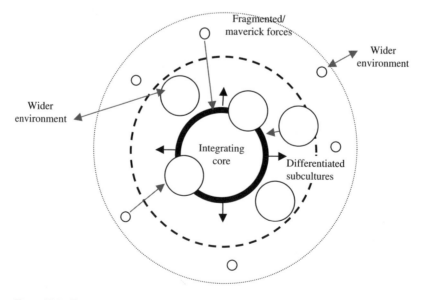

Figure 15.1   The culture of a strategic organization as a stable but moveable, or adaptive, nucleus

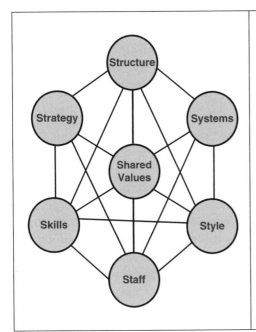

- *Strategy:* What is it and how is it implemented?

- *Structure:* How is the company organised? What processes does it employ to get things done?

- *Systems:* How does the company operate on a day-to-day basis?

- *Skills:* What are the organization's core competencies?

- *Staff:* What is the 'demographic' make-up of important personnel categories within the firm?

- *Style:* What is the symbolic behaviour of management and which behaviours does it consider important?

- *Shared Values:* Which values define company culture and corporate identity?

Figure 15.2 McKinsey's 7-S framework (adapted from Pascale and Athos, 1981, © McKinsey and Co.)

and fragmenting forces in your culture. If they aren't present then it may be time to encourage them.

One effective way to challenge strong (or Icarus) type cultures or to actively encourage differentiating and fragmenting forces is to play around with, or 'subvert', the traditional culture frameworks that have become prevalent since the 1980s. The first and still best known of these is the McKinsey 7-S framework. This was first mentioned in *The Art of Japanese Management* in 1981 but the model was actually 'born' at a meeting of Richard Pascale and Anthony Athos with their fellow McKinsey staffers Peters and Waterman in 1978. Subsequently, it also appeared in *In Search of Excellence*.

Frameworks like the 7-Ss, or Johnson and Scholes' Cultural Web, emphasize consistency. Each component should reinforce the others to ensure an integrated and unified set of 'shared values' or a cultural 'paradigm'.

But as Thomas Kuhn explained in *The Structure of Scientific Revolutions*, substantial creative progress comes from 'paradigm shifts' rather than paradigm maintenance. And, in our experience, if one wants to promote creative strategizing it can be useful to actively seek to inject a little differentiation and fragmentation into the mix occasionally.

For example, instead of hiring staff that fit the mould or the 'description of important personnel characteristics', hire, and then support, somebody *other* than that, somebody who might inject different skills or challenge and fragment the existing style. Start telling and promoting stories of a different 'hue', which seem to go against the grain of how the organization has viewed itself before, and let these challenge existing rituals and lead to differentiated structures in different parts of the organization.

Theorists in cultural studies have long argued for such a relationship between culture and sub-culture. Raymond Williams described the interplay between dominant, emergent and residual cultures, with the dominant culture continually being reshaped by what came before it (residual) and what threatened to succeed it (emergent). Dominant cultures succeed by being open enough to change without falling apart. We would argue the same applies for a strategic organization. If strategic organization is to connect with innovation and entrepreneurship, its culture needs to allow space for the influence of unfamiliar emergent or divergent creative subcultures, rather than imposing its own shared values. The culture of a strategic organization is thus one that maintains itself by knowing, but then challenging and questioning, its own identity, to ensure that it continues to adapt.

The 2nd Virtue: Democracy and Dictatorship: Meritocratic Politics

In the domain of politics, the virtue for strategic organization to steer for is meritocracy. Dicta-torship, whilst having some short-term benefits in terms of providing a clear focus, eventually exhausts its own possibilities. And full or direct democracy, while a noble aim, can become a rab-ble without strong leadership. As the Shakespearian 'fool' character, Barry, in the popular British television series *Auf Wiedersehen, Pet* once said, 'democracy is the system where everybody gets what nobody wants'.

We have already noted the need to allow new ideas to percolate upwards from further down the organization. In Part I of this book, we related the story of the photocopying assistant who responded to the 'any ideas?' memo from the CEO with a proposal for double-sided printing. But this was just one of around 300 ideas received from across the organization, of which thirty were selected for further investigation. The remaining 270 were rejected outright. We have also noted the danger of over-democratic decision making, particularly the over-reliance on focus groups which have often blocked rather than encouraged innovation in fields as diverse as car design and television.

Meritocracy, as an organizational virtue, requires two main elements. First, a meritocracy requires a means of *knowing* about good creative ideas when they emerge. It needs what Stafford Beer, perhaps the most underrated organization and systems theorist of the 20th century, called an 'algedonic signal'. The word algedonic is the combination of the ancient Greek words for pain and pleasure. Beer presents his 'viable systems model' as a biological alternative to the conventional mechanistic organization chart view. The organization is seen as a living system, designed for long-term survival, consisting of five components: identity, research/marketing, operations management, regulation and operational elements. Running through each of these parts must be an algedonic signal. This signal will alert the highest levels to anything indicating a serious sense of opportunity or threat (pleasure or pain), in the same way that an animal's nervous system triggers an instinctive response to stimuli such as food or danger.

The second element in a virtuous meritocracy is a good way of *evaluating* these ideas and further sponsoring or developing those deemed meritorious. Companies like Walt Disney make much of their ability to tap into employee creativity – what is less clear is how they evaluate and adapt their employees' suggestions, turning novel ideas into creative acts which are novel *and* valuable. Again this organizational virtue connects with the other dimensions of creative strategy. Across the creative industries, the ability to recognize a good idea is very often more valuable than the ability to have a good idea – without evaluation, the best innovations will pass away unnoticed. And as we noted in Part II, evaluation is the critical point in the development of an entrepreneurial enterprise and self-evaluation can be the turning point in an entrepreneurial career. The leader who selectively promotes ideas and people from below is also evaluating in a meritocracy. The virtue of meritocracy thus becomes one of the conditions and criteria for a strategic organization.

Test this out for your organization. Ask yourself: if somebody in your organization had a really good innovative idea or an idea that would help solve a problem by fruitfully adapting an existing innovation, how would we find out about it? Then ask yourself: Having received that idea how would we evaluate its merits and develop it if it was deemed worthy of further development? If the answer to either question is unclear, then work remains to be done towards the second virtue.

The 3rd Virtue: Naive and Expert: Deutero-Learning

To say that expert knowledge is useful to an organization is an obvious statement. For this reason it is easy to justify investing in it. But most of the innovations we referred to in Part I of this book stem from more 'naive', untrained or undisciplined thinking (or at least the combination of naivety with expertise). If you want your organization to encourage further innovation then a 3rd virtue to aim for is the blending of expertise with an irreverent questioning of the received wisdom of experts.

As long ago as 1974, Chris Argyris and Donald Schön proposed the concepts of 'single-loop', 'double-loop', and 'deutero' or 'second system' learning which can help us explain why the 3rd virtue is important to creative strategy.

- SINGLE-LOOP or 'adaptive' learning focusses on incremental change. This type of learning solves problems but ignores the question of why the problem arose in the first place. The expert's ability to quickly outline action strategies can be very useful here.

- DOUBLE-LOOP or generative learning focusses on transformational change that changes the status quo. It uses feedback from the consequences of past actions to question assumptions or the 'governing variables' underlying current views. Such questioning benefits from an open or a 'naive' mindset. Argyris and Schön found double-looped learning to be an essential skill for higher-order creativity. From the perspective of creativity theory this corresponds to a distinction between problem-solving (single-loop) and problem-finding (double-loop) – in order to be genuinely transformative, creative thinking needs to reframe the question, not just find the answer.
- DEUTERO-learning, which we are advocating here as an organizational virtue, is about developing a secondary system to make organizational learning better by seeking to improve *both* single- and double-loop learning. It is the ability to both enact and challenge the rules of a game. Deutero-learning may be seen an application of Einstein's dictum: 'The significant problems we face cannot be solved at the same level of thinking we were at when we created them. You have to rise above it to the next level.'

The virtue of deutero-learning requires us to think bisociatively, identifying connections *between* different frames of reference, not just within them. It can be related to the leader's ability to envision strategy by sussing or mapping an organization from a different perspective. Very often this new perspective can be achieved by playing people out of position. In sports, for example, having a heavy sprinter pushing a bobsled, a baseball pro analysing the way a cricket team fields, or a handball player working with a soccer goalkeeper on throwing will create some effective questioning of past practices, and, subsequently, new action strategies.

Think back to how rugby union was fundamentally changed by the positioning of the New Zealand winger Jonah Lomu at the 1995 World Cup. Lomu's physique combined the size of a flank forward and the strength of a prop. But his speed encouraged his coaches to try the unprecedented step of playing him as a winger. And as they learned how the game could be played differently from this experiment they reorganized and fine-tuned his team's offensive and defensive strategies around his strengths and weaknesses. This resulted in a number of new strategies and ploys that have become a part of most team's arsenal in international rugby. Usain Bolt, who would have been considered the wrong build for speed in the past, has done some similar things recently in sprinting.

Similar learning can occur from playing people out of position in more conventional organizations. The theme is developed in Bob Sutton's book *Weird Ideas That Work*. Sutton's $11\frac{1}{2}$ weird ideas use the perspective of the non-expert to question expert knowledge (see below).

Sutton's ideas have precedents. Thomas Edison liked to ask potential new recruits unusual questions such as: how is leather tanned?; where is the River Volga?; or, what is the finest cotton grown? McKinsey & Company is famous for asking questions like: how many pigs are there in China? And Microsoft tests potential recruits by quizzing them: how would they weigh a jet plane without scales?; which way should the key turn to unlock a car door?; or why are manhole covers round rather than square?

BOB SUTTON'S 11 $^1/_2$ WEIRD IDEAS THAT WORK

(1) Hire smart people who will avoid doing things the same way your company has always done things.

($1\frac{1}{2}$) Diversify your talent and knowledge base, especially with people who get under your skin.

(2) Hire people with skills you don't need yet, and put them in untraditional assignments.

(3) Use job interviews as a source of new ideas more than as a way to hire.

(4) Give room for people to focus on what interests them, and to develop their ideas in their own way.

(5) Help people learn how to be tougher in testing ideas, while being considerate of the people involved.

(6) Focus attention on new and smarter attempts whether they succeed or not.

(7) Use the power of self-confidence to encourage unconventional trials.

(8) Use 'bad' ideas to help reveal good ones.

(9) Keep a balance between having too much and too little outside contact in your creative activities.

(10) Have people with little experience and new perspectives tackle key issues.

(11) Escape from the mental shackles of your organization's past successes.

Source: Sutton, 2007

The answers to these questions are not important. What is important is changing the way people think about the processes and structures they use to answer such problems. As Peter Senge's landmark book *The Fifth Discipline* makes clear, effective creative thinking requires that implicit mental models are regularly exposed and questioned in the light of changing circumstances.

The 4th Virtue: Subjective and Disembodied: Development from Everywhere

In Part 3 we noted the goal set by Procter and Gamble's CEO to source 50% of its innovations outside of the company. The target is less important than the underlying signal it sends, that ideas should come from both outside and inside the organization. If they are coming from diverse places, then the interaction between those ideas will lead to further new ideas. Relying exclusively on outsourcing or on internal innovation is less likely to trigger this interaction.

The need for balance in this regard may be illustrated by looking at the rise of the use of external consultants to develop an organization's strategy. Not only may the overuse of similar consultants lead to diminishing returns as strategies are homogenized (see Chapter 6) and lead to an over-emphasis on expertise (see the 3rd virtue above), such a dependency or 'addiction' can also diminish the motivation and capabilities of those inside your organization. If all of the interesting problems your organization faces are passed on to outside consultants, the people inside your organization miss out on the development opportunities that such problems present. Hence, it can be worth testing, from time to time, whether you are overly dependent on consultants (see the box below).

This is not to say that using external consultants is a bad thing. Sourcing ideas entirely from within will lead to insular, parochial and overly subjective thinking. Consultants can add a great deal of value if used in moderation, and used in combination with internal staff so that a contest of ideas and learning opportunities can be shared and held onto by the organization as capabilities that can be used again.

ARE YOU ADDICTED TO CONSULTANCY? TEST YOURSELF

Ask yourself the following questions to find out whether you're over-using consultants:

1. Can you say when you expect your consultant will be leaving the premises permanently?

YES/NO

2. Do you have a good reason for not using somebody internal or not taking someone on as staff to fulfil the consultant's role?

YES/NO

3. Do you have a defined objective for the consultancy you've employed?

YES/NO

4. Do you ask your consultant for advice on matters other than the task for which you hired them?

YES/NO

5. Do your employees refer to the consultant as the 'owner' or 'manager' of the initiative?

YES/NO

Answer 'yes' to the first three questions and 'no' to the last two and you're likely to be using consultants sensibly. 'No' to the first three and 'yes' to the last two means you're using consultants as a crutch rather than as a defined and useful part of your business.

Adapted from 'Lost the ability to think for yourself?' by Guy Clapperton, *The Guardian*, 27 October 2006.

Our organizational virtues depend upon balance or finding the middle-way. Just as there is a danger of becoming too reliant on external consultants, so too there is a danger of blocking out external voices. Wayne Burkett's *Wide-angled Vision* describes a number of what he calls external 'saviours-in-waiting', people who could (if asked) tell a company what it needs to hear. People on the inside often find it difficult, or not expedient to tell the company what it needs to hear. Disgruntled customers; upstart competitors; rogue employees; and fringe suppliers can all offer these insights. Burkett goes on to question the recent tendency to bring strategic suppliers 'inside the tent' in order to cement relationships and achieve efficiencies. Strategic supplier relationships are not likely to function as any more than a mirror to your organization. Fringe suppliers that are challenging to deal with may be far more useful sources of new strategic insights. While these saviours-in-waiting may not always be right, and you need not follow what they say, a virtuous organization should be able to listen to what they have to say and think through how they should respond.

In Part I we examined how 'market innovations' and 'boundary innovations' combine the insights of existing and potential customers with those inside the organization. Duncan Angwin's book *The Strategy Pathfinder* cites examples of how companies as diverse as Land Rover, Levi's and Build-a-Bear generate new ideas by actively training people how to drive off-road, helping them to design their own clothes, or getting them to build their own soft toy. Not only does this help develop a greater sense of ownership among customers, thereby increasing switching costs, it allows the organization to build an information system that can help shape future product ideas.

In *The New Age of Innovation*, C.K. Prahalad and M.S. Krishnan take this thinking further towards what they call 'co-creation'. Co-creation allows customers, organizations and sometimes suppliers to work together to design new approaches, products, and even pricing. Prahalad and Krishnan cite one example where health insurance premiums for somebody with diabetes could be reset continually based on a monitoring of a person's vital signs and compliance with a regime of diet, exercise and medication. An early version of such a model is being used by ICICI Prudential in India. As we noted in Part I, co-creation is increasingly influential in the creative and media industries. Consumers are increasingly involved in remixing music and uploading promotional videos (Lily Allen, Radiohead), co-producing films through social networking sites (*Faintheart, Snakes on a Plane*), or acting as co-promoters and distributors (*The Age of Stupid*). Co-creation, through social networks or 'sharing' sites like YouTube, makes a significant contribution to music, films, newspapers, videogames and advertising.

Co-creation can also occur through 'crowdsourcing' whereby problems faced by an organization are put out on the World Wide Web to see if anybody 'out there' may be able to provide interesting solutions. The case of Industrial Research Limited, included in Part I of this book as an example of 'learning innovation', showed how 'problemsourcing' can be used in this way to learn about potential clients.

The 4th virtue lies in balancing internal capabilities and external forces. Consultants, saviours-in-waiting, co-creation and crowd-sourcing all offer clues and ideas for innovation and strategy – provided they are used in moderation. The virtuous organization needs to connect and test the subjective ideas of insiders against the disembodied voices of outsiders. This can be achieved by setting up moderating structures, which encourage interaction and learning, rather than allowing one set of voices to drown out the others.

The 5th Virtue Distracted and Blinkered: A Multi-Tasking Orientation

Our 5th virtue of organization finds a balance between people being too distracted and too blinkered. While much has been written recently on the perils of distractions at work (e-mail and cell phones chattering and twittering away constantly), distraction may not always be a bad thing. According to Gary Marcus, author of *Kluge: The Haphazard Construction of the Human Mind*, humans are essentially interruption-driven because evolution has made us highly alert to respond to signals and change to aid survival. 'We're not built to stay on task', he contends.

Whether or not we are biologically wired for distraction, it is certainly true that people like it. We know it would be sensible to only receive e-mails a couple of times a day (and it's easy enough to set our systems just so) but most people like to keep a more regular eye on the in-box. Computer programs like Adblock have not been as popular as expected, partly because people couldn't be bothered to install it, and partly because they don't mind the occasional pop-up ad.

But not only are we biologically and temperamentally drawn to distraction, moving between things or multi-tasking is also good for creativity. Just as playing people out of position encourages double-loop learning distraction, so moving between the task at hand and something else can help what Koestler refers to as 'thinking aside' or the kind of 'double-mindedness' that he relates to creative thinking. Henri Poincaré refers to a process of 'incubation', where we relax our conscious mind and allow our sub-conscious or 'back brain' to work on a problem in the background. This helps explain the value of giving people more than one task at a time, of the chief executive spending a day on the shopfloor, or a videogames developer going out bowling. These breaks from routine can heighten certain senses, diminish assumed barriers and lead to fruitful new relations or associations between planes of thought. It might even be important to take forty winks now and again (see the box below).

But too much distraction is not a good thing. It can lead to disjointedness, frustration and nothing ever being completed. Indeed, while humans may have always been distracted beings, people in past eras never had to cope with so much beeping, ringing and buzzing. Sometimes we need to put the 'blinkers' on. Gloria Mark, a professor of informatics at the University of California at Irvine, monitored thousands of hours of workplace behaviour. She found that most workers now switch gears every few minutes, and once they're distracted, it can take nearly half an hour to get back on track. 'When you see the hard numbers, it kind of hits home how bad [distraction today] really is.' The virtuous organization must also protect employees from over-distraction.

SLEEP ON IT

Give your brain a break, and it will find hidden connections

How does your brain manage to see both the trees and the forest? A new study suggests that getting the big picture requires some downtime and, for an extra boost, a night of sleep.

The ability to recognize hidden relations among our memories, a characteristically human feature, is vital for solving problems in creative ways. To understand how this 'relational memory' develops, a team of researchers from Harvard Medical School and McGill University presented students with pairs of abstract images in which one image was considered 'greater', then asked them to guess the hierarchy of the images in new combinations.

Subjects tested 20 minutes after the learning period performed no better than chance – their brains had not yet been able to figure out new connections. Those who were tested after at least 12 hours, however, were much more successful in detecting the hidden relations. And participants who had slept during their time away from testing outperformed the other groups in the most difficult inferences.

'The process of binding memories together evolves over time', says neurologist Jeffrey Ellenbogen, a member of the research team. As we sleep or focus on other tasks, our brain forges connections in the background, fitting newly learned information into a bigger picture. One more reason why you should sleep before taking an exam: connecting the dots takes time.

By Graciela Flores, from the August 2007 edition of *Scientific American Mind*

Technology is being developed that can aid this. One IBM prototype is an instant-messaging answering machine known as IMSavvy that allows messages to tap gently at your door and be politely deferred: a bit like having a protective but well-mannered butler. The programme can sense when you are busy by your typing and mouse patterns. It protects your focus by putting such messages 'on hold' and politely telling would-be interrupters you are not available, when you might be able to get back to them and suggesting ways they can get through to you should the matter be urgent.

But movement toward the 5th virtue does not need to be so high-tech. It can be aided by simply asking this question of your co-workers. Do you have the right amount of variety in your work to keep your interest up without feeling run-ragged? A virtuous organization should adjust accordingly, by recognizing and rewarding a distinction between 'on task thinking' and 'one task thinking'. A multi-tasking orientation contributes both to the bisociative process of strategic innovation, but also to the diligent-dilettante paradox of strategic entrepreneurship. Distraction and concentration can work together – for example, breaking the routine can help us to refocus on the task. If we are to generate ideas *and* act on them, we need to balance eclecticism against single-mindedness.

The 6th Virtue: Open Planned and Closed Planned: Ambidextrous Architecture

In 2001, the financial services company Egg's call centre in Derby, England, was nominated as one of the UK's 'most creative and feel good offices for the digital age'. This was a surprising result, given that call centres were supposed to be the 21st century's sweat-shops and that Derby lacked what one might call a 'feel good' reputation. But Egg's call centre was designed to be different.

With the opportunity to design and build from the ground up on a greenfield site, Egg's vision was to create a vibrant and fun call centre that would accommodate over 1000 people. Its express purpose was to help attract and retain the highest quality personnel. Instead of relying on existing models, Egg's design consultants set about talking to potential staff members aged between 18 and 23 (a typical age for new call centre employees) in order to find out what sort of work environment would appeal to them.

The result is a huge white aircraft hangar-like building that looks like half an egg sliced lengthwise. It has almost no internal walls, office furniture is configured to enable people to cluster together in teams and to enable employees to re-configure it as they see fit, and no set seating plan. In each of the four corners of the building are recreational spaces based around different themes (for example, a sports area with room for ball-games, pinball and so on and a relaxing Mediterranean café) that staff can use depending on their mood.

But Egg are by no means alone in opening and loosening up the workplace. Many trace the beginnings of this workplace architectural revolution to the invention of Apple computers. Apple made much of their not being IBM. They didn't make computers for IBM-type people and they didn't work like IBM employees. No corporate uniforms, no strict timetables, no rigid job descriptions, no formal chains-of-command and time-weary procedures, no sitting alone in an allocated box. This was played upon in Apple's early advertising for models like the Macintosh and it has become an integral part of Apple's identity (including the more recent 'I'm a Mac'/'I'm a PC' campaign). Following Apple's lead, executives began to dress-down on Fridays, or to replace their suits and ties with chinos and soft collars on a more permanent basis. New terms like 'open-plan' and 'hot-desking' entered the language, and more and more workspaces contain 'chill-out rooms' and fitness centres.

The open plan revolution redressed the imbalance caused by the 20th century's first workplace mavericks. Ninety years ago workplace architects, inspired by F.W. Taylor's 'Scientific Management' doctrine, sought to rationalize the workplace and design out all vestiges of individuality. They built in order to maximize sterility and order. Modernism henceforth became the business world's architectural style of choice and offices came to resemble filing cabinets. By the 1980s the backlash that Apple personified was long overdue.

But by the end of the 20th century things had loosened up so much that for many the lines between work and play were becoming increasingly imperceptible. In 2001, a British report entitled 'Tomorrow's Workplace: Fulfilment or Stress?' envisaged the office of the future as a 'recreational centre', where the toys and tasks differed little from those found at home. Product designers began responding to the blurring of these boundaries too. Industrial designer Sam Hecht claimed that he was no longer sure if there was any difference: 'It [became] very hard to distinguish between objects for the home and for the office.'

The same period witnessed a blurring between work-time and play-time, with employees finding it increasingly difficult to determine whether they are at work or not. Thanks to 'advances' in information technology, for many the workday now begins when they begin their commute, not when they sit down at their desk. For others, it never really ceased as they are constantly available on the end of a cell phone and most homes now contain a computer and an e-mail connection in a 'home office'.

Although not specifying exact working hours has become the norm for an increasing class of workers, it is generally understood that most 'white-collar jobs' (an increasingly anachronistic term given the relaxation of dress codes) consume more and more of people's time. As Madeline Bunting's book *Willing Slaves: How the Overwork Culture is Ruining Our Lives* explains, in many parts of the labour market 'the boundaries between work and play have been eroded: work is play, work is your hobby. Work becomes the organizing principle of your life.' This is a notable feature of the 'no-collar' workplaces in the creative industries, where self-exploitation, especially among the young, is dressed up as the freedom of 'flexible' working, and after-work 'socialising' is a compulsory extension of the working day.

We may now be witnessing a backlash against the backlash. As with most doctrines, the open plan revolution has perhaps gone too far. In a recently published essay called 'Game Over! Back to Work', Jonathan Bell claims that the modern office is beginning to resemble a playpen. Not only may all of this just be a ruse to increase productivity – to fool jaded employees into thinking that their company loves them so much that it wants them to have fun, so that these employees, in turn, feel that they owe the company – it may also be a ruse that doesn't actually work. Hence, we may not be too far away from 'rediscovering the worth of workspaces that are workspaces rather than romper rooms'.

In different ways, both Bunting and Bell question whether opening of the work space is necessarily a good thing. Indeed, the 5th virtue outlined how important being distracted or taken away from one's work task is for creativity. If people never really leave work, or only leave to partake in work-sponsored diversions with their co-workers, then their minds may not be free-associating enough. Moreover, says Bell: 'It may be time to recognize that [the majority] do not find identity and purpose in vintage PacMan machines and bean bags. Innovations like hot-desking fail to recognize that most of us want a permanent workstation that allows us to get our job done. We are starting to realize that long hours spent in the office playing table football are not useful or clever. Many of us love our work [but] don't need side-shows or soft furnishings to keep the relationship alive.'

One advertising agency that we spoke to with regard to *Creative Strategy* has now got rid of its pinball machine and set up what it calls a 'library' (where employees can escape from the open plan office) – a sign perhaps that Bell's arguments are gaining ground.

Indeed, Bell believes that a new generation of offices will emerge that acknowledge that good ideas can come from people having the freedom to congregate, but at the same time recognize that a good office is about allowing individuals to focus on doing their jobs quickly and cleanly. 'It's a century since Frank Lloyd Wright's Larkin Building was completed in Buffalo, New York', concludes Bell. 'This was perhaps the first modern office building. And here was order and communality, efficiency and common purpose. He may have been on to something.'

We would concur. Some creative tasks are solitary. Others are collaborative. The virtuous organization should be made up of a combination of open and closed spaces.

As with all Aristotelian virtues, there is no general law as to what the balance of open and closed space should be. This depends on the organization and the communities in which they act. Because of the need for confidentiality and concentrated thinking, legal and accounting practices and universities will veer toward more closed spaces. Advertising agencies will be more open. And it depends on the organization's position or strategy within its industry. For example, it would not suit IBM to be as loose and open as Apple. And it depends on how the industry or company is moving. For example, in recent years many banks have sought to redesign their branches to make them more conducive to relationship building and co-creating products and services with customers to help build trust and loyalty in an age of greater informality. But, once again, there is a point where this might go too far. When the bank branch becomes too open its image as a solid and secure organization may be compromised and those relationships actually diminished.

This same ambidextrous logic should be applied to blending remote and on-site working. Remote working provides many benefits. But while it may be the 'new thing' or the flavour of the moment, it may not be useful to take it too extremes. There have been many examples of organizations diminishing themselves through outsourcing to excess (notably in the broadcasting industry), and, on a smaller scale, the technology that keeps people connected may never supply the creative energy and productivity supplied by a room full of fellow workers.

Finally, it can also help if there are spaces in between the open and closed spaces. Creativity, as we have already seen, is often sparked at the juncture. There is a reason why Microsoft has white boards in the corridors. One advertising agency has deliberately encouraged chance encounters and corridor conversations by siting its print department at the furthest part of the building. People have to walk through other departments to get there and may well make a new connection along the way.

Encouraging people to move between different spaces is good for the minds of employees, but it's also good for the body (which, it turns out, is good for the mind too). A recent interview with famous dance choreographer Twyla Tharp in the *Harvard Business Review*, entitled 'Creativity Step by Step', asked what her advice would be for executives looking to enhance their creative thinking. 'The first thing I'd say', explained Tharp, 'is get moving. Because one of the things I think I have to offer people is the knowledge that using your body makes your brain work better. Movement stimulates our brains in ways we don't appreciate – a fact we're learning more and more about from neuroscientists.' This same learning is being drawn upon by those encouraging education boards to reverse recent trends that have seen schoolchildren do less exercise in exchange for more academics. Creativity requires different spaces and space to move.

The 7th Virtue: Static and Flux: Poised for Change

Octavio Paz, Mexican poet, writer, and diplomat, once said that 'Wisdom lies neither in fixity nor in change, but in the dialectic between the two.' The final virtue of strategic organization relates to the domain of change. The virtuous or strategic organization must steer a course between all change and no change. It must be self-assured enough to demonstrate a *poise* that makes it ready for change if change is needed but ready to resist change for change's sake. There must be a sense of urgency, as we outlined in Chapter 8, but this urgency should not result in a lack of composure.

At the beginning of Chapter 8 we used a quotation from *Alice in Wonderland*'s Queen of Hearts to encourage the thinking of 'impossible things' as a spur for innovation. But there is another side to the Queen that has parallels to the way that many organizations have carried on over the past twenty years.

You may remember *Alice in Wonderland*'s croquet game. It degenerates into chaos because the Queen keeps changing the rules. Many employees probably feel like the players in that game as their organizations continue to impose upheaval after upheaval and they run from pillar to post never reaching any desired state because the playing field keeps being redrawn. This applies especially to organizations in the public sector – schools, hospitals and social services – which are continually bombarded with new structures and systems with each change in political regime or fresh government initiative.

A number of studies in the private sector also point to people being overwhelmed by the sheer volume of organizational change initiatives, resulting in such initiatives doing more harm than good. Christopher Bartlett and Sumantra Ghoshal may have been the first to claim that levels of change now in many instances outpace the human capability to cope with change. But there are many others who that back this up.

One of the more compelling studies in this regard resulted in a book called *When Too Much Change is Never Enough*. Its authors, Anna Bodi, Glenn Maggs and Don Edgar from the Centre for Workplace Culture Change in Australia, concluded that many organizations are caught in a perpetual cycle of organizational fads as they try to keep pace with competitors. But their people become increasingly cynical and disillusioned as fads are applied like recipes from an endless cookbook, to the point that little useful change is achieved. We've paraphrased Bodi et al.'s subsequent recommendations for the effective management of change below:

- Avoid fad surfing: 'the practice of riding the crest of the latest management panacea and then paddling out again just in time to ride the next one'.
- Adopt the dictum that change management is the art of the pilot and not the autopilot. This means having the courage to actually lead and manage in an age of instant answers. The critical tasks in this respect are selecting a course from among the many options available, ensuring their choices make up a coherent whole, and making adaptations and changes in course when they are needed – and then learning from experience.
- Accept that organizations which aspire to fundamental change must change the fundamentals. Managers must share a preparedness to review continually the basic features of their businesses and adapt them to changing circumstances. But they must do so by balancing the need for change with the need for continuity. In other words, they have to recognize that a prerequisite for adding value is maintenance of the existing strengths of the enterprise.

Rather than risk undermining the reasons for the organization's success, the virtuous organization should seek to surf the good things that already exist within the organization and build around these, rather than seeking to surf around trends originating somewhere else. It is not that the elements of what the organization has done in the past should not be questioned. It is rather that they should be appreciated before weighing up whether to discard them. Indeed, Bodi and her colleagues recognize that sometimes fundamental change will be necessary – but all too often the organization has been too exhausted by trivial and unnecessary changes to seize the opportunity when it is most needed.

The virtue of being poised for change is, we believe, related to an interesting finding from a recent study done on which popular management approaches have exhibited the greatest longevity. A survey of the forty year archive of the journal *Long Range Planning* (strategic management's longest running journal), showed that only one approach had been consistently applied in a widespread manner over a period greater than ten years. Total quality management, business process reengineering, developing a vision, all came and went relatively quickly. But scenario planning has had a significant influence over nearly thirty years. We believe that this is due to the fact that scenario planning does not tell an organization what it should do, nor does it tell organizations how they should change or what that change should be. Rather, scenario planning is a framework to help people ready their minds for the inevitability of some form of change.

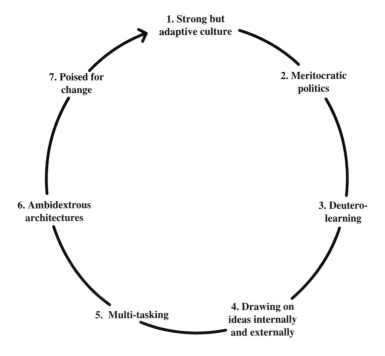

Figure 15.3   A virtuous circle of strategic organizational virtues

Being poised in the face of the many pressures for change that organizations now face is not easy to do. It requires a self assuredness. This relates back to notions of centred leadership that we described in Part III and also to the 1st virtue, that of having a clear but adaptive cultural identity. This brings us full circle with respect to the seven virtues of strategic organization (and we present this 'virtuous circle' in Figure 15.3). But it also relates to having a clear sense of what the organization's particular context and strategy is; which takes us forward to the final chapter of *Creative Strategy*.

CHAPTER 16

Strategic Organization: Where Creative Strategy Ends (and Begins Again)

I am a great lover of these divisions and generalizations, they help me to speak and think.

Plato, *Phaedrus*

T hroughout the course of this book, we have emphasized that creative strategy, through innovation, entrepreneurship, leadership and organization, requires an ability to switch between opposing mindsets. Organization is the medium through which an enterprise's particular switches can be either facilitated or prevented.

The virtuous 'golden mean' in strategic organization is not therefore some perfect compromise which irons out differences into a smooth consensus. As we described at the start of this book, this search for 'one best way' has been one of the limitations in management resulting in much unproductive conflict between opposing 'schools' of strategy in academic management and a destructive pursuit of alternating fads in management practice. This is the essence of Danny Miller's *Icarus Paradox* – too much of anything, even if we are flying high, will eventually cause us to crash and burn. Rather the organizational virtues we have described in the previous chapter depend upon an ability to switch in between organizational vices. To be ambidextrously focussed and loose, and thus strategically creative, our organizations must develop capabilities on both sides of a spectrum, not merge into a single model or attitude somewhere in the middle.

To give one example of a strategic organizational virtue in practice, many organizations have experimented with different office spaces, from 'hot desking' to 'open plan' to virtual environments. Yet some of the most stimulating spaces seem to be those which encompass multiple environments, allowing employees to switch between the buzz of an open office to private meeting rooms or reflective spaces for solitary concentration. When BBC Worldwide moved into new offices in 2009, the specially designed working environment included themed meeting rooms, flexible workspaces which could be reconfigured using a 'blocking and stacking' system, workstations (35% of staff do not have a desk), spaces for relaxation and reflection and informal caféareas as well as more conventional offices and desks. The offices were designed to reflect BBC Worldwide's brand and culture, but above all to allow for different modes of working for a very diverse workforce, many of whom had experienced the excesses of 'open' and 'closed' office designs in the past and called for something different.

In this chapter we consider how each loose-focussed organization should encompass different organizational characteristics and positions rather than fixing on a generic 'one best way'. We then conclude by considering how organizing fits within the overall pattern of creative strategy, arguing that successful organizations are continually regenerating themselves, triggering a new cycle of innovation, entrepreneurship, leadership and re-organization.

Organizing for Creative Strategy: Getting the Particular Balance Right

If an organization's strategy is its message, then the structure which facilitates the delivery and renewal of that message is the medium. Linking the message to the medium is thus the key to organizing for creative strategy. And, because creative strategies, as we outlined at the beginning of this book, must be different, organizational structures, and the way the seven virtues are pursued, should be different too. Let's look at some broad ranging examples of how this relationship plays out, paying particular attention to two key contextual variables, which our discussion on Aristotle in Chapter 14 advised us to remember: the fit between organization and strategy, and the fit between organization and what we might call competitive context.

In literature, an organization that suits the message leads to greater creative effect. Some of humanity's most influential books have combined a powerful message with an innovative structure that suits that message. While some may not like what some of these books have created, there can be little doubt that they have created a lot – partly because of the fit between medium and message:

- Confucius's philosophy lent itself to pithy sayings that populate *The Analects* whereas Plato's philosophy was better suited to the looser more wandering style of what we now call 'Socratic dialogue'.
- The *New Testament*'s four loosely similar but different versions of the life of Christ enable this to appear both more convincing as a factual narrative and also more mysterious, allusive and subject to interpretation and re-interpretation.

- The *Qur'an*'s clear structural divisions into thirty *juz* and seven *manazil* enable monthly and weekly readings which make it more memorable and recitable.
- While many potentially revolutionary essays were written in the 19th century, the focussed 'ten points' at the core of Marx's *Communist Manifesto* is a structure perfectly suited to clearly communicate and garner support for any plan: from a revolution to a clearly defined marketing strategy in PowerPoint.

In football, the same is true. A good fit between organization and its particular capabilities and purpose enables punching above one's weight:

- The 4-2-4 formation was developed in Hungary and Brazil in the 1950s to combine a strong attack with a strong defence in such a way that supported their relatively fitter and more skilled footballers to unlock the tight defences of traditionally stronger but more conservatively-minded opponents.
- The 'total football' styles of the great teams of the 1970s from the Netherlands and West Germany, where the emphasis was upon the fluid turning of defence into attack, was supported by a 4-3-3 formation.
- In more recent years, expanded World Cups have allowed in teams of what might be termed lesser attacking skill, leading to a number of managers (such as Guus Hiddink of Australia in 2006) employing a tighter, more crowded 3-6-1 formation to stifle and frustrate attacking opponents in the hope that they may pinch draws or single goal victories.

The point here is that none of these literary or sporting formations is inherently superior to the others – each is adapted to the unique characteristics and intentions or strategies they express.

Based on this principle of diversity between and within organizations we can begin to see how different organizations will line up differently with regard to looseness, focus and the individual virtues themselves. Obviously, smaller organizations, creative teams or skunk-works within wider organizations can aim looser than bigger, more conservative bureaucracies. But there may be other contextual nuances too. The football examples started to highlight how the particular fit between organization and competitive context is important. We can illustrate this by looking at some examples from the world of business:

- The strategic innovations at General Motors under Alfred Sloan were supported by a particular model of organization. The decision to produce cars with different levels of styling and quality was delivered through Sloan's innovative decentralized multidivision (M-form) federation. That federal structure was perfectly suited to a group of semi-independent brands (Chevrolet, Pontiac, Oldsmobile, Buick and Cadillac) targeting different markets with updated styling every year, where buyers could be kept in the 'family' as their buying power and preferences changed as they aged. Just as GM offered a greater level of product diversity and pricing than Ford's Model-T, GM recognized the need to go looser than Ford in culture, politics, learning, idea development, multi-tasking, architecture and their attitude to change. But not too loose. The organizational architecture meant that the different brands were complementary rather than competing. GM's virtuous golden mean was still loose-tight, but the balancing point had shifted a few degrees looser than that of Ford.

- More recently, Nike has gone looser in order to re-invigorate its capacity to innovate, after a period when it seemed to be losing its creative edge. Instead of structuring the business around tight product categories – shoes, apparel, equipment – the company moved towards a loosening overlay of three activity groups – sports, tribes and activities. But Nike won't make the mistake of going too loose, into realms that do not fit its core values and capabilities. Here too the company learned from past mistakes (anybody remember the Nike produced movie called *Spacejam*?). For Nike then, the virtuous mean was prompted by its internal history and a knowledge of its vices.
- Philips, which by its own admission has struggled to assemble the right collection of businesses and the organization with which to run them, has moved from loose and complex, toward simpler and more focussed by jettisoning two of its divisions and refocussing a leaner company structure around three: consumer technology, lighting and health care. Following on from this, it recently invited all of its 125,000 workers worldwide to stop work on what was dubbed 'Simplicity Day' and spend the time coming up with ideas as to how Philips could simplify and tighten up the way it did things even further.
- Toyota, meanwhile, after a period veering toward the tight end of the scale, with an aim for 'world cars' and global practices, is now seeking what the company sees as a perfect balance of loose and tight (or, to use their terms, integration and expansion). They describe their forces for organizational integration that *stabilize the company's expansion and transformation* as being:

  - Values from the founders
  - Up-and-in people management
  - Open communication

- And their forces of organizational expansion in order to *lead the company to instigate change and improvement* are described as:

  - Setting impossible goals
  - Encouraging local customization and
  - Promoting experimentation

- This balance dovetails with the company's newly espoused strategy of 'learning local and acting global' as they look to increase the self-reliance of overseas manufacturing facilities and to develop good ideas from anywhere.

Organizational virtues are relative to a specific context – where one organization might need to move towards a more fluid, spontaneous structure, another might need clearer boundaries. Edward de Bono cautioned that whilst lateral thinking might unlock the capacity to generate new ideas by loosening up a 'tight' bureaucratic structure, an artist might have the opposite problem – too many ideas, not enough structure.

As these examples show, the circle of virtues we outlined in Chapter 15 does not tell how, exactly, one must organize for creativity, rather they provide a framework, a process of division and generalization to use Plato's conception from the *Phaedrus*, that can be used to think about and discuss what your best organizational structure might be in order to suit your organization's particular creative identity. The key thing to bear in mind is that you or your team can develop a simple

Table 16.1 Organizational virtues that fit

Organizational Virtue Fit	Strategic Purpose	Competitive Context	Organization
Communist Manifesto	Revolution	Increased political awareness and mobilization Fluid political and social environments Many 'manifestos for change' emerging	Easy to understand 10 point plan at the core of the argument
Hungary and Brazil	Win more often with limited resources	Large competitors have become more conservative and predictable Changes in pitches and equipment make free-flowing skills easier to implement	Free-flowing 4-2-4
Philips	Increase focus and simplicity to reduce costs without harming innovative culture	History of loose structure to foster innovation has led to increased costs and complexity	Three clear divisions enable inviting ideas from everywhere in a more focussed way
Your Organization	?	?	?

articulation or picture of the company's strategy organization. You can, in other words, fill in the boxes at the bottom of Table 16.1 in such a way as to make clear how the virtues need to be developed to achieve a good fit with your organization's particular purpose and context.

Organizing Creative Strategy

We have looked at organization as the fourth stage in a cycle which began with innovation. Innovative ideas are driven forward by entrepreneurial attitudes and capabilities, and these ideas and personalities are orchestrated by leadership and eventually consolidated into organizational forms. And to prevent this organization from turning in on itself and succumbing to organizational vices, the cycle must start again, with a new wave of innovation and entrepreneurship reinventing the organization. More broadly then, this whole cycle is itself a form of organization, one which allows for the different paradoxes and juxtapositions described throughout this book. Organization is thus not just a steady state but a dynamic process of organizing – just as strategy depends on strategizing, so the creative processes of innovation, entrepreneurship and leadership need to be actively organized. First, there must be space for different types of creative behaviours – discovering, creating, diligence, dilettantism, envisioning, interacting, focus and looseness – to co-exist. Secondly, these different creative behaviours must be brought together in productive relationships – connected, not merged.

Organization is therefore both the end and the beginning of creative strategy. It is the end point as a creative idea evolves into an entrepreneurial project, channelled by creative leadership into a sustainable organization. But it is also the interchange through which all of the creative processes described in this book originate, a conduit through which the creative process of paradoxical think-ing can pass. Organizing to promote creative strategy means allowing space for several creative behaviours to coexist, whilst at the same being tight enough to contain and channel them to the next stage. This loose-tight structure is the organizational equivalent of the creative mind's 'tol-erance for contradictions' noted at the start of this book, and Fitzgerald's 'first-rate intelligence' with which we began our discussion of strategic organization.

Strategic organization is also transformational firstly in the sense of reorienting and recontex-tualizing the raw components of creative strategy into new formations, secondly in the sense of self-transformation. At the start of this book we referred to Boden's comment that creative thinking transforms the generative system or conceptual space within which it occurs – it does not merely answer the question, it reframes the problem. According to Boden this transformation of the field in which creativity occurs is incremental, through a continual process of 'boundary tweaking'. This reorganization is also self-transformational – in order to transform the market, industry or field the organization also ends up reinventing itself. This brings us to the final point about strategic organization and creative strategy – creative strategy is iterative, not linear, contin-ually circling back on itself through successive loops of innovation, entrepreneurship, leadership and (re)organization.

So we return to the beginning of our cycle and to the point of this book. While the discussion in *Creative Strategy*'s prologue led us to define the content of creative strategies as:

innovative plans, positions, patterns, perspectives and ploys that add value,

and the outcomes of good creative strategies as being:

greater orientation, animation and integration that results in transformation and rethinking within an organization and beyond,

a process for developing creative strategies remained unclear.

Initial research led us to see that this process would involve connecting understanding of innova-tion, entrepreneurship, leadership and organization and that each of these elements would need to be strategic: or mindful of how they would integrate with one another. Further investigations at the beginning of the project that led to this book revealed that each of these four elements should draw upon bisociative thinking, much like creativity itself. We presented these four bisociations in Chapter 5 as a creative strategy 'helix', reproduced below. However, what remained to be teased out was how the bisociations might work in practice. The remainder of *Creative Strategy* puts flesh on these bones.

In PART I, we saw how Strategic Innovation (SI), and the heart of creative strategy, required the bisociation of discovery and creation toward developing the new and original. We explored how SI could be given greater purpose if aimed toward six degrees of innovation: (1) adding value; (2) reducing cost; (3) increasing volume; (4) developing better market relations; (5) shifting conventional boundaries; or (6) developing more effective ways of learning. And, we discovered (and created) five preconditions that can help foster SI:

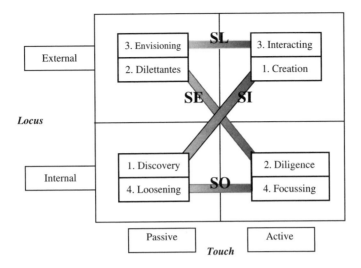

Figure 16.1 The creative strategy helix

- Diversity
- Naivety
- Curiosity
- Urgency, and
- Thinking beyond 'best practice'

★ ★ ★

In PART II, we found that getting good strategic innovations off the ground and off to market required the coordination of five entrepreneurial phases or angles:

- Recognition
- Development
- Evaluation
- Elaboration, and
- Launching

We discovered that one of the real problems with conceptualizing or enacting Strategic Entrepreneurship (SE) was that the first two angles required quite opposite characteristics or emphases from the last two (and the third a blend of these opposites). Strategic Entrepreneurship begins with the unfettered opportunism of the dilettante and progresses through diligent application. Realizing this should make it easier to promote the necessary dilettante and diligent aspects of Strategic Entrepreneurship at the appropriate points. And our three profiles of entrepreneurial journeys furnished a 'mix tape' of additional insights.

★ ★ ★

In PART III, we outlined how balancing the necessary Strategic Leadership (SL) bisociation of envisioning over and above and interacting in the 'nitty gritty' required positioning oneself not at the top or at the front but in the middle. In order to conceptualize how this works in practice we created a Strategic Leadership Keypad which showed how good strategic leaders in creative enterprises shift between and join four positions or 'keys':

- Linking with the outside
- Sussing or distilling the organization's strategic essence
- Promoting good ideas (or people or disciplines or practices), and
- Mapping out desirable futures and pathways for getting there

Our four tales of Strategic Leadership demonstrated how the Keypad could be used to understand the key tasks for a creative leader in a range of circumstances.

In PART IV, we discovered the need to move beyond specific traits and principles of organizational excellence and replace this emphasis with a focus on generic virtues which should be matched to the particular purposes, capabilities and contexts of each organization. These virtues for organizing for creative strategy are:

- A strong but adaptive culture
- Meritocratic politics
- Deutero-learning
- Drawing on ideas internally and externally
- Multi-tasking
- Ambidextrous architectures, and
- Being poised for change

Strategic Organization (SO) is the last twist of the creative strategy helix: the final act. But it should not be the end or where creative strategizing stops. It is the closing act, or the act that completes the circle (or figure 8) in order to accelerate going round again. Its aim is to create an environment in which creative strategy – innovation, entrepreneurship, leadership and organization – is created and recreated, again and again.

Relatedly, the frameworks that we have developed in this book, in search of a process for creative strategy, are designed not as a checklist or a formula, but as processes of division and generalization that can help you to speak and think, question, discover, create, rejuvenate, and give momentum to creative strategy, in the many and varied enterprises that matter to you.

THE ROYAL SHAKESPEARE COMPANY
ACT IV : THE ORGANIZATIONAL ACT

A true ensemble requires dynamic difference. The most successful open-source projects on the web have involved extremely diverse and different skills. If you have the same skills rushing towards the project they'll bump into each other...

Michael Boyd, Artistic Director of the RSC, 8 June 2008

Organizational slack and intensity are both necessary to the creative process. In the case of rehearsal, this dynamic depends upon the organizational culture within which decisions are made. As with our first organizational virtue, rehearsals seek a culture which balances between disintegration and homogeneity of values and intentions. Intensity and focus build energy and momentum, but can shut out new ideas and new people. However a slack, open culture creates space for new ideas and new players, but may be harder to unite into a coherent purpose or focus.

The British director Tim Supple has spoken to us of his need to 'control the culture within which decisions are made' and to create a 'culture of seeing'. He relates this shared culture to the bank of sense-memories, described by Stanislavski, which actors draw upon to develop their roles. In the case of *Richard III*, the company's culture had developed through their work together on the preceding plays in the RSC Histories cycle. This legacy of shared experience, relationships and knowledge was a significant asset for both actors and audiences across the cycle, and a resource which the company continued to invest in through the rehearsal period. The director also went out of his way to create a specific culture for this particular play, by linking to a set of cultural and political reference points, as we discussed in our previous Leadership Act. This culture accumulates through what Supple and Mendes refer to as a 'core understanding' of the play, reinforced through the kind of motifs and shorthand communication noted in the previous Act. This conceptual framework was as real to the actors as the physical boundaries provided by the set and the dimensions of the stage, indicated in the layout of the rehearsal room.

By controlling the culture within which decisions are made, the director can alternately loosen or tighten the actors' frame of reference. The paradox of creative freedom is that the 'slack' of open conversation and improvisation depends upon the security and reassurance of an underlying consensus; conversely the focus achieved in later rehearsals is intensified because shared understanding of the play has been earned through repeated testing and experiment. In the early rehearsals, the frame is set very wide; the slack of the rehearsal encourages experimentation and divergent thinking. As the rehearsals progress, the boundaries around the rehearsal tighten; the timetable speeds up, the physical business of props and staging introduces a new set of constraints, actors and director begin to anchor the scene around specific moments of action or dialogue.

The paradox of 'loose-tight organization' in the rehearsal room centres on what Tim Supple describes as 'a mutually understood territory of impulses'. This is not a fixed interpretation of the text, but a shared understanding of the structures and concepts within which the play will be interpreted. This basic understanding of the themes, impulses and emotions of the play provides a framework within which multiple meanings and interpretations can be given free rein during the phase of experimentation, and a shared set of criteria against which later, more detailed decisions can be tested during the phase of enactment. As Supple comments on his production of *Midsummer Night's Dream*, 'you could argue that the definition of good theatre is freedom within a confined space'.

The organizational virtues of a 'loose-tight' organization extend outwards beyond the rehearsal room to the development of 'ensemble principles' across the RSC as a whole.

First of all, ensemble bridges the extremes of 'loose' individualism and 'tight' over-centralisation. And in line with the fourth virtue, seeking a balance between ideas which are 'disembodied' or overly subjective, Boyd argues that a successful organization needs to be open to 'ideas from the coal face' whilst at the same time integrating these ideas into collective engagement. There is a danger here of setting up a 'false ensemble' which squeezes out the diversity of individual voices. Equally organizations can succumb to an irresponsible 'cult of individualism'. As in rehearsal, the golden mean depends upon trust. Mutual trust keeps open the lines of communication between the people who initiate ideas and the people who invest in ideas, allowing entrepreneurial risk-taking to connect with collective resources and impetus, and steering between the vices of conformity or recklessness.

Secondly, an ensemble organization forces its members to be multi-skilled and resourceful – our fifth organizational virtue. People tend to stay with the RSC for a long time. This means that individuals have to generate their own dynamism, rather than 'just being yourself in different situations'. At its worst, Boyd acknowledges the company might be seen as a 'career terminus' – but at its best, by pushing change from within rather than from external adaptation, people can grow into different roles in the organization, just as they do in the acting company. Boyd believes the continuity of the organization provides a framework for individual change, allowing people to grow within it. This in turn encourages loyalty and commitment. From our perspective, the possibility of inhabiting multiple roles rather than retreating into a single position is what drives the dynamic process of creative strategy. From Boyd's perspective, ensemble requires an engagement of the whole self, not just specialist skills and partial commitment. This whole engagement releases the multi-tasking and paradoxical thinking of creative strategy rather than locking us into one specialist function or position.

Architecturally, we have already referred to the RSC's use of a 'community-minded architecture' to reengineer its relationship with the wider community of the town and region. Our sixth organizational virtue referred to the open and closed architecture of the organization. Here Boyd sees the RSC organization both opening out and closing in. The architecture of the new auditorium is designed to be welcoming and friendly, but also to bring the audience together, 'to inhabit the same space and time'. In his New York speech, Boyd elaborated on the importance of 'one-room theatre' and site-specific work in establishing a shared space for actors and audience, engendering the collective engagement necessary to Boyd's vision of theatre. But the new building is also sym-bolically open to the town. Historically there has always been a divide between the Stratford of the RSC and the Stratford of fish and chips, ice-cream and feeding the ducks – Boyd sees the new building as signalling the start of a new relationship with his neighbours. Executive director Vikki Heywood agrees that audiences are more involved in the work the company is producing and is about to produce, and not just through community and education projects. A social network extends outwards from the company to the wider community and at the centre there is a genuine interest in what audiences think and how they approach the theatre.

Heywood also comments on the organizational architecture of the RSC. When she first arrived at the RSC she attempted to loosen up some of the hierarchical and departmental structures – breaking down 'silos' between departments, delegating responsibility and accountability, making the senior management team more accessible, introducing a learning programme with internal workshops run by staff members, improving communication between managers and staff (and vice versa). Less tangibly, Heywood describes a 'system of behaviours' through which people can work together effectively and feel that they belong to a larger project beyond their individual and immediate goals. 'People need to see the whole picture – it's not just about the sound or the lighting, or the box office. Problem-solving is something we can do across the organization, not just a job for senior management.' Heywood compares the by and large 'happy and engaged' staff today with the more dysfunctional and hierarchical culture when she first arrived at the RSC.

But has this 'loosening up' gone too far? We have projected a series of paradoxes and contradic-tions throughout this book and argued that the ability to switch between them is essential to a 'creative' strategy. In organizations we have claimed that organizational virtue depends upon navigating between organizational vices. Readers might at this point be a little sceptical. How are these paradoxes and oppositions to be negotiated other than through muddy compromise? What happens when a loose, democratic organization has to deal with a financial crisis or an unruly employer? What happens when the 'loose-tight' paradox erupts into open conflict? Should a leader not impose order rather than allowing diversity and democracy to threaten harmony and unity?

Boyd responds by comparing this dynamic to the expanding and contracting of the human heart. The heart must open up to draw in the blood – new ideas, new people – but must also contract to push the blood around the body. The heart is a strong muscle and contraction is a robust movement, sometimes pushing people in directions they do not want to go. But without at the same time opening to harvest their ideas and spirit, the show of force is an empty gesture. And without this double movement – a loosening and tightening of organizational discipline, pumping ideas through the system – the organization will suffer what Boyd calls 'a collective aneurysm'.

Of course such an approach invites conflict. The continuity and commitment of the ensemble mean facing one's demons, individually and collectively, rather than politely ignoring them in the knowledge that the next project will be different. If two of Boyd's actors fall out in rehearsal, the tensions cannot be ignored or deferred, and will spill over into other parts of the organization – after all, the actors are going to be together for two and a half years. So the two of them must deal with their differences. Boyd comments that 'we live in a conflict-averse society, and by avoiding commitment you can avoid conflict'. In this scenario he believes that the tensions between the two actors and the need to address them will yield better performances. It is their commitment to the ensemble which prevents them from brushing the issue aside.

The ability to harness and work with conflict – rather than attempting to smooth it out – is essential to many of the creative processes and paradoxes we have described in this book. We have argued that to achieve a virtuous balance, the strategic organization must recognize its vices. In this case the RSC's ensemble provides a framework in which differences can be managed and explored. The models of innovation, entrepreneurship, leadership and organization we are advocating in this book involve bridging very different organizational cultures and individual mindsets. Boyd acknowledges that dealing with such culture clashes and personal antagonisms involves 'some pain'. But we share his belief that such conflicts can be creative, feeding dynamism and change.

Boyd's fellow leader agrees. Vikki Heywood distinguishes 'ensemble' from a cosy togetherness. Previously new recruits were welcomed into the RSC 'family', a phrase which Heywood identifies as a 'terrible shorthand' for conformity and consensus. A workplace where everybody agrees is after all unlikely to bring out the best in us. Whether in the rehearsal room or the boardroom, creative tensions can spark new ideas – and if everybody instantly agrees to the first suggestion, we may never have the chance to consider the next one.

Heywood and Boyd are also in agreement that the ensemble approach will not work with every organization. It happens to fit with the RSC's ethos and practice as a theatre company. It connects the company back to its Shakespearean history. Shakespeare's 'King's Men' worked as an ensemble, and Shakespeare the writer allowed his vision to be shaped by the improvisations of his actors. He was a creative discoverer, reinventing other people's stories and making them his own; he was a diligent craftsman as well as a dilettante 'picker up of unconsidered trifles' – traces of scientific knowledge and contemporary politics are scattered through the texts. The idea of an ensemble of actors informed the RSC's early years under Peter Hall and Peter Brook. It is appropriate then that the RSC should rediscover an organizational form which fits with its history and heritage.

The RSC's particular organizational virtues reflect its purpose and context. Heywood argues that for a publicly funded organization like the RSC, 'producing good work is not enough. The organization has to be significant.' The ensemble provides a coherent set of values which extends beyond the success or failure of specific projects – what managers would call a brand, and Boyd prefers to call an 'identity'. The loosening of the organizational structure has created a tighter sense of unity – staff, customers and stakeholders recognize an organization they want to be part of. For Boyd the true measure of the ensemble's success or failure will be manifest in its artistic output. By bringing arguments and questions into the open and engaging different perspectives, the ensemble organization releases the innovative processes and entrepreneurial energies in the rehearsal room, led by a director who knows when to loosen or tighten the reins. Organizational problems, failures and vices – what Boyd calls 'mistakes' – help us to discover organizational virtues. The RSC ensemble releases tensions rather than resolving them. Such an approach may not fit with every organization. But for the RSC, this is the source of its dynamism, providing the impetus to move around the creative strategy loop of innovation, entrepreneurship, leadership and organization.

'SPARK-NOTES'

- The 'loose-tight' organization in the rehearsal room is manifest in a 'culture of seeing' which is loose enough to allow individual risk and experiment and tight enough to integrate individual perspectives into a coherent vision.
- For the RSC organization as a whole, the loose-tight organization of the ensemble maps onto the organizational virtues described in this chapter.
  - **Ideas from everywhere (4th virtue):** Ideas come from all parts of the organization – from inside and outside artistic team, from the top and 'from the coal-face'.
  - **Multi-tasking (5th virtue):** The continuity and commitment required by an ensemble means that all members of the organization (not just the actors) must expand their repertoire, multi-tasking rather than over-specializing and growing into their role rather than being distracted by too many commitments.
  - **Loose and tight architecture (6th virtue):** the physical architecture of the new building, and the symbolic architecture of the organization open up to new ideas and new people, but also bring people together whether as actors and audiences or as colleagues.
  - **Meritocracy (2nd virtue):** the leadership must steer a virtuous course between democracy and dictatorship, knowing when to open up to new ideas and when to push the company in a new direction.
- **Ensemble** organization opens up **conflict** rather than repressing it. Conflict and difference can be a source of **creativity** in rehearsals and in the organization. This fits with Koestler's description of creativity as a **bisociative** process which requires us to embrace paradox and complexity – it also fits with this book's overall model of **creative strategy**.
- **Ensemble** is an organizational form which **fits** with the RSC's ethos and purpose, not a model for **best practice**. Every organization will have to discover its own virtuous balance between vices.
- The RSC's strategic organization supports the other dimensions of its **creative strategy**, as a source of **innovation** and **entrepreneurship** and reflecting its approach to **leadership**.

ACT V : CURTAIN CALL

The fifth act is where Shakespeare's plays end, often in marriage or death. Shakespeare's *Richard III*, the final part in the Histories cycle, ends with a new beginning as Richmond introduces the new Tudor regime which emerges from years of war at home and abroad – in Boyd's production the moment is given added weight as the actor delivering the final lines is recognizable as the impetuous young Hotspur and as the son killed by his father in the earlier plays, now speaking with a hard-won maturity.

Boyd's own journey since taking over the company in 2003 has followed a similar trajectory of triumph from adversity, marrying commercial success with cultural relevance and laying to rest the company's troubled past. Over the last seven years, the RSC's creative strategy has encompassed artistic renewal and managerial change.

The journey takes us back to a question with which we started this book: what is the relationship between commerce and creativity, and how can we see creative thinking and strategy working in partnership, rather than at loggerheads?

Artistically, the impetus of the RSC's creative strategy has ignited fresh innovations. The ensemble model has been extended, with a new group of actors working on a new set of plays, beginning with *As You Like It* in 2009. The company has expanded its range by inviting in new associate directors and forging links with younger, more 'experimental' theatre companies as well as international partners; this follows the company's Complete Works festival in 2006 which invited companies from all over the world to present their interpretations of Shakespeare's plays. From 2009, the repertoire has been broadened to encompass new work inspired by Shakespeare's plays and a new season of plays from Russia and Eastern Europe. In future seasons, Boyd plans to balance the repertoire evenly between Shakespeare and promoting the creation and discovery of new and original writing. At the same time, the RSC has been reaching out to new markets through its programmes for schools and young people (including the innovative – and very popular – 'Stand up for Shakespeare' scheme), and by touring to popular venues like London's Hackney Empire and the Latitude Festival.

All of this sees the RSC confidently expanding beyond the Shakespearean canon to encompass new ideas, new talent and original writing – as if the company's 'Shakespearean' identity is no longer bounded by the plays themselves, but to a vision of theatre and the contemporary world which attempts to recapture the spirit behind those plays and distil that essence for a modern audience. The RSC is opening up – and discovering a renewed relevance and renewed interest from the public.

Commercially and organizationally, Boyd's ensemble principles are now explicitly embedded in everything the company does; from the actors to the administrators there is greater dynamism,

Figure 16.2 Creative reorganization: the new Royal Shakespeare Theatre takes shape on the banks of the River Avon in Stratford

creative energy, enthusiasm and a renewed sense of identity and pride. It is as if management is imitating art, driven by an individualized sense of innovating the 'RSC way', rather than art being corralled into imitating management 'best practice'.

Boyd has overseen the turning around of an inherited deficit of £2.8 million in 2002 into an eventual surplus. But the financial transformation, like the artistic one, has been a result of steady hard work and attention to detail in addition to dynamism, change and flashes of brilliance – a process continued under Heywood's stewardship following her appointment in 2004.

At the end of 2010, the company will move into its new theatre in Stratford, a building project which has continued on schedule and on budget alongside the company's artistic renaissance (and in the midst of a global recession). The new building will realize Boyd's vision of 'community-minded architecture' with public spaces and a riverside walkway, and the thrust stage will bring audiences and actors closer than ever before. In the meantime, despite the temporary loss of one of its auditoria, the company has continued to perform at the box office, bringing in £9.2 million for the 2007–08 season and selling over half a million tickets in Stratford, London and on tour, including 32,000 people coming to see Shakespeare for the first time. The new building is expected to host its first performances in 2011. It will be a fitting monument to the RSC and its current leadership – a massive commercial investment, an innovative artistic vision, and a bold entrepreneurial reinvention of the past, reigniting the organization's creative future.

Sources and Suggested Further Reading

Prologue: When Strategy Meets Creativity

Chapter 1: False Separations and Creative Connections

Our discussion of creativity as a paradoxical process derives from Arthur Koestler's *The Act of Creation*. However, seeing such a duality at the heart of creation can be traced back to Nietzsche's *The Birth of Tragedy* (where he explores and makes the case for the co-existence of Apollonian and Dionysian forces), subsequently back to ancient mythology and most culture's pre-historical creation myths.

The core of Koestler's definition of creativity is *bisociation*, a surprising connection between two habitually disconnected frames of reference. For a further discussion of Koestler's concept of bisociation and its relation to other fields and disciplines, see Mark Turner's edited collection *The Artful Mind* (2006).

We began to explore the false opposition between 'creatives' and 'executives', in the light of the need for bisociation on both fronts, in works such as the book *Images of Strategy* (Cummings and Wilson, 2003 – in particular in the chapter 'Strategy as Creativity' by Bilton, Cummings and Wilson) and the book *Management and Creativity* (Bilton, 2007).

For a critique of the business rhetoric of 'creativity' in academic literature, see Craig Prichard's 2002 article, 'Creative Selves? Critically Reading "Creativity" in Management Discourse'. Thomas Frank (1997), Jim McGuigan (2009) and Philip Schlesinger (2007), all present further examples of the misappropriation of 'creative' rhetoric by business leaders.

The 'first texts that sought to define what strategy was' are generally seen to be Igor Ansoff's *Corporate Strategy* (1987) and Alfred Chandler's *The Visible Hand* (1977).

The quotation from Aaron De Mey is taken from the article 'Make-up Magician', *New Zealand Herald*, 27 May 2009.

The idea that the 'net generation' is no longer interested in strategy is expressed by Michael Porter in his 2006 article 'Strategy and the Internet'. More recent works such as Erickson (2009) and Tapscott (2009) offer broader and more nuanced views of the differences exhibited by Gen Y, and the ways in which they are not that different after all.

The reference to 'antipreneurs' comes from an article 'Meet the Antipreneurs' in the SmallBiz supplement of *BusinessWeek*, 20 June 2008.

Chapter 2: What is Creativity?

There are several good accounts of current theories of creativity – two wide-ranging books which encapsulate current thinking are R. Keith Sawyer's *Explaining Creativity* and Robert Weisberg's *Creativity: understanding innovation in problem solving, science, invention and the arts*. Less recent but still an excellent source for clear definitions and insights are Margaret Boden's two works *Understanding Creativity* and *Dimensions of Creativity*. The latter includes her discussion quoted in this chapter of P-creativity and H-creativity, and her arguments about creative thinking working within and ultimately transforming a 'bounded conceptual space' (Boden, 1994, pp. 75–117).

Theories of creativity range from personality or trait-based approaches (e.g. Gruber and Davis, 1988) and the psychometric tests developed by E.P. Torrance (Torrance, 1974) through to cognitive approaches such as Sternberg (1988), through to today's emphasis on sociocultural models of creativity as a collective process (Sawyer, 2003). However, a common feature has been the element of paradox or duality, between opposing traits, thinking styles or group members (Bilton, 2007).

For a discussion of the importance (or rather unimportance) of intention in definitions of artistic creativity, see the first chapter of John Carey's *What Good are the Arts?* (2005). And for a critical account of the notion of creative genius, see Negus and Pickering (2004), Weisberg (1986) and Howe (1999). Philip Sandblom (1992) and Kay Jamison (1996) discuss the relationship between creativity and mental illness.

The best known sociological account of creativity is the American sociologist Howard Becker's *Art Worlds* (1982). Csikzsentmihalyi (1988) discusses the relationship between the domain or field and individual creativity. Janet Wolff (1993) takes this a stage further arguing that creativity and creative reputation are social constructs, with no real autonomous meaning. The first two chapters draw out the core of her argument. All of these approaches are directly or indirectly influenced by Bourdieu's sociology of culture – Bourdieu's 'Field of Cultural Production' provides a useful introduction (Bourdieu, 1993).

Less overtly academic but perhaps more stimulating for a general reader are two edited collections of quotations and first hand accounts of creativity. Rothenberg and Hausman (1976) trace debates about creativity back to the time of Aristotle and Plato. Brewster Ghiselin (1985) introduces accounts by writers of their creative process, glossed by a thoughtful editorial commentary.

The text box on 'The Power of Bisociation' refers to an article by Jennifer George and Jing Zhou and also draws on Csikzsentmihalyi (1997).

Throughout the book, we refer to creativity as a paradoxical process which cuts across viewpoints and disciplines. From an empirical perspective, this relates to the argument that creative people are often most active at the edges of networks (Gardner, 1999). This has been confirmed in studies of 'boundary-spanning' creativity in various fields (Mumford and Gustafson, 1988), including scientific research (Kasperson, 1978) and product design (Sutton and Hargadon, 1996).

Chapter 3: Uncreative Strategy

Our critical view of strategy reflects earlier writing in books such as *Recreating Strategy* (Cummings, 2002), *Images of Strategy* (Cummings and Wilson, 2003), and *The Strategy Pathfinder* (Angwin, Cummings and Smith, 2007 – particularly the last chapter of this work entitled 'Maverick Strategy'). Our discussion in this chapter also draws on several works by Henry Mintzberg, which are referenced in the notes on Chapter 4.

Some of the criticisms of the discipline of 'strategic management' in this chapter are developed in one of Mintzberg's earlier works, *The Rise and Fall of Strategic Planning* (1994), whilst the more formal approach to strategy which is being criticized here is that which has filtered into mainstream strategy textbooks which have drawn on some aspects of founding works such as Igor Ansoff's *Corporate Strategy* (1987) and Alfred Chandler's *The Visible Hand* (1977).

The reference to and quotation from Paul Feyerabend relates to *Against Method* (also worth reading in this regard is his *Farewell to Reason*), whilst the references to James Dyson come from an interview with the *Irish Times'* 'Innovation' supplement from June 2007.

A rich account of the 'culture change' at the BBC under Greg Dyke's leadership can be found in Georgina Born's detailed sociological account of regime change at the BBC (Born, 2004).

The Vonnegut quotation is taken from his novel *Player Piano*.

Erich Poettschacher's discussion of the self-peceptions of creative entrepreneurs has been published in the *International Journal of Entrepreneurship and Innovation* (Poettschacher, 2003) and more recently in an article in the *International Journal of Cultural Policy* (Poettschacher, 2010). Teresa Amabile's research into the correlation between intrinsic motivation, self-belief and creativity are included in her articles 'How to Kill Creativity' (Amabile, 1999) and 'Within Me, Without You' (Amabile 1990). Alfred Bandura's arguments about self-efficacy beliefs – and the importance of childhood experiences in building up this resource of self-belief in creative abilities – is contained in Bandura (1997). His argument that formative experiences of power and control help us to overcome failure and disappointment in later life seems especially pertinent to artists, writers and film-makers (thanks to Warwick PhD student Claudia Chibici-Revneanu for drawing our attention to this). Lying behind all of these is Maslow's work on motivation and self-actualization; a good way into this is to read his chapter on 'Creativity in Self-Actualising People' in Maslow (1968).

The Honda case study draws upon Richard Pascale's 1985 account in *Harvard Business Review* – the article is reproduced as a case study in Mintzberg and Quinn (1996).

The educational theories of Jerome Bruner and Jean Piaget are referred to in greater detail in Chapter 12. In management literature, the power of visual communication is best represented by Gareth Morgan's work, notably *Imaginization,* and in Mintzberg's work on 'organigraphs' (Mintzberg and Van der Heyden, 1999).

We also refer in this chapter to the linking of organizational strategy with organisational culture, in particular to the work of Blake and Mouton (1972). It would be invidious to single out particular works from the voluminous literature on organizational culture from a theoretical perspective – but the authors we have found particularly useful include Edgar Schein, Mats Alvesson and Andrew Pettigrew. From a more empirical perspective, several works have examined the 'strong, integrated culture' of Japanese firms underpinning the success of Japanese manufacturing, especially among Japanese car makers like Toyota and Nissan during the 1970s. Western firms were encouraged to mimic this Japanese model, with a resulting 'Japanization' of management culture. One of the most influential of these works was William Ouchi's *Theory Z,* published in 1981.

The distinction between creativity and 'mere novelty' derives from Margaret Boden (1994) and is further developed in Chapter 6 of Bilton's *Management and Creativity.* Sawyer's assertion that the sociocultural model of creativity has become the dominant paradigm for thinking about creativity is from Sawyer (Sawyer, 2006, p. 4).

The discussion of Business Process Re-Engineering and of management's lack of a sense of its own history is contained in Chapter 3 of Cummings' *Recreating Strategy.*

The article linking the narrowing of references in scientific papers to a reduction in creativity is James Evans' 'Electronic Publication and the Narrowing of Science and Scholarship', published in the 18 July 2008 edition of *Science.*

Chapter 4: A More Creative View of Strategy

The three part definition of strategy and of creativity in this and preceding chapters is partly inspired by Andrew Pettigrew's three distinctions between strategy process, strategy content and strategy context, which were later adopted by Bob De Wit and Ron Meyer (2004).

The 'more creative view of strategy' in this chapter is mainly derived from Mintzberg. The Five Ps of strategy can be found in *The Strategy Process* (Mintzberg and Quinn, 1996) and the various schools of strategy are detailed in *Strategy Safari* (Mintzberg et al., 1998). In *Stategy Safari* Mintzberg and his co-authors don't just classify the different 'schools' of strategy, they also argue for a more 'eclectic', less single-minded approach to strategy – an argument with which we would surely concur. An interesting discussion of Mintzberg's theories of strategy in a more overtly 'creative' context can be found in Björkegren (1996).

Karl Weick's description of orientation and animation in strategy can be found in his 1987 chapter 'Substitutes for Strategy'. This discussion is further developed in the opening chapter of *Images of Strategy* (Cummings and Wilson, 2003).

The concept of teleology and its applications to management and organization is described and advocated in Tsoukas and Cummings' 1997 paper 'Marginalization and Recovery: The Emergence of Aristotelian Themes in Organization Studies'.

Chapter 5: Creating and Discovering a Creative Strategy Process

This chapter draws together ideas from the prologue including several of the sources already noted above. The chapter also introduces the RSC case study. The principles of ensemble at the RSC were set out by Michael Boyd in a speech at the New York Public Library on 20 June 2008, entitled 'Making Theater and New Communities', available online at http://www.nypl.org/research/calendar/prog/lpa/video/index.cfm?vidid=7. The RSC ensemble project as a model for management is also the subject of a research project by Demos, led by John Holden, Robert Hewison and Samuel Jones, due for publication in 2010.

Part I: The Innovative Act: Discovery and Creation

Any search on Amazon or Google Scholar will reveal a frightening amount of work that has been published over the past few decades relating to innovation. As we outlined in our introduction to the book we make no claim to comprehensive coverage of this literature, the three chapter sub-heads below list and describe the works that we have explicitly referred to in this part of the book, and, on occasion, some ideas as to how a reader may trace some of the tangents, which we only partially went down, further. Before this, however, we would offer just two recommendations of general source material relating to strategic innovation. The first is any book by John Bessant (Bruce and Bessant, 2001; Bessant and Tidd, 2005; Tidd and Bessant, 2009; Bessant, 2009). More than anyone else, we believe that John covers the field in an extremely intelligent and accessible way. Second, if one wants a good review of the current academic literature, a concise and insightful guide is provided in Schlegelmilch et al. (2003).

Chapter 6: The Bisociations of Strategic Innovation

The concepts of 'creation' and 'discovery' as sources of innovation reflect different approaches to the innovation process as much as differences in the outcome. A similar distinction, between 'making' and 'finding' respectively, is highlighted in Gordon Becker's essay (Becker, 1990). Creation is more in tune with the modern, secular tradition of Western art, requiring artists to originate new ideas from within; discovery is closer to Eastern traditions of art, and to pre-secular cultures.

David Galenson's categorization of painters as 'conceptual innovators' and 'experimental innovators' follows a similar logic to our distinction between creation and discovery. According to Galenson, conceptual innovators like Picasso conceive a new style of painting – 'I paint objects as

I think them, not as I see them.' Conceptual innovation is thus akin to our category of 'creation'. Conceptual innovators often produce their best work in their twenties, failing to build on their early success. Experimental innovators build their oeuvre more incrementally – Galenson cites Cézanne as a painter who patiently experimented with the craft of painting throughout his career, working empirically to represent the world as he saw it – like our 'discoverers' and unlike Picasso, Cézanne claimed to 'seek in painting' (Galenson, 2005).

In the management literature there is a similar distinction between different aspects of innovation, the breakthrough concept and then the incremental application and adaptation of innovative ideas (Kirton, 1991; Kauffman, 2004). In science too, creativity theorists distinguish between scientific discovery as a logical, rational process and an opposing argument promoted by Karl Popper, Max Planck and Albert Einstein that knowledge derives from imagination and intuition, not empirical research (Simonton, 2003, p. 475).

Chapter 6 draws upon two differing arguments for the importance of innovation. Theodore Levitt's 'The Globalisation of Markets' (Levitt, 1986) assumes that innovation centres on a compelling product idea – further innovations in the way this product is presented to different markets merely tinker with and so dilute that product's appeal. Chris Anderson's 'Long Tail' (Anderson, 2004; 2006) argues that innovations in the technologies of production and distribution have broken the supremacy of global 'one size fits all' products, especially in the creative industries. With a long tail of books, music and movies to choose from, consumers are increasingly susceptible to market innovations – new patterns of delivery, word of mouth from other customers, 'information about information' channelling consumer taste. Whilst Levitt's theory has been overtaken by lower costs of customization and 'just-in-time' response to consumer demand, his arguments still resonate in contemporary context, for example in television, where consumers tend to resist 'overchoice' and converge around a narrow range of hit programmes rather than fragmenting across niche channels and interests (Barwise and Ehrenberg, 1988). Conversely Anderson's ideas have been subject to continuing debate among those who feel he has oversold his argument (Wu, 2006)

Chapter 6 also draws upon Philip Nattermann's evidence that 'best practice' in strategy leads to diminishing returns as firms converge on a single approach to technology, production or strategy (Nattermann, 2000).

The argument that design innovation is linked to strategic differentiation and hence to improved financial outcomes draws on data and examples cited in publications published by the UK Design Council reports (see http://www.designcouncil.org.uk/ and http://www.designcouncil.org.uk/Design-Council/3/Publications/)

The argument that innovation can proceed from deliberation, preparation and collective effort rather than individual genius is developed by Weisberg (Weisberg, 2006; 1986). Weisberg also presents a more comprehensive analysis of the Watson and Crick's discovery of DNA and Picasso's *Guernica* referred to in this chapter.

Our arguments about the originality of movie sequels connects to a broader argument that 'originality' in film often results not from deviating from traditions but from working within them

(Petrie, 1991). For more recent views see 'Return of the Sequel', by Robert Welkos (*Oakland Tribune*, July 9 2004); and 'I Think We've Seen this One Before', by Ryan Gilbey (*The Guardian*, 15 June 2007). Our search on the number of sequels on a year-to-year basis was carried out through http://www.imdb.com/keyword/sequel.

For both sides of the story with respect to the perspective of Edison versus Tesla the following two books are very good: *Edison: Inventing the Century* by Neil Baldwin and *Tesla: Man out of Time* by Margaret Cheney.

Chapter 7: The Six Outcomes of Strategic Innovation

The chapter's theoretical framework draws on Kim and Mauborgne (2005) and on Porter (1985). In order to be consistent with our argument and terminology, we have preferred the term 'strategic innovation' to Kim and Mauborgne's 'value innovation' – as explained in Chapter 6, we define strategic innovation as an innovation which is transformative and valuable and this fits with Kim and Mauborgne's definition of 'value innovation'.

Several works are referred to in the chapter which have redefined or reconfigured our understanding of Porter's value chain. Many of these works highlight the growing importance of consumers as innovators and co-creators of value. The concept of 'value constellation' was developed in the *Harvard Business Review* in 1992 (Normann and Ramirez). A further rethinking of the value chain is driven by a perception that today's consumers are more powerful and active. Chris Anderson's *The Long Tail*, Jeff Howe's *Crowdsourcing* and Joseph Surowiecki's *The Wisdom of Crowds* show innovation happening at the consumer's end of the value chain, and show how businesses are using consumer creativity to reinvent and reposition products and brands. In the creative and media industries there is a more optimistic view of consumer creativity, with consumers producing and distributing products on their own terms, supported by emerging technologies such as social networking websites, interactive digital media and Web2.0 tools – these possibilities are celebrated through neologisms like 'wikinomics' (Tapscott and Williams, 2006) and 'we-think'(Leadbeater, 2008). Whether or not this democratization of production and distribution is sustainable is open to question, with many of these innovations being absorbed back into more conventional business models.

Sources utilized to illustrate the case examples in this chapter include 'Weird Science: 101 inventions' (*Cream Magazine*, No. 113, 2008); Simon Garfield's *Mauve*, 'Momofuku Ando' (*The Economist*, 20 January 2007); 'Is This Detroit's Last Winter?'by Bill Saporito, (*Time*, 4 December 2008 – this contains the quotation from Prof. Speer); 'Detroitosaurus wrecks' (*The Economist*, 6 June 2009); Max McKeown's *The Truth about Innovation*; David Ellyard's *Who Invented What When*; 'Thrills without frills' (*Financial Times*, 25 June 2007); 'Special report on cars in emerging markets' (*The Economist*, 15 November 2008); Angwin et al.'s *The Strategy Pathfinder*; Cummings and Wilson's *Images of Strategy*; http://www.tompeters.com (a generally excellent source for interesting ideas and developments with respect to innovation in management from around the word; http://www.ponoko.com; Gardener's term 'the nostalgia cycle' is taken from the Gilbey article from *The Guardian* mentioned under resources for Chapter 6; other sources include Evans and Wurster's *Blown to Bits*; Seth Godin's *Survival Is Not Enough*; 'Mark Twain's Big Mistake', by Paul Collins (*New Scientist*, 3 December 2005); Michael Schrage's *Serious Play*; Amar Bhidé's *The Venturesome Economy*; and Douglas Brinkley's *Wheels for the World*.

Chapter 8: Sparking Strategic Innovation

The chapter lists five perspectives necessary to spur the innovation process. This is our own categorization, but each draws inspiration from other sources.

The 'diversity' perspective refers to Abrahamson and Freedman's *A Perfect Mess*, Frans Johansson's *The Medici Effect* and Joseph Ellis' *Triumphs and Tragedies at the Founding of the Republic*. All of these books highlight the correlation between innovation and the diversity or mess which allows for unexpected connections and interactions to occur.

Our exploration of the importance of 'naivety' connects with Michael Schrage's *Serious Play*, mentioned at the end of the previous chapter, and to Pat Kane's *Play Ethic*, and Mihaly Csikszentmihalyi's *Creativity: flow and the psychology of discovery and invention*, as well as referring to an interview with Michael Stedman in *Recreating Strategy* (Cummings, 2002).

Our discussion of 'curiosity' is partly inspired by an analysis of Barack Obama's inauguration speech, entitled 'Curiosity Makes a Comeback' by William Hoffman, available online at: http://www.scienceprogress.org/2009/02/curiosity-makes-a-comeback/

The focus on 'urgency' derives from John P. Kotter's writing (Kotter, 1995; 2008). It is also indebted to McKeown's *The Truth about Innovation*.

The discussion of learning from failure and 'worst practice' refers to Richard Watson's 2008 article 'Celebrate Failure' (*Fast Company*, 8 July 2008) as well as to Tom Peters' concept of 'fast failing' (http://www.tompeters.com). Our bad band names are derived from http://www.spinner.com, which does a yearly update. The bad brand names are from our own experience.

The notion of 'promising practice' is the subject of a current research project by Chris Voss of the Advanced Institute of Management (AIM) in London. 'Next practice' is introduced in *Recreating Strategy* (Cummings, 2002). For a review of worst, good, promising and next practice, see Angwin et al. (particularly Chapter 11, 'Maverick Strategy').

Part II: Strategic Entrepreneurship: Dilettantes and Diligence

Chapter 9: The Five Angles of Strategic Entrepreneurship

The '50 greatest entrepreneurs' list in the box in the introduction of this chapter is taken from *Success* magazine's June/July 2008 issue.

The five angles of entrepreneurship draw upon Webster's taxonomy of entrepreneurial types (Webster, 1977). Like Webster, we present these angles as stages in a process rather than as entrepreneurial traits or individual characters. The idea of different phases and characteristics converging in a productive system is also present in much of the literature on creative teams (e.g., Kirton, 1991; Sykes, 2008) and in creativity theory. Sawyer describes the importance of creative 'field-switching' (Sawyer, 2008, p. 64), and refers to Howard Gruber's 'network of enterprises' to characterize the way that creative people work across multiple fields (Gruber and Davis, 1988). The ability to work across the edges of different capabilities connects with Gardner's theory of multiple intelligences (Gardner, 1984; 1999).

CASIS analysis is covered in more detail in Chapter 5 'Perfect Positioning' in Angwin et al. (2007).

Our Richard Branson case box draws from an article from November 2008's edition of *Entrepreneur* magazine (pp. 58–62).

Our differentiation of a 'zone of risk' and a 'zone of exploitation' is also implicit in much creativity theory, from De Bono's distinction between 'lateral' and 'vertical' thinking (De Bono, 1995) to Weisberg's categories of 'divergent' and 'convergent' thinking (Weisberg, 1986). Whereas De Bono emphasizes the divergent, 'dilettante' aspects of the creative process, Weisberg emphasizes the deliberate, 'diligent' aspects of the process. However, in this chapter we argue that both elements are necessary.

The paper by Alvarez and Barney that we cite is 'Discovery and Creation: Alternative Theories of Entrepreneurial Action', from the first issue of the new journal *Strategic Entrepreneurship Journal*. This is already evolving into the premier academic journal on the subject and we would highly recommend that anybody interested in surveying the latest rigorous research in the field explore its contents.

The creative thinking exercises come from Adams (1979); the six thinking hats are described in De Bono (1995) and in more detail in De Bono (1990).

As with Part I on Strategic Innovation, we do not profess to cover the whole field of writing on Strategic Entrepreneurship in our chapters here, but we would recommend two books in particular for those who want to do further reading: from a management angle Peter Drucker's classic *Innovation and Entrepreneurship*; and from a creative industries angle *Entrepreneurship in the Creative Industries*, edited by Colette Henry.

Chapter 10: Three Angular Journeys of Entrepreneurship

The chapter is based on interviews rather than written sources. The Nick Hornby case makes reference to Hornby's link on the Penguin website (http://www.penguin.co.uk) which also contains a link to his blog.

The case on Trelise Cooper is co-authored with Deb Cumming and uses an additional quotation from an article called 'Kiwis on the Catwalk' from *The Economist* (28 February 2008).

The 2008 survey of online music quoted at the start of the chapter was conducted by Will Page (Chief Economist for the MCPS – PRS Alliance) and Andrew Bud (Executive chairman of MBlox), and presented at the Telco 2.0 conference in December 2008. Their research, cited in *The Guardian* on 20 December 2008, questioned the notion of the 'long tail' in music, noting that 80% of tracks available online sold nothing at all, while 80% of revenues were accounted for by just 3.8% of tracks – a dramatic reassertion of the old 80:20 rule of a hit-based economy.

At the end of the chapter we refer to the RSC actor Richard Cordery's account of his acting technique (Smallwood, 2004).

Part III: Strategic Leadership: Envisioning and Interacting

Chapter 11: Leading from the Middle

Much of the writing on leadership highlights the need for leaders to inhabit different leadership styles according to different situations (Bass, 2006; Grint, 2000). Typically this is set out as an evolutionary progression, towards a less directive, more consultative and engaging leadership style. Rather than mark out a single course, we argue that leaders must continually switch between leadership positions – something we consider to be common in sport but less understood in business.

Marcus Aurelius is best known in popular culture through being the Emperor at the time the movie *Gladiator* was set. His *Meditations*, a treatise on what he had learned about being a leader having had this destiny thrust upon him, has been a well-regarded text throughout history, but one which has tended to ebb and flow in and out of popularity. There are a number of good translations, but the one we use here is Walter J. Black's.

'All roads lead to the middle' is inspired by Aurelius's *Meditations*, a recent article in *Scientific American Mind* by Stephen Reicher and his co-authors, and Badaracco's (2002) argument for 'leading quietly'.

Arie De Geus is best known for his work on scenario planning, but his book *The Living Company* presents an excellent and easily digested summary of the rise of the knowledge age.

'Working with the wisdom of crowds' obviously leans heavily on James Surowiecki's book of similar name. His comments about the failing of global markets in the GFC are taken from an article entitled 'It's the stupid economy' from New Zealand's *Sunday Star Times* (26 April 2009), by Kate Camp. The research showing how one person making a crowd of guesses is better than a person making a single guess was conducted by Edward Vul and Harold Pasher (2008). It is also worth relating this stream of thought to the recent championing of 'crowdsourcing' (Jeff Howe coined the term and his book is well worth reading).

Our section on gut instinct and intuition draws on Malcolm Gladwell's *Blink*, but also those works that inspired and informed Gladwell, in particular those by Gigerenzer and Gershon. We also make reference to the recent very good book by Tichy and Bennis. We also draw heaving on Gladwell's earlier book *The Tipping Point* in the section following this.

'The power of networks...' adds to *The Tipping Point* logic by drawing on two recent *Harvard Business Review* articles on networking by Uzzi and Dunlap (2005) and Byham (2009). See also 'Blossoming Brains' (*The Economist*, 17 August 2007) and *The Social Atom* by Mark Buchanan.

The expansion from IQ, to many Qs, is influenced by the work in this area by the Lominger organization (see Robert W. Eichinger and Michael M. Lombardo on the 'The 6 Qs of Leadership').

Our section on post heroic leaderships draws on the article by Reicher et al. from *Scientific American Mind* and refers to the influential work of James McGregor Burns (particularly the book *Leadership*). It also notes Jim Collins' popular books *Built to Last* and *From Good to Great*. It draws quotations from a recent interview with Collins in *Business Week* (25 August 2008); and the opinion piece 'Jeff Immelt: GE's model of a modern CEO' by Joe Nocera and published in the *International Herald Tribune* on 9 June 2007.

A defence of 'middle management' and their importance in strategy development is made in *Recreating Strategy* (Cummings, 2002) and *Building Strategy from the Middle: Reconceptualizing Strategy Process* by Floyd and Woolridge (2000).

The 'crisis' in cultural leadership alluded to in this chapter is described by Hewison (2004); for a different perspective see also Bilton, Cummings and Wilson (2003).

Chapter 12: The Strategic Leadership Keypad

The 'keypad' is developed primarily from our experience of working with and observing leadership in a wide range of organizations, but through the discussion of the keypad's parts we refer to a number of works. These include A.G. Lafely's *Harvard Business Review* article and the power-interest matrix (explained in more detail in Angwin et al., 2007, Chapter 2) which we draw upon to explain Key 1.

Key 2, the sussing key, uses elements from organizations like Prudential, Hewlett-Packard and the New Zealand police, which are described in Angwin et al., 2007 (Chapter 7), Dru's book *Disruption* and Godin's books *Survival is Not Enough* and *Purple Cow*. A good book on how leaders can and should create evocative narratives is Jacobs' *Management Rewired*.

The 3rd key utilizes examples referred to earlier in the book; while the 4th key is based largely on Cummings and Angwin (in press). The example from Bob Brett is based on an interview conducted in 2007. The Ben Rich example is described in the book *Skunk Works* by Rich and Leo Janos. The research on children being helped by using hand gestures when doing maths is reported in 'A handwaving guide to arithmetic' (*Economist*, 21 February 2009).

Chapter 13: Shifting Keys: Leadership as Envisioning and Interacting

Three of the four case studies in the chapter have a sporting connection, albeit indirectly so in the case of Bill 'Coach' Campbell.

The Campbell case uses several quotations from 'The Secret Coach', an article written by Jennifer Reingold, which appeared in the 21 July issue of *Fortune* magazine in 2008.

The Billy Beane story was brilliantly told by Michael Lewis in *Moneyball*; in this and his other book, *Blindside*, Lewis combines an analysis of American sport with insights into leadership and business. Our version of the Beane story also includes elements from 'Heavy Hitter', an article by Ron Kroichink from the August 2008 issue of *Diablo* magazine, and an interview with Beane conducted by Bill Jordan and posted on the bizofbaseball.com site on 17 June 2007.

We wish to point out that the inclusion of cases on Arsène Wenger and Nick Hornby in the one book is mostly a coincidence: we are not hardcore Arsenal supporters (hopefully the inclusion of the contrast with Alex Ferguson attests to this). The article from the *Irish Times* which we refer to in this regard is 'Old masters pumped by same pursuit' by Michael Walker published on 18 April 2009.

For further connections between sport and leadership, we can also recommend the book by cricketer Ed Smith (Smith, 2008), and Mark De Rond's book on rowing (De Rond, 2008).

Part IV: Strategic Organization: Focussing and Loosening

Chapter 14: From Principles of Excellent Organizations to Organizational 'Virtues'

This chapter takes as its starting point Peters and Waterman's *In Search of Excellence*, which, despite being panned by a wide range of critics in recent time, is, we believe, a ground-breaking book. Certainly their 'loose-tight' principle has stood the text of time. Peters' frank confessions about the development of the book are from 'Tom Peters's True Confessions' (*Fast Companys* 19 December 2007).

The comments from Eric Schmidt are taken from a discussion involving Schmidt and Andy Grove of Intel on YouTube. This is the link although it may not be there by the time you are reading this book: http://www.youtube.com/watch?v=Q1qoDY-gjKY

The image from Edison's Menlo Park notebooks is from the excellent and freely available collection that has been compiled and digitized by Rutgers University: http://www.edison. rutgers.edu/digital.htm.

For a useful review of the academic literature with regard to new terms to express SLT forms see David Barry and Claus Rerup's 'Going Mobile' (2006). Our discussion on the re-evaluation of bureaucracy as an organizational form draws on the last works of Harold Leavitt: *Why Hierarchies Thrive* and *Top Down*.

Danny Miller's *The Icarus Paradox* is a good companion/antidote to *In Search of Excellence* and a work that is still widely cited.

Aristotle's thoughts on virtue, ethics and the rule of the mean are (conveniently) developed in the one volume *The Nichomachean Ethics* (there are many good translations). For a good additional primer try *Aristotle's Ethics* by J.O. Urmson. This thinking is applied to business ethics in Daniel Nyberg's 'The Morality of Everyday Activities: Not the Right, But the Good Thing To Do', and Stephen Cummings' chapter 'Strategy as Ethos' (Cummings and Wilson, 2003).

Chapter 15: Seven Virtues of Strategic Organization

The 'first virtue' part of this chapter makes reference to the following works: Pascale and Athos's *The Art of Japanese Management*; Gioia et al.'s *Organizational Identity, Image and Adaptive Instability*; Frost et al.'s *Reframing Organizational Culture*; Kuhn's *Structure of Scientific Revolutions*; and Raymond Williams' *Marxism and Culture*.

The 'second virtue' section cites the first series of popular British television comedy *Auf Weidersen, Pet*, which is still widely available on DVD, and Stafford Beer's *Designing the System for Organizations*. Beer's systems are often updated, although they are still not widely known or utilized; the latest attempt to make them more popular is the very good *Fractal Organization: Creating Sustainable Organizations* with the *Viable System Model* by Patrick Hoverstadt.

The 'third virtue' discussion builds upon Argyris and Schön's classic *Theory in Practice: Increasing Professional Effectiveness*. For an update on developments with regard to deutero-learning see Visser's *Deutero-Learning in Organizations*. Also utilized here are Bob Sutton's *Weird Ideas that Work* (his *Weird Rules of Creativity* is also worth looking at) and Peter Senge's *The Fifth Discipline*.

Our discussion on the fourth organizational virtue utilizes ideas from Guy Clapperton's article 'Lost the Ability to Think for Yourself?' (*The Guardian*, 27 October 2006); Wayne Burkan's *Wide Angle Vision*; Angwin et al.'s *Strategy Pathfinder*; and Prahalad and Krishnan's ideas with regard to co-creation from the book *The New Age of Innovation*.

The 'fifth virtue' draws on Gary Marcus' *Kluge: The Haphazard Construction of the Human Mind* and also the ideas of Henri Poincaré. Poincaré was a 19th century mathematician who described his discovery of a complex mathematical formula while travelling on a bus for a sight-seeing trip (Boden, 1992, p. 25). The story is told by Boden together with other famous examples of artistic and scientific discovery occurring between sleep and wakefulness, from Kekulé's discovery of the structure of benzene molecules while dozing in front of the fire to Coleridge's dream of 'Kubla Khan'. Poincaré was also interested in the psychology of discovery and the philosophy of science and developed a four-part model to explain creativity based on preparation, incubation, illumination and verification. The model is explored by Margaret Boden (Boden, 1992, pp. 25–39) and has been very influential in subsequent theories of creativity, including Koestler's theory of bisociation.

The boxed example on the powers of 'sleeping on it' is taken from the article 'Sleep on it' by Graciela Flores (*Scientific American Mind*, August/September 2007). This relates to other ideas advanced in the book *Distracted* by Maggie Jackson. The references to Gloria Mark's studies are taken from the article 'May We have Your Attention Please?' (*BusinessWeek*, 23 June 2008).

The 'sixth virtue' notes the idea of the 'no-collar workplace', examined by Richard Florida in *The Rise of the Creative Class*. Also referred to in this section are Madeline Bunting's *Willing Slaves* and the study 'Tomorrow's Workplace: Fulfilment or Stress' by Michael Moynaoh and his collaborators, which was part of the government funded 'Tomorrow Project' (this is now difficult to obtain although it is often referred to in other works); Jonathan Bell is contributing architecture editor at *Wallpaper* magazine, his article 'Game Over! Back to Work' is from a 2007 issue of *Wallpaper*. Choreographer Twyla Tharp's 'Creativity Step by Step' appeared in the *Harvard Business Review* in 2008.

The advertising agency which replaced its pinball machine with a library is Naked Communications in London; the agency with the long and winding road to the print office is HHCL, another 'hot' creative agency in London.

The final virtue cites the important work by Bartlett and Ghoshal which is used as a starting point for the chapter 'Navigating Change' in the book *Strategy Pathfinder* (Angwin et al., 2007). This chapter provides good background on the loose/tight change + continuity approach to strategic change advanced here. The Octavio Paz quotation is also from that chapter. *When Too Much Change is Never Enough: Stories of Organisational Change* is a little known but very good Australian study by Anna Bodi, Glenn Maggs and Don Edgar. The final part of this section makes reference to Cummings and Daellenbach's study of the forty year history of the journal *Long Range Planning* (2009).

Chapter 16: Strategic Organization: Where Creative Strategy Ends (and Begins Again)

The description of BBC Worldwide's offices and the response from staff members is based on an interview with Fiona Eastwood, Head of Marketing Planning at BBC Worldwide.

On the importance of fit between organization and creativity the following works are interesting. For a further look at how the structure of influential books is almost as important and their context see Andrew Taylor's *Books that Changed the World*.

Alfred P. Sloane's memoir *My Years with General Motors* is a testament to American organizational creativity and innovation. For more on Nike's structural development see the case study 'Trouble in Beaverton' in *Recreating Strategy* (Cummings, 2002). Philips' move toward organization simplicity is described in 'The Complex Task of Simplicity' by Adam Smith (*Time*, 21 February 2008). For more on Toyota's organizational paradoxes see Takeuchi et al.'s 'The Contradictions that Drive Toyota's Success'.

Boden's description of boundary-tweaking and transforming the conceptual space comes from her *Dimensions of Creativity* (1994, pp. 79–84; see also Boden, 1992, pp. 4–5). The correlation between creativity and 'tolerance for contradictions' was highlighted by Frank Barron in his 'Psychology of the Imagination' – echoing the Fitzgerald quote at the start of Part IV, Barron found that creative individuals 'are more at home with complexity and disorder than most people'.

Finally there is a growing literature on organizational creativity – for example Wang and Yang's 'Organizational Creativity', Rosabeth Moss Kanter's 'When a Thousand Flowers Bloom' and Amabile's 'A Model of Creativity and Innovation in Organizations'. Jane Henry's edited collection *Creative Management and Development* includes articles by several authors referred to in this book and represents a good primer on the subject. The journal *Creativity and Innovation Management* is another excellent source.

References

Abrahamson, Eric and Freedman, David H. (2006) *A Perfect Mess: The hidden benefits of disorder*, London: Weidenfeld and Nicolson.

Adams, James L. (1979) *Conceptual Blockbusting: A guide to better ideas*, New York: London: W.W. Norton.

Alvarez, Sharon and Barney, J. (2007) Discovery and Creation: Alternative theories of entrepreneurial action, *Strategic Entrepreneurship Journal*, **1**(1), 11–26.

Amabile, Teresa M. (1988) A Model of Creativity and Innovation in Organizations in *Research in Organizational Behaviour*, **10**, 123–67.

Amabile, Teresa M. (1990) Within You, Without Me: The social psychology of creativity in M.A. Runco and R.S. Albert (eds), *Theories of Creativity*, Sage.

Amabile, Teresa M. (1997) Motivating Creativity in Organisations: On doing what you love and loving what you do, *California Management Review*, **40**(1), Fall: 39–57.

Amabile, Teresa M. (1998) How to Kill Creativity, *Harvard Business Review*, **76**(5), **77**(12). Also available in *Harvard Business Review on Breakthrough Thinking*.

Anderson, Chris (2004) The Long Tail in *Wired*, 12.10 available online at http://www.wired.com/wired/archive/12.10/tail.html.

Anderson, Chris (2006) *The Long Tail: How endless choice is creating unlimited demand*, London: Random House Business.

Angwin, Duncan, Cummings Stephen and Smith, Chris (2007) *The Strategy Pathfinder: core concepts and micro-cases*. Oxford: Blackwells.

Ansoff, H. Igor (1987) *Corporate Strategy* – revised edition – first published 1965, London: Penguin.

Argyris, Chris and Schön, Donald A. (1974) *Theory in Practice: Increasing professional effectiveness*, Oxford, England: Jossey-Bass.

Badaracco, Joseph L. (2002) *Leading Quietly: An unorthodox guide to doing the right thing*, Boston MA: Harvard Business School Press.

Baldwin, Neil (1996) *Edison: Inventing the century*, New York: Hyperion.

Bandura, Albert (1997) *Self-efficacy: The exercise of control*, New York: W.H. Freeman.

Barry, David and Rerup, Charles (2006) Going Mobile: Design considerations from Calder and the Constructivists, *Organization Science*, **17**, 262–76.

Barron, Frank (1958) The Psychology of Imagination, *Scientific American*, **199**, 255–61.

Barwise, Patrick and Ehrenberg, Andrew (1988) *Television and its Audience*, London: Sage.

Bass, Bernard M. and Riggio, Ronald E. (2006) *Transformational Leadership*, Mahwah NJ: Erlbaum.

Becker, Gordon M. (1990) Making it or Finding it in Mark A. Runco and Robert S. Albert (eds), *Theories of Creativity*, London: Sage Publications, pp. 168–81.

Becker, Howard (1982) *Art Worlds*, Los Angeles: UCLA Press.

Beer, Stafford (1995) *Designing the System for Organizations*, Oxford: John Wiley & Sons.

Bessant, John and Tidd, Joe (2007) *Innovation and Entrepreneurship*, Oxford: John Wiley & Sons.

Bessant, John (2009) *Innovation*, London: Dorling Kindersley.

Bhidé, Amar (2008) *The Venturesome Economy: How innovation sustains prosperity in a more connected world*, Princeton, NJ: Princeton University Press.

Bilton, Chris (2007) *Management and Creativity: From creative industries to creative management*, Oxford: Blackwells.

Bilton, Chris, Cummings Stephen and Wilson, David (2003) Strategy as Creativity in Stephen Cummings and David Wilson (eds), *Images of Strategy*, Oxford: Blackwells.

Björkegren, Dag (1996) *The Culture Business: Management strategies for the arts-related business*, London: Routledge.

Blake, R.R. and Mouton, J.S. (1972) *How to Assess the Strengths and Weaknesses of a Business Enterprise*, Austin, TE: Scientific Methods Inc.

Boden, Margaret (1992) *The Creative Mind: Myths and mechanisms*, London: Abacus.

Boden, Margaret A. (1994) What is Creativity? in Margaret Boden (ed.) *Dimensions of Creativity*, Cambridge MA/London: MIT Press/Bradford Books, pp. 75–117.

Bodi, Anna, Maggs, Glenn and Edgar, Don (1997) *When Too Much Change is Never Enough: Stories of organisational change*, Warriewood, Australia: Business & Professional Publishing.

Boltanski, Luc and Chiapello, Eve (2005) *The New Spirit of Capitalism*, London: Verso.

Born, Georgina (2004) *Uncertain Vision: Birt, Dyke and the reinvention of the BBC*, London: Secker and Warburg.

Bourdieu, Pierre (1993) The Field of Cultural Production in Pierre Bourdieu (ed.) *The Field of Cultural Production*, Cambridge: Polity Press, pp. 29–74.

Brinkley, Douglas (2003) *Wheels for the World*, London: Penguin.

Bruce, Margaret and Bessant, John (2001) *Design in Business*, London: Financial Times/Prentice Hall.

Buchanan, Mark (2007) *The Social Atom*, New York: Bloomsbury Press.

Bunting, Madeline (2004) *Willing Slaves: How the overwork culture is ruling our lives*, New York: HarperCollins.

Burkan, Wayne (1996) *Wide Angle Vision: Beat your competition by focusing on fringe competitors, lost customers and rogue employees*, New York: John Wiley & Sons.

Burns, James Macgregor (1978) *Leadership*, New York: Harper Row.

Byham, William C. (2009) Start Networking Right Away (Even if You Hate It), *Harvard Business Review*, **87**(1) (January), 22.

Carey, John (2005) *What Good Are the Arts?* London: Faber.

Chandler, A. (1977) *The Visible Hand: The managerial revolution in American business*, Cambridge, MA: Harvard University Press.

Cheney, Margaret (2001) *Tesla: Man out of time*, New York: Simon & Schuster.

Collins, Jim and Porras, Jerry I. (1994) *Built to Last: Successful habits of visionary companies*, New York: HarperBusiness.

Collins, Jim (2001) *Good to Great: Why some companies make the leap . . . and others don't*, New York: HarperBusiness.

Csikszentmihalyi, Mihaly (1988) Society, culture, and person: A systems view of creativity in R.J. Sternberg (ed.) *The Nature of Creativity: Contemporary psychological perspectives*, New York/Cambridge: Cambridge University Press), pp. 325–39.

Csikszentmihalyi, Mihaly (1997) *Creativity: Flow and the psychology of discovery and invention*, New York: Harper Perennial.

Cummings, Stephen and Angwin, Duncan (in press) Stratography: The art of strategic communication, *Sloan Management Review*.

Cummings, Stephen and Daellenbach, Urs (2009) A guide to the future of strategy? A history of Long Range Planning, *Long Range Planning*, **42**(2), 234–63.

Cummings, Stephen and Wilson, David (eds) (2003) *Images of Strategy*, Oxford: Blackwells.

Cummings, Stephen (2002) *Recreating Strategy: Management from the inside out*, London/Thousand Oaks/New Delhi: Sage.

De Bono, Edward (1990) *Six Thinking Hats*, London: Penguin.

De Bono, Edward (1995) *Serious Creativity*, London: HarperCollins Business.

De Geus, Arie (1997) *The Living Company*, Boston MA: Harvard Business School Press.

De Rond, Mark (2008) *The Last Amateurs: To Hell and Back with the Cambridge Boat Race Crew*, Cambridge: Icon Books.

De Wit, Bob and Meyer, Ron (2004) *Strategy: Process, Content, Context*, London: ITP.

Dru, Jean-Marie (1996) *Disruption: Overturning conventions and shaking up the marketplace,*, New York: Wiley.

Drucker, Peter (1994) *Innovation and Entrepreneurship*, Butterworth Heinmann.

Eichinger, Robert W. and Lombardo, Michael M. (2006) The 6 Qs of Leadership, *Lominger in Focus*, 12.

Ellis, Joseph J. (2007) *American Creation: Triumphs and tragedies in the founding of the republic*, New York: A.A. Knopf.

Ellyard, David (2006) *Who Invented What When*, Sydney: New Holland.

Erickson, Tamara (2008) *The Generation Y Guide to Thriving at Work*, Harvard Business Press.

Evans, James (2008) Electronic Publishing and the Narrowing of Science and Scholarship, *Science* **321**(5887), 18 July, pp 395–399.

Evans, Philip and Wurster, Thomas S. (2000) *Blown to Bits: How the new economics of information transforms strategy*, Boston MA: Harvard Business School.

Feyerabend, Paul (1987) *Farewell to Reason*, London: Verso.

Feyerabend, Paul (1988) *Against Method*, London: Verso.

Florida, Richard (2002) *The Rise of the Creative Class: And how it's transforming work, leisure, community and everyday life*, New York: Basic Books.

Floyd, Stephen and Woolridge, Bill (2000) *Building Strategy from the Middle: Reconceptualizing strategy process*, London: Sage.

Frank, Thomas (1997) *The Conquest of Cool: Business Culture: Counterculture and the rise of hip consumerism*, Chicago: University of Chicago Press.

Frost, Peter J., Moore, Larry F., Louis, Meryl Reis and Lundberg, Craig C. (1991) *Reframing organizational culture*. Newbury Park CA; London: Sage Publications.

Galenson, David W. (2005) *Old Masters and New Geniuses: The two life cycles of artistic creativity*, Princeton, NJ: Princeton University Press.

Gardner, Howard (1984) *Frames of Mind: The theory of multiple intelligences*, London: Heinemann.

Gardner, Howard (1999) *Intelligence Reframed: Multiple intelligences for the 21st century*, New York: Basic Books.

Garfield, Simon (2000) *Mauve: How one man invented a colour that changed the world*, London: Faber & Faber.

George, Jennifer and Zhou, Jing (2007) Dual Tuning in a Supportive Context: Joint contributions of positive mood, negative mood, and supervisory behaviours to employee creativity, *Academy of Management Journal*, **50**(3), 605–22.

Gershon, Michael D. (1998) *The Second Brain*, Harper Collins.

Ghiselin, Brewster (ed.) (1952) *The Creative Process: A symposium*, University of California Press, 1985.

Gigerenzer, Gerd (2007) *Gut Feelings: The intelligence of the unconscious*, London/New York: Penguin.

Gioia, Dennis, Schultz, Majken and Corley, Kevin (2000) Organizational Identity, Image and Adaptive Instability, *Academy of Management Review*, **25**, 63–81.

Gladwell, M. (2000) *The Tipping Point: How little things can make a big difference*, Little Brown: London.

Gladwell, M. (2005) *Blink: The power of thinking without thinking*, Allen Lane: London.

Godin, Seth (2002) *Survival Is Not Enough: Zooming evolution and the future of your company*, London: Simon & Schuster.

Godin, Seth (2009) *Purple Cow: Transform your business by being remarkable – new edition*, New York: Portfolio.

Grint, Keith (2000) *The Arts of Leadership*, Oxford: Oxford University Press.

Gruber, Howard and Davis, S. (1988) Inching our way up Mount Olympus: The evolving-systems approach to creative thinking in R.J. Sternberg (ed.) *The Nature of Creativity: Contemporary psychological perspectives*, New York/Cambridge: Cambridge University Press), pp. 243–70.

Henry, Colette (ed.) (2007) *Entrepreneurship in the Creative Industries*, Cheltenham, UK: Edward Elgar.

Henry, Jane (ed.) (2006) *Creative Management and Development*, 3rd edition, London/Thousand Oaks CA: Sage.

Hewison, Robert (2004) The crisis of cultural leadership in Britain, *International Journal of Cultural Policy*, **10**(2) (July), 157–66.

Hoppe, Klaus D. (1994) Affect, Hemispheric Specialisation and Creativity in Melvin P. Shaw and Mark A. Runco (eds) *Creativity and Affect*, Norwood, NJ: Ablex, pp. 213–24.

Howe, Jeff (2008) *Crowdsourcing: How the power of the crowd is driving the future of business*, London: Random House Business Books.

Howe, Michael (1999) *Genius Explained*, Cambridge: Cambridge University Press. http://www2.warwick.ac.uk/fac/soc/wbs/research/csme/research/working_papers/wp92.pdf.

Hoverstadt, Patrick (2008) *Fractal Organization: Creating sustainable organizations with the Viable System Model*, Oxford: John Wiley & Sons.

Jackson, Maggie (2008) *Distracted*, Prometheus Books.

Jacobs, Charles (2009) *Management Rewired: Why feedback doesn't work and other surprising lessons from the latest brain science*, New York: Portfolio.

Jamison, Kay R. (1996) *Touched with fire: Manic depressive illness and the artistic temperament*, New York: Free Press.

Jenkins, H. (2006) *Convergence Culture: Where old and new media collide*, New York: New York University Press.

Johansson, Frans (2004) *The Medici Effect: Breakthrough insights at the intersection of ideas, concepts and cultures*, Boston, MA: Harvard Business School Press.

Kane, Pat (2004) *The Play Ethic: A manifesto for a different way of living*, Basingstoke: Macmillan.

Kanter, Rosabeth Moss (1988) When a Thousand Flowers Bloom, *Research in Organizational Behaviour*, **10**, 123–67.

Kasperson, C.J. (1978) Psychology of the Scientist: XXXVII. Scientific Creativity: A relationship with information channels, *Psychological Reports*, **42**, 691–4.

Kauffman, Geir (2004) Two Kinds of Creativity: But which ones? *Creativity and Innovation Management*, **13**(3), 154–65.

Kim, W. Chan and Mauborgne, Renée (2005) *Blue Ocean Strategy: How to create uncontested market space and make the competition irrelevant*, Boston, MA: Harvard Business School Press.

Kirton, M.J. (1991) Adapters and Innovators – why new initiatives get blocked in J. Henry (ed.) *Creative Management*, Sage Publications/Open University Press.

Koestler, Arthur (1976) *The Act of Creation*, London: Hutchinson [1964].

Kotter, John F. (1995) Leading Change: Why transformation efforts fail, *Harvard Business Review*, March/April, **73**(2), 59–67.

Kotter, John F. (2008) *A Sense of Urgency*, Boston, Mass: Harvard Business Press.

Kuhn, Thomas (1996) *The Structure of Scientific Revolutions* 3rd edition. Chicago; London: University of Chicago Press.

Lafley, A.G. (2009) What only the CEO can do, *Harvard Business Review*, May, 54–62.

Leadbeater, Charles (2008) *We-think*, London: Profile.

Leavitt, Harold and Kaufman, Rhonda (2003) Why hierarchies thrive, *Harvard Business Review*, March–April.

Leavitt, Harold (2004) *Top Down: Why hierarchies are here to stay and how to manage them more effectively*, Boston, Mass.: Harvard Business Press.

Lessig, Laurence (2008) *Remix: Making art and commerce thrive in the hybrid economy*, London: Bloomsbury.

Levitt, Theodore (1963) Creativity is Not Enough, *Harvard Business Review*, August, **80**(8), 137–44.

Levitt, Theodore (1986) The Globalisation of Markets in Theodore Levitt (ed.) *The Marketing Imagination*, New York/London: Free Press/Macmillan.

Lewis, Michael (2003) *Moneyball: The art of winning an unfair game*, New York: W.W. Norton & Co.

Lewis, Michael (2007) *Blindside: Evolution of a game*, New York: W.W. Norton & Co.

Marcus, Gary (2008) *Kluge: The haphazard construction of the human mind*, New York: Houghton-Mifflin.

Maslow, Abraham H. (1968) *Toward a Psychology of Being* (2nd edition), New York: Van Nostrand Reinhold.

McGregor, Douglas (1960) *The Human Side of Enterprise*, London: McGraw-Hill.

McGuigan, Jim (2009) *Cool Capitalism*, Pluto Press.

McKeown, Max (2008) *The Truth about Innovation*, Harlow/New York: Pearson/Prentice Hall.

Miller, Danny (1991) *The Icarus Paradox: How excellent companies bring about their own downfall*, Harper Business.

Mintzberg, Henry (1994) *The Rise and Fall of Strategic Management*, Hemel Hempstead: Prentice Hall.

Mintzberg, Henry, Quinn, James Brian and Ghoshal, Sumantra (1996) *The Strategy Process*, New Jersey: Prentice-Hall.

Mintzberg, Henry and Van der Hayden, Ludo (1999) Organigraphs: Drawing how companies really work, *Harvard Business Review*, September/October 1999.

Mintzberg, Henry, Lampel, Joseph and Ahlstrand, Bruce (1998) *The Strategy Safari: A guided tour through the jungles of strategic management*, Englewood Cliffs, NJ: Prentice Hall.

Morgan, Gareth (1993) *Imaginization: The art of creative management*, Newbury Park CA/London: Sage.

Mumford, M.D. and Gustafson, S.B. (1988) Creativity Syndrome: Integration, application, and innovation, *Psychological Bulletin*, **103**, 27–43.

Nattermann, Philip (2000) Why Best Practice does not Equal Best Strategy, *McKinsey Quarterly*, **2**(1).

Negus, Keith and Pickering, Michael (2004) *Creativity, Communication and Cultural Value*, London/Thousand Oaks CA: Sage.

Nyberg, Daniel (2008) The Morality of Everyday Activities: Not the right, but the good thing to do, *Journal of Business Ethics*, **81**, 587–98.

Ouchi, William (1981) *Theory Z: How American business can meet the Japanese challenge*, London: Addison-Wesley.

Pascale, Richard and Athos, Anthony (1981) *The Art of Japanese Management*, New York: Warner.

Peters, Thomas (1988) *Thriving on Chaos: Handbook for a management revolution*, Basingstoke: Macmillan.

Peters, Thomas and Waterman, Robert (1982) *In Search of Excellence: Lessons from America's best-run companies*, New York and London Harper Row.

Petrie, Duncan J. (1991) *Creativity and Constraint in the British Film Industry*, Basingstoke: Macmillan.

Pettigrew, Andrew (2003) Strategy as Process, Power and Change in Stephen Cummings and David Wilson (eds) *Images of Strategy*, Oxford: Blackwells.

Plato (1987) Ion in *Early Socratic Dialogues*, Trevor J. Saunders (ed.), Harmondsworth: Penguin, pp. 47–65.

Poettschacher, Erich (2005) Strategic creativity: How values, beliefs and assumptions drive entrepreneurs in the creative industries, *International Journal of Entrepreneurship and Innovation*, **6**(3), 177.

Porter, Michael (1985) *Competitive Advantage: Creating and sustaining superior performance*, New York; London: Free Press.

Porter, Michael (2006) Strategy and the Internet, *Harvard Business Review*, March, **79**(3), 62–78.

Prahalad, C. and Krishnan, M.S. (2008) *The New Age of Innovation: Driving cocreated value through global networks*, McGraw-Hill Professional.

Prichard, Craig (2002) Creative Selves? Critically Reading Creativity in Management Discourse in *Creativity and Innovation Management*, **11**(4), 265–76.

Norman, R. and Ramirez, R. (1993) From Value Chain to Value Constellation, *Harvard Business Review*, July-August, 65–77.

Reicher, Stephen D., Haslam, S. Alexander and Platow, Michael J. (2007) The New Psychology of Leadership in *Scientific American Mind*, **18**(4) (August/September 2007), 22–9.

Rich, Ben R. and Janos, Leo (1996) *Skunk Works: A personal memoir of my years at Lockheed*, Bay Back Books.

Rifkin, Jeremy (2000) When Markets Give Way to Networks in Jeremy Rifkin (ed.) *The Age of Access*, London: Penguin, pp. 16–29.

Rothenberg, Albert and Hausman, Carl R. (1976) *The Creativity Question*, Durham, NC: Duke University Press.

Sandblom, Philip (1992) *Creativity and Disease: How illness affects literature, art and music* (7th edition), New York/London: Marion Boyars.

Sawyer, R. Keith (2003) *Group Creativity: Music, theatre, collaboration*, Mahwah, NJ: Erlbaum.

Sawyer, R. Keith (2006) *Explaining Creativity*, Oxford: Oxford University Press.

Schlegelmilch, Bodo, Diamantopoulos, Adamantios and Kreuz, Peter (2003) Strategic Innovation: The construct, its drivers and its strategic outcomes, *Journal of Strategic Marketing*, **11**, 117–32.

Schlesinger, Philip (2007) Creativity: From discourse to doctrine? *Screen*, **48**(3), October, 377–87.

Schlesinger, Philip (2010) The Most Creative Organisation in the World: The BBC, 'creativity' and 'management style', *International Journal or Cultural Policy*, **16**(2), (forthcoming – July 2010).

Schrage, Michael (2000) *Serious Play: How the world's best companies stimulate to innovate*, Boston, MA: Harvard Business School Press.

Schumpeter, Joseph A. (1939) *Business Cycles: A theoretical, historical and statistical analysis of the capitalist process*, New York: McGraw Hill.

Senge, Peter (1990) *The Fifth Discipline: The art & practice of the learning organization*, London: Random House.

Simonton, Dean K. (2003) Scientific Creativity as Constrained Stochastic Behavior: The integration of product, person and process perspectives, *Psychological Bulletin*, **129**(4), 475–94.

Sloan, Alfred P. (1965) *My Years with General Motors*, Macfadden-Bartell.

Smallwood, Robert A. (ed.) (2004) *Players of Shakespeare 6: Essays in the performance of Shakespeare's history plays*, Cambridge/New York: Cambridge University Press.

Smith, Ed (2008) *What Sport Tells Us About Life*, London: Penguin.

Sternberg, Robert J. (1988a) A Three-facet Model of Creativity in R.J. Sternberg (ed.) *The Nature of Creativity: Contemporary psychological perspectives*, Cambridge University Press, 1988 repr. 1997), pp. 125–47.

Storper, Michael (1994) The Transition to Flexible Specialization in the US Film Industry: External economies, the division of labour and the crossing of industrial divides in Ash Amin (ed.) *Post-Fordism: A reader*, Oxford: Blackwell, pp. 195–226.

Surowiecki, James (2005) *The Wisdom of Crowds*, New York: Anchor Books.

Sutton, Robert I. (2001) The Weird Rules of Creativity, *Harvard Business Review*, Sept, 94–103.

Sutton, Robert I. (2007) *Weird Ideas That Work: How to build a creative company*, New York: Free Press.

Sutton, Robert I. and Hargadon, A. (1996) Brainstorming Groups in Context: Effectiveness in a product design firm, *Administrative Science Quarterly*, **41**, 685–718.

Sykes, Nigel (2008) Envisioning, Enabling and Enacting: Metamorphosing the enterprise, *Working Paper 92*, Centre for Small and Medium Enterprises, Warwick Business School.

Takeuchi, Hirotaka, Osono, Emi and Shimizu, Norihiko (2008) The Contradictions that Drive Toyota's Success, *Harvard Business Review*, June, 96–104.

Tapscott, Don (2009) *Growing Up Digital: How the Net generation is changing your world*, McGraw-Hill.

Tapscott, Don and Williams, Anthony D. (2006) *Wikinomics: How mass collaboration changes everything*, London: Atlantic Books.

Tharp, Twyla (2008) Creativity Step by Step, *Harvard Business Review*, April, 47–51.

Tichy, Noel M. and Bennis, Warren (2007) *Judgment: How winning leaders make great calls*, Portfolio.

Tidd, Joe and Bessant, John (2009) *Managing Innovation: Integrating technological, market and organizational change*, Oxford: John Wiley & Sons, 4th edition.

Torrance, E.P. (1988) The Nature of Creativity as Manifest in its Testing in R.J. Sternberg (ed.) *The Nature of Creativity: Contemporary psychological perspectives*, Cambridge University Press, 1988 repr. 1997), pp. 43–75.

Tsoukas, Haridimos and Cummings, S. (1997) Marginalization and Recovery: The emergence of Aristotelian themes in organization studies, *Organization Studies*, **18**, 655–83.

Turner, Mark (ed.) (2006) *The Artful Mind: Cognitive science and the riddle of human creativity*, Oxford/New York: Oxford University Press.

Urmson, J.O. (1988) *Aristotle's Ethics*, Oxford: Blackwell.

Uzzi, Brian and Dunlap, Shannon (2005) How To Build Your Network, *Harvard Business Review*, December, **83**(12), 53–60.

Visser, M. (2007) Deutero-Learning in Organizations: A review and a reformulation, *Academy of Management Review*, **32**, 659–67.

Vul, Edward, and Pashler, Harold (2008) Measuring the Crowd Within: Probabilistic representations within individuals, *Psychological Science*, **19**, 645–7.

Webster, Frederick (1977) Entrepreneurs and Ventures: An attempt at classification and clarification, *Academy of Management Review*, **2**(1), January, 54–61.

Weick, Karl (1987) Substitutes for Strategy in J. Teece (ed.) *The Competitive Challenge*, Cambridge, MA: Balinger.

Weisberg, Robert (2006) *Creativity: Understanding innovation in problem solving, science, invention and the arts*, Hoboken NJ: John Wiley and Sons.

Weisberg, Robert W. (1986) The Myth of Divergent Thinking in Robert W. Weisberg, *Creativity: Genius and other myths*, New York: W.H. Freeman.

Williams, Raymond (1977) *Marxism and Literature*, Oxford: Oxford University Press.

Williams, Wendy M. and Yang, Lana T. (1999) Organisational Creativity in Robert J. Sternberg (ed.) *Handbook of Creativity*, Cambridge: Cambridge University Press.

Wolff, Janet (1993) *The Social Production of Art*, Basingstoke: Macmillan.

Wu, T. (2006) The Wrong Tail: How to turn a powerful idea into a dubious theory of everything, *Slate*, 21 July, http://www.slate.com/id/2146225.

Index

Index compiled by Annette Musker